Mastering

Interviews and
Group Discussions

FOURTH EDITION

Forewords
VS Bejoy
Director, AIMA

Anurag Vohra
Managing Director, Royal Bank of Scotland

Mastering
Interviews and
Group Discussions

FOURTH EDITION

Dinesh Mathur VSM
Wing Commander (Retd.)
Indian Air Force

CBS Publishers & Distributors Pvt Ltd

New Delhi • Bengaluru • Chennai • Kochi • Kolkata • Mumbai
Hyderabad • Jharkhand • Nagpur • Patna • Pune • Uttarakhand

ISBN: 978-93-86478-56-6

Fourth Edition: 2018
First Edition: 2011
Second Edition: 2012
Reprint: 2014
Third Edition: 2016
Revised and Abridged Edition: 2017

Published by Satish Kumar Jain and produced by Varun Jain for

CBS Publishers & Distributors Pvt Ltd
4819/XI Prahlad Street, 24 Ansari Road, Daryaganj, New Delhi 110 002, India.
Ph: 23289259, 23266861, 23266867   Website: www.cbspd.com
Fax: 011-23243014   e-mail: delhi@cbspd.com; cbspubs@airtelmail.in.

Corporate Office: 204 FIE, Industrial Area, Patparganj, Delhi 110 092
Ph: 4934 4934   Fax: 4934 4935   e-mail: publishing@cbspd.com; publicity@cbspd.com

Branches

- **Bengaluru:** Seema House 2975, 17th Cross, K.R. Road,
  Banasankari 2nd Stage, Bengaluru 560 070, Karnataka
  Ph: +91-80-26771678/79   Fax: +91-80-26771680   e-mail: bangalore@cbspd.com
- **Chennai:** 7, Subbaraya Street, Shenoy Nagar, Chennai 600 030, Tamil Nadu
  Ph: +91-44-26680620/26681266   Fax: +91-44-42032115   e-mail: chennai@cbspd.com
- **Kochi:** Ashana House, No. 39/1904, AM Thomas Road, Valanjambalam, Ernakulam 682 016,
  Kochi, Kerala
  Ph: +91-484-4059061-65   Fax: +91-484-4059065   e-mail: kochi@cbspd.com
- **Kolkata:** 6/B, Ground Floor, Rameswar Shaw Road, Kolkata-700 014, West Bengal
  Ph: +91-33-22891126, 22891127, 22891128   e-mail: kolkata@cbspd.com
- **Mumbai:** 83-C, Dr E Moses Road, Worli, Mumbai-400018, Maharashtra
  Ph: +91-22-24902340/41   Fax: +91-22-24902342   e-mail: mumbai@cbspd.com

Representatives

• Hyderabad	0-9885175004	• Jharkhand	0-9811541605	• Nagpur	0-9021734563
• Patna	0-9334159340	• Pune	0-9623451994	• Uttarakhand	0-9716462459

Printed at Mudrak, Patparganj, Delhi, India

to
_____

the fond memory of our dear son
Umang
who was a special child, confined to bed.

His ever-smiling face,
despite his tremendous suffering,
has encouraged me to
work under most difficult circumstances.

He was a beautiful flower that bloomed for only
17 years, but his fragrance shall linger
in our hearts forever.

Foreword

To be successful in any academic or career environment, the candidates should have the right knowledge, skill and attitude sets. The knowledge level could be assessed through academic achievements or test results. However, skill and attitude components can be ascertained only through direct interaction with the candidates. To this end, group discussion (GD) and personal interview (PI) are the two tools which are time-tested and being extensively used for job recruitment as well as for admissions to higher professional education.

A large segment of the candidates lack the much needed information and source of guidance for GD and PI. This handicap can quite often lead to non-achievement of the right career/course in time despite the necessary potential in the candidates.

Wing Commander (Retd.) Dinesh Mathur has made great efforts to bring out a candidate-friendly publication to help out the aspirants from various segments of the society despite their urban–rural divide and/or technological divide.

This book provides critical hints, practical tips and guidance to the candidates to enhance their performance in GDs and PIs. I am confident that the candidates will find this book very helpful in preparing for GDs and PIs.

VS Bejoy
Director
All India Management Association (AIMA)
New Delhi

Foreword

Mastering Interviews and Group Discussions is a new and detailed guidebook compiled by Wing Commander Dinesh Mathur for students seeking admissions in various management institutes or seeking entry level jobs. Most selection processes entail GD/PI as essential tests to screen or select candidates. I am confident that the book would be of immense help to a wide set of readers, since not only does it provide a detailed analysis to highlight critical success factors, it also provides refreshingly new insights into the same, and with that it stands out from a lot of existing books on similar subjects. The book lays required stress on brushing-up general awareness and acquiring skills to effectively participate in GD/PI phase of the selection process. The book is quite easy to read, which is a no mean task given the subject area, and I would encourage readers to absorb it in its entirety.

Anurag Vohra
IIM Calcutta Alumnus
Managing Director
Royal Bank of Scotland
International Banking Technology Support

Preface to the Fourth Edition

This is the thoroughly revised and updated edition of the book which focuses on laying the foundation of the planned strategy to face interviews successfully and effectively participate in competitive group discussions. Towards this aim, in Unit I a step-by-step approach to face interviews has been adopted to facilitate easy and fast track assimilation of this strategy by the students. Comprehensive tools for preparation and essential tips for putting forth an improved performance have been included.

In Unit II of this book, detailed analysis to highlight critical success factors to crack group discussions (GDs) have been included. Mock GDs and expert comments highlight the finer aspects which provide crucial tips to ensure a winning performance. The book includes detailed discussions on 27 significant current topics based on most recent developments in various fields of generic interest. It is hoped that comprehension and adequate practice of discussing these topics would sufficiently equip the students in their preparation for effective participation in GDs. Comprehensive lists of 500 Frequently Asked Interview Questions and 200 suggested GD topics have also been included in this book for easy reference and guidance of students. However, students should make efforts to gather sufficient information and relevant data on these topics to update their knowledge base.

This book aims to serve as a handy yet authentic *guide* to all students who have to face interviews and participate in group discussions as a part of the selection/screening process for various entrance examinations as well as entry level jobs. There is a huge demand for a comprehensive book on the preparation for interviews and group discussions. Hence this effort.

Wing Commander **Dinesh Mathur** VSM (Retd.)

A-3/110, Janakpuri, New Delhi 11 0058
Mobile: 9811281391
email: dmmathur21@gmail.com

Acknowledgments

Since the book includes discussions on a large variety of topics, the job entailed rummaging through voluminous data and scattered commentaries on current topics published in daily newspapers like *The Hindustan Times* and *The Times of India* and various other journals, to extract relevant information. As obviously, such information cannot spring from any one source or an individual.

I would like to sincerely thank Madhvi and Sadhvi for helping me collect the material from various sources in the preparation of the manuscript. Finally, I thank my wife Malka for extending the much needed support to complete this book despite severe constraints of our lives.

Contents

Unit I
Interviews

Unit II
Group Discussions

Part I
Concept of a Group Discussion and
How to Effectively Participate in a Group Discussion

Part II
Mock Group Discussions

Part III
Detailed Discussions on Significant Current Topics

Part IV
Suggested Topics for Preparation and Revision

Unit I

Interviews

Interview Fundamentals

Introductory Notes

Getting interviewed by an interviewer or a group of interviewers is both unusual and an unsettling experience. The very thought of getting interviewed and thus becoming a victim in the hands of interviewer(s) may put a person into a state of considerable discomfort, often accompanied by anxiety and animated suspense. Candidates complain that their throats go dry, voices choke and there is excessive sweating while they undergo an interview. This is precisely so, since one is not quite familiar with the course of developments that he/she may encounter while facing

> While getting interviewed is markedly stressful, facing an interview is both science and art.

a selection interview. Fear of landing in an unknown and difficult situation grips the person involved. Most certainly, interviewing is not merely talking or holding an informal conversation, but often a much serious business, with lot at stake. If you do not perform well, you may lose a chance of going to your dream MBA institute or grab the desired job.

Owing to above uncertainties involved in an interview situation, it makes tremendous sense for the interviewee to get acquainted with the process as well as content of an interview. It is now fairly well established that facing an interview is an art, but to prepare for an interview one certainly needs a focused scientific approach. Thus, preparation and subsequently appearing for an interview involve both art and science. In this regard, intricacies of art and logical approach of science come together.

Distinctions between a Normal Conversation and Interview

With a view to appreciating the common process and content of an interview, it is both appropriate and essential to distinguish between a normal conversation and a typical interview situation. First of all, the prime factor that distinguishes the interview from a normal conversation is the very basic structure of the interview. Interviews are carefully conducted with a planned opening and closing and comprehensive probing in between. Secondly,

> Interview is a planned conversation aiming to collect essential information about the candidate.

while a normal conversation may not always aim at seeking information from the interviewee, an interview pointedly aims at seeking sufficient and specific information about the interviewee. Thirdly, to take part in a general conversation, one may not need any sort of preparation, while the interviewee as well as the interviewer/interviewers essentially need adequate preparation to face and conduct an interview respectively. In fact, preparation undisputedly remains the key for a meaningful and successful selection interview.

Yet, another distinguishable feature between a normal conversation and an interview is the formalized turn taking in talking that is strictly enforced during the conduct of an interview. It implies that the interviewer is required to pose a variety of questions and the interviewee is supposed to offer or attempt answering these questions. This situation is certainly not reversible, unless of course, the interviewer himself allows or encourages the interviewee to ask questions. On the other hand, during an informal conversation, no such formal turn-taking is enforced and one is permitted to express his/her views on the subject as and when necessity to do so is felt. In fact, besides all these aspects, while the outcome of an informal conversation may not be at all significant, the result of a selection interview would lead to selection or rejection of a candidate for a job/assignment, which may even change the entire course of life of that person.

> Interview is a formal occasion but its process is usually informal. Informal process ensures spontaneous flow of information from the candidate.

It is now widely realized, that purposeful interviews are conducted in a formal setting, but deliberately in an informal manner. This is precisely so, since informal mannerism markedly facilitates easy and natural flow of information from the interviewee. These are some of the significant distinguishable features between a normal conversation and an interview.

Significance of Interview as Part of a Selection Process

- Even though interviews have been widely used to gather all kinds of information about a person for varied purposes, yet, utilization of interviewing technique as an integral part of a selection process, has been clearly noteworthy.
- Selectors use interviews to gain crucial information about a candidate to assess his/her suitability to undergo a course of study or perform a job. An effective personal interview provides the much needed data about the personality and competence aspects of the candidate.

> A written exam does not reveal many personality and competence aspects of a candidate.

- A candidate who has performed well in a written entrance examination, is not necessarily the best person to be selected and, that is where the significance of interview emerges, i.e., in assessing a person's finer qualities.
- A written test mainly reveals a number of mental abilities of a person, but interviewing a candidate brings out various behavioural aspects.
- Inputs gathered from personal interview complement and supplement the information that is obtained from other assessment tools/tests.

- Like vibrant music is the mainstay of a dance party, interviews have now become the mainstay of an effective screening/selection process.

> Posing synthetic situations in an interview brings out personality traits and leadership qualities of a candidate.

- To bring in an element of stress during the interview, often synthetic situations are posed. Synthetic situations may relate to the contents of the proposed course of study, or to routine situations/activities of the job profile of a manager.

Defining an Interview

An interview is an interaction between two or more individuals with exchange of words as the main medium. Purpose and aim of this exchange is to make sure that relevant and sufficient information about the candidate is obtained to decide his/her selection/rejection for a course of study or assignment.

One of the most popular and apt definition describes an interview as "A personal face-to-face meeting and conversation between two or more persons with the object of gaining information about that person".

Another definition of a selection interview could be "A physical interface between interviewer(s) and interviewee with the objective of assessing the interviewee's potential for a purpose".

TYPES OF INTERVIEW

Interviews conducted as a part of selection process to select MBA aspirants usually are not that elaborate and probing as job interviews. Yet, it will be worthwhile for the candidates to become acquainted with various formats of interviews.

Interviews are now conducted for a number of reasons. Purpose of an interview would, by and large, guide the way in which it should be conducted. Some of the more popular forms of interview which are frequently used these days are enumerated below:

a. *Direct interviews:* This type of interview is normally used to elicit large amount of information or data from the candidate in a short time. Questions on varied subjects are fired at the candidate in rapid succession. Such interviews are generally resorted to verify certain facts as a part of the selection process, especially for lower or middle level assignments.

b. *Indirect interviews:* Interview of this type allows a person to speak freely and frankly about himself/herself or about some issue without many interruptions from the interviewer(s). Such interviews are often held as a part of selection process for high-level jobs.

c. *Patterned interviews:* Methodology adopted to conduct this type of interview attempts to encompass most positive aspects of Direct as well as Indirect variety of interviews. This type of interview allows desired coverage as well as judicious utilization of time of the interviewer(s). This category of interview is the Evaluation Interview that is conducted in the Defence Services Selection Boards for selection of officer cadre.

d. **Stress interviews**: Emphasis in this type of interview is on simulation of appropriate stressful situations to check the stress management of the candidate. Currently, usage of Stress Interviews is on the rise in the Corporate World.

e. **Panel interviews**: In this kind of interview, a panel of specialists assembles to interview a candidate. A typical example of this interview is the one which is presently conducted by the Union Public Service Commission (UPSC) for Civil Services, i.e., high-level jobs like IAS/IFS/IPS, etc. This type of interview mainly checks mental abilities of the candidate, but has some distinct limitations in adequately assessing behavioural aspects.

f. **Group interviews**: This kind of interview is resorted to mainly segregate candidates of a large group. Often, such interviews are conducted in the initial part of a screening test much before the main selection process commences.

g. **Exit interview**: This type of interview is essentially conducted at the time of physical departure of an employee from the work place after the individual takes the final decision to relinquish his/her job. The purpose of this interview is to collect significant information, which provides an insight into critical weak areas of functioning in the organization.

h. **Interview pattern for MBA entrance tests**: It has been observed that interviews conducted as a part of selection for MBA Entrance Tests are a mix of Patterned Interviews and Stress Interviews. While, in the beginning of such interviews, requisite information about the candidate in terms of his/her academic record, social environment, spare time interest/hobbies and achievements in extra curricular activities and sports etc., are collected, towards the end of the interview, some synthetic situations related to the job profile of a manager are often posed. This pattern of interview helps the interviewer to easily assess the personality and stress bearing capabilities of the candidate.

Unit I Interviews

Communicating with the Employer: Your Manners, Conduct and Etiquette

While, you are searching for a job, you must ensure that you project yourself as someone who is quite familiar with civilised rules of communication and display correct manners and etiquettes. Interview is an assessment of your personality, and manners and etiquettes are very much a part of your personality. You project a part of your personality while you communicate with your recruiter. Remember, even if you reply all questions asked during an interview correctly, there are other factors which also work to improve your chances of selection. Correct correspondence etiquettes play an important role in this regard. Let us now discuss some ways to ensure effective and correct communication with your employer.

E-mail Communications

- You might have opted for any kind of e-mail ID for your personal correspondence, it is recommended you keep an impersonal e-mail ID for your interactions with your recruiter. For example, e-mail ID like love XYZ @ abc.com would be appropriate for your personal use but not for dealing with your employer.
- You must scan your e-mails before sending to the recruiter to ensure they are free of any virus. An infected mail will positively work against you and annoy the recruiter.
- In case, you have exchanged a few mails with your recruiter, it would be considered prudent, if you send your e-mail in the 'reply mode' so that the recruiter can refer to your earlier correspondence, if he/she so desires. This would assist him in handling your case expeditiously and with ease.
- Be prompt in replying to the e-mails sent by your recruiter. In normal course of action e-mail should be replied within 48 hours. In case you anticipate any delay, do send an SMS and thereafter reply at the earliest.
- Like when you send your resume as a hard copy, do attach a brief covering letter with your CV, when you send your resume through e-mail as well. The covering letter should highlight your profile in a few lines to quickly attract the attention of the recruiter.

Telephone Interviews

- A job seeker usually keeps two or three job profiles for job specifications given by the recruiter. It would, therefore, be appropriate to keep a track of such resumes by organising their despatch to respective recruiters. This would be handy in case you suddenly receive a call for facing a telephone interview. In other words, you must know which jobs profile you had sent to which recruiter before you get connected for the telephone interview.

- Usually, one tends to become informal while talking on telephone. Remember to remain formal with the interviewer, while you reply to his questions during telephone interview, as you remain formal, when you give interview face to face.

- A per the current practice, an interviewer will ask you. "Is it a good time to talk" or "Can we talk for a few minutes". Make sure you say 'yes', only if you are in a position to talk without getting disturbed. If you are not able to talk, you can ask for an excuse politely and then get back to the interviewer at the earliest.

- Make sure that your caller tune and your mail message convey that you are a professional and a mature person. Your messages which give out excessive personal details about you should be carefully avoided.

Follow-up after the Interview

- Do not annoy the recruiter by calling or sending an e-mail more than once a week after your interview gets over. If you call the recruiter more frequently, you will be projecting yourself as an impatient person who also lacks maturity.

- To display your courtesy and mannerism you must thank the interviewers after the interview gets over and must also mention that you are quite keen to get this job.

- At times, it happens that before you receive any communication conveying your selection after the interview, you may receive selection message for a better job and you may then decide to give up your candidature for this job. In that case, you should still thank the interviewer for his effort and time to keep your options open for a subsequent opportunity. To convey your withdrawal it would be more appropriate to send an e-mail rather than calling up the interviewer.

- Finally, it is significant, 'What' you convey to your interviewer but it is perhaps equally important 'how' you convey your ideas. In this regard, your communication skills as well as good etiquettes assume increased importance. Interviewers clearly observe your mannerism to assure that you fit into the culture of the organisation you intend joining. Therefore, display correct manners and etiquettes to grab your dream job.

4 What Interviewers Look for and Criteria of Selection in an Interview

As a general practice, HR people brief the interviewers about the specific job profile and skills/traits that are required in a candidate to execute a task efficiently and effectively. A set of designated skills/traits are essentially needed in a candidate to perform a job as per organisation's planning. However, we have compiled twelve personality traits, which are essentially required in a candidate to become a good manager. These traits are quite relevant for selection interviews for a job or admission to a prestigious institute for higher learning. Generally speaking, interviewers look for:

A dozen qualities interviewers look for

1. Candidates who can express their ideas clearly and effectively.
2. Candidates who are reasonably self-confident of themselves.
3. Candidates who possess above-the-average academic achievements, and practical intelligence.
4. Candidates who have a clear goal to achieve, be it for better career prospects or becoming an entrepreneur, etc.
5. Candidates who are fairly motivated and enthusiastic to achieve their goals.
6. Candidates who can think and plan in a systematic manner.
7. Candidates who are reasonably aware of their environment and happenings – especially about developments in the fields of business and economy.
8. Candidates who are inquisitive and keen to learn.
9. Candidates who can assert but can also willingly work in a team/group.
10. Candidates who display leadership qualities and possess a pleasing personality.
11. Candidates who take initiative and show distinct dedication towards tasks assigned to them.
12. Candidates who are willing to put in that extra bit of hard work with a smile and shoulder responsibilitites.

Criteria of Assessment in Interviews

1. Interviewers ask a host of searching questions to assess a number of qualities and competencies of candidates. These qualities pertain to personality aspects as well as mental abilities of an aspiring candidate.

2. Broadly, interviewers look for the following attributes in the personality of the candidate:

> During an interview, a candidate's finer qualities of personality emerge rather easily.

   a. Physical appearance and bearing.
   b. Self-confidence.
   c. Grasp, imagination and mental alertness.
   d. An eye for detail.
   e. Inquisitiveness to learn more.
   f. Communication skills.
   g. Ability to analyse a problem/situation in a logical/systematic manner.
   h. General awareness about things around.
   i. Current affairs with special emphasis on developments in various fields.
   j. Team spirit and cooperation.
   k. Sense of responsibility.
   l. Leadership skills.
   m. Decision making abilities.
   n. Planning and organising abilities.
   o. Cheerfulness and stress management.
   p. Physical and mental stamina.
   q. Intellectual honesty.
   r. Determination.
   s. Overall impact of personality of the candidate.

3. Interviewers besides posing a series of questions, observe the candidates' body language closely to assess the above mentioned abilities of the candidate.

Unit I Interviews

Essential Preparation Required to Face an Interview

It is common knowledge that most candidates find facing an interview far more intimidating than appearing in a written examination. Three main factors are responsible for this kind of a situation. Firstly, interview format remains typically subjective and does not have a set syllabus, therefore, despite putting in requisite hard work, the element of uncertainty keeps bothering the candidate. Secondly, during an interview situation, the candidate is always required to correctly answer questions instantly as there is hardly any time to brood or recall. Finally, owing to the close proximity of the interviewer, the entire perso-

> Going through an interview is certainly an intimidating experience and focussed preparation is the key to success during an interview.

nality of the candidate is fully exposed and the interviewer keenly observes the candidate in an attempt to assess a host of qualities. All these three factors jointly put considerable pressure on the candidate and, therefore, effective preparation, that is needed to face an interview, assumes increased significance. In this regard, focused steps as explained further, must be initiated by the candidate keeping the time factor for each activity in view. Sound preparation is essentially the key to get over those pre-interview jitters.

A. Know your Institute/Corporate/Organisation

If you have selected an organisation out of so many, it is logically expected that you know the background of that company or institute. It would be handy to visit the website of the institute/corporate and read its brochure rather thoroughly to collect requisite information on the following aspects:

- What is the location of the institute or various locations of the company?
- A brief history.
- Any special features.
- Some aspects of the institute or company for which it is known.
- Details of the company in terms of business and corporate objectives, etc.
- Advantages of doing a particular course of study from this institute or working in the company.
- Financial status and business prospects of the company.

B. Refreshing Academic Achievements of Graduation/ Postgraduation Level

- As interviewers cross-check the knowledge base of the candidate in the area of his/her speciality in academic field, the candidate should broadly brush up the important topics pertaining to his/her academic qualifications or field of specialisation.

> To show depth of knowledge and an eye for detail, you must revise basics of your academic background.

- More often than not, questions based on practical application of certain fundamentals, rules or concepts are posed to check the depth and clarity of thoughts of the candidate.
- Do brush up your definitions, important formulas and principles, etc.
- Questions are generally asked to assess grasp, imagination and an eye for detail of the candidate and whether, he/she is able to apply theoretical knowledge in the practical field.
- As basically management is an activity which encompasses so many practical aspects, questions on practical aspects/ situations are quite relevant for candidates who seek admissions to various MBA institutes or entry level jobs.

C. Updating Information Base

- A reasonably intelligent and smart candidate must be aware of the environment he/she lives in.
- One must be sufficiently inquisitive to know as to what all goes in his/her town/state/country/world.
- Knowing 'what' is happening is not considered adequate, but the ability of the candidate to answer as to 'why' something is happening will be considered acceptable by the interviewers. One needs to acquire in-depth knowledge in terms of background and other details of a situation to answer 'why' questions.
- There is a definite need for the candidate to cultivate reading habits to update their information base about current affairs prior to facing the interview. Candidate must read one national daily (The Times of India, The Hindu, The Hindustan Times, etc.)

> Get to know happenings around you and revise general awareness thoroughly. Must read one national newspaper daily and glance through a few informative magazines.

sufficiently in detail quite sometime before the interview is scheduled.
- Information about current affairs needs to be augmented by reading some of business related magazines and other journals like Yojna, India Today, Frontline, Outlook and Competition Success Review, etc.
- To update information on economic aspects, one should refer to one financial newspaper and one economic survey.
- Watching TV channels and other TV programs, where analysis of news is being telecast, would also be quite relevant during the preparation phase.

Unit I Interviews

- The candidate must essentially collect sufficient data on developmental and economic activities in India and abroad.
- Other important topics on which a candidate must collect latest information include, political affairs, noteworthy technological advances, corporate information, social/cultural issues and sports, etc.
- Candidate must cultivate the habit of analyzing information on a wide spectrum of topics to gain self-confidence.

D. Making Short Notes on Latest Information

- Identify source of data on a number of current topics and then prepare short notes for easy reference and assimilation.
- Prepare short notes as it may not be feasible for the candidate to revise the entire chunk of information he/she collects during the preparation phase.
- Short notes are a handy tool to revise the information just before the interview.
- Refer to these notes frequently to update information, refresh memory and gain confidence.

E. Displaying Knowledge of what you Claim

- Prior to the interview, a candidate usually lists his/her achievements in the field of academics, extra-curricular activities, sports and experience gained, etc. Interviewers usually verify these claims.
- You should authenticate these claims by producing certificates of merit or photographs.

> Brief notes on a variety of topics are quite handy during the preparation phase.

- It would be in order to attach photocopies of your certificates with your CV and original certificates must be neatly arranged in a folder and carried with you during the interview for verification, if required.
- Brush-up your knowledge about your hobbies and other extra-curricular activities including sports. Interviewers feel that, if you are a reasonably intel-

> Be ready to prove your achievements that you claim during the interview. Get to know more about your hobbies/sports.

ligent person, what you practice frequently, should be known to you better than others.

F. Expressing Ideas Effectively

- Often, candidates are able to acquire requisite knowledge, but have problems with their power of expression–especially in English.
- While, it is essential to acquire sufficient information as well as communicate the same to the interviewer(s), it is equally

> Make effective efforts to improve your communication skills. Speak clearly and confidently.

desirable that this information is conveyed in a simplistic yet effective manner to leave the right impression on the interviewer(s).

- 'What' you convey in an interview is significant but 'how' you convey is no less important.
- Improving communication skills is a time consuming process and cannot be undertaken in a jiffy.
- Reading on a variety of topics, listening and practicing to speak over a reasonable time is considered mandatory.
- If, your communication skills really bother you most of the time, then you must listen to TV/Radio news and discussions on a regular basis. Undergoing a short course in spoken english from a reputed institute would also not be a bad idea.
- Speaking in front of a mirror everyday for a few days really helps.

G. Organising Mock Interviews

- Having taken the above mentioned steps to adequately prepare yourself to face an interview, this is the right time to organize mock interview sessions to polish your skills.
- This should be done in an institute in a formal setting, and in case that is not feasible, having a mock interview session

> Polish your communication skills during practice interview sessions to gain self-confidence.

with your friends or elderly family members would also be quite useful.
- Organizing at least two formal practice interview sessions is strongly recommended before facing the real interview.
- During these mock sessions, the candidate must practice answering the Frequently Asked Questions (FAQs) as well as other commonly asked questions.
- Appearing in mock interviews will boost a candidate's self-confidence and will also help tackling stress.
- After participating in a few mock interview sessions, a candidate will feel more confident and can thereafter face an interview panel as well.

Unit I Interviews

Facing an Interview

If the candidate prepares as highlighted in the previous chapter, he/she should be adequately ready to face an interview. A positive frame of mind at this juncture is the key to success.

Getting Ready

- Ascertain and note down the time and venue of the interview and make sure that you arrive at the designated place at least 10–15 minutes before. | Be punctual and carry your CV and required documents in a folder. |
- Don't schedule other appointments too close to your interview time. These extra minutes would take care of unexpected situations like traffic delays or other out-of-the-blue emergencies.
- Do carry your documents, CV and relevant certificates in a folder and a **working** pen in your **shirt** pocket.
- Do not carry your mobile phone while appearing for the interview, even though it is switched off.

Dress Code and Entry

- Interview is a formal interaction so the candidate must put on a formal dress for this occasion.
- Essentials of cleanliness and neatness are certainly important.
- Good taste in clothing is the best guide. Put on decent and sober clothes and avoid very colourful or trendy attires. Choose colours and styles that have universal appeal. | Dress formally for an interview and must avoid casual attires. |
- Men should wear a decent shirt and trousers. Wearing a tie will make your dress definitely formal.
- If the occasion or weather demands, a blazer or suit may be used. For UPSC interviews, which are generally held in summers, a light coloured suit is desirable. Since, interviews are generally conducted in a small room, perfumes and scents should be sparingly used.
- Sports shoes, jeans, T-shirts and other informal clothes must be avoided. Men must put on leather shoes with laces.
- Ensure your clothes are clean and well-ironed. Accessories and shoes should be polished, in good condition and subtle.

- Women candidates should not put on bright colours and avoid making a fashion statement. Only bare essential jewellery and make-up is recommended for use during interviews. A decent formal dress or light coloured saree and blouse is considered quite acceptable. Women candidates must avoid heels during the interview session.

- *A warning:* Do not borrow clothes or use dresses that are ill-fitting and those that you are not used to. This will certainly appear odd and will work against your self-confidence.

- Even though the attire displays your attitude and reveals your personality, the candidate should not unduly worry about too many details. An attractive personality and reasonably good academic record would overcome most hurdles.

- Do seek interviewer's permission before entering the room by saying 'May I come in Sir/Madam' and greet the interviewers as appropriate. If, the time of interview is before 12:00 hrs in the morning, you should greet with a 'Good Morning Sir(s)/ Madam and subsequently, 'Good Afternoon or Good Evening' as required.

> Seek permission to enter the interviewers' room, greet them and occupy your seat only when offered.

Handshake

- Candidate should not take the initiative to shake hand with the interviewer and must wait for the interviewer to extend his hand for a handshake. A handshake can form a winning first impression or ruin it. It is a powerful means of establishing initial link with someone you do not know. Handshake should neither be too strong nor too weak. While a limp or awkward handshake, called a 'fish handshake', creates a poor impression on the interviewer, extra strong handshake portrays display of overconfidence or power. After holding the interviewer's hand, just give two smooth pumps with shake coming from the elbow. Your posture and body language add to your appearance. Finally, a handshake should be coupled with a head nod, smile and a keen eye contact. All this would make you look confident. Remember not to present a sweaty palm or too many large rings on your hand.

- Wait, until you are offered a chair before you sit down. Let the interviewer start the discussion. If, the interviewers are themselves standing, wait for them to sit down before occupying your seat.

- Sit erect in your chair with a slight lean forward displaying your keenness to take part in the interview process.

- Display reasonable enthusiasm while you talk and maintain a cheerful disposition.

First Impression

- In an interview situation, first impressions have their significance, since, they set the tone for early stages of the interview and thus first impressions cannot be left to chance. In any case, one never gets a second chance to make the first impression. It has been established that about 55% of first impression of a person

> You never get a second chance to make that first impression, yet, performance during the entire interview remains crucial.

is formed by his/her appearance and 38% by the way one speaks.

- Being on time, being dressed appropriately, the pace at which you walk, your handshake, your appearance and being prepared, all contribute in making that first impression.

- There is a general consensus that, a candidate feels more confident if the first few minutes go off well and conversely, very nervous, if he/she is unable to handle those first few minutes.

- Some interviewers feel that impression just before leaving, is perhaps more lasting compared to the first impression. This is called "recency effect" or "parting shot".

- High caliber and mature interviewers, who come to conduct interviews for jobs or admissions to premier institutes like IIMs, etc., assess candidates on much more than first or last impressions.

- After making the first impression, the performance of the candidate throughout the interview is considered important.

Opening the Interview

- In the beginning of the interview, most interviewers try to put the candidate at ease by asking a few questions, which may not put much stress on the candidate. These questions may relate to an opportunity given to the candidate to introduce himself/herself, or talk about some other familiar activities of the candidate. Thus, speaking out on a familiar subject, in the beginning of the interview, gives certain amount of confidence to the candidate to collect his/her thoughts.

- While introducing yourself, emphasise only on vital characteristics and do not waste time on aspects which are already mentioned in your resume/admission form. Do highlight your family back ground, academic profile, hobbies/extra-curricular activities, games, reading habits and ambitions, etc., while you talk about yourself. You may also mention some of your strong likes and dislikes.

- Do mention your significant achievements, but in a short way. There is no need to give a detailed account of your all achievements.

Questioning to assess Knowledge and Personality

- Interviewers may, thereafter, ask a variety of questions depending upon the purpose of the interview. All such questions (more than 500 in number) have been included in the Chapter of 'Frequently Asked Questions'. These questions may relate to academics, technical knowledge, extra-curricular activities, grasp, imagination, hobbies, and general awareness, etc.

- Further, to get a good idea about the candidate's desirable conduct during an interview, students **must** carefully read the Chapters on the topics, "Do's and Don'ts" and "Tips on Body Language".
- Listen to the questions carefully and only then reply. Let the interviewer finish the question before you start answering.
- If you have not understood a question, politely ask the interviewer to repeat the question.
- As far as possible, avoid giving 'one-word' answers, as they look very abrupt. At least reply in a full sentence.

Closing the Interview

- When the interview is about to be over, at times, the interviewer may give an opportunity to the candidate to ask one or two questions. Be sure to ask right type of questions in such a situation. By asking such question, you can display your keen interest to join the company or a course of instruction. Your question(s) may touch upon the following clarifications:
  a. Work culture of the organization including working hours, etc.,
  b. Job contents or responsibilities,
  c. Career prospects,
  d. Reporting chain,
  e. Learning and training opportunities provided by the company,
  f. Clarifications on performance appraisal/assessment, etc.
- When the interviewer(s) indicates that the interview is over, the candidate should thank the interviewer(s) with a slight lean forward and leave the room.

Unit I Interviews

Do's and Don'ts of an Interview

The interviewer does not know you, but you are required to make an impression about yourself. From what you wear to how savvy you are about the job or institute you wish to join, and how you express yourself, and about so many little things you may not even think about, can ruin your chances of getting your job or admission in your dream institute. A list of important do's and don'ts have been, therefore, compiled so that you steer clear of committing glaring interview mistakes and put your best foot forward.

   i. *Express clearly*:
   - Be brief, logical, consistent and rational.
   - Deliberately avoid making sweeping or generalized statements.
   - Try and avoid discussing controversial political or religious issues and be tactful while dealing with such matters.

  ii. *Stay cool*:
   - You should politely defend what you say with due respect to the views of the board.
   - Even if the interviewer makes an attempt to provoke you by interrupting you or differing with you, you must stay cool and maintain a cheerful profile.

 iii. *Avoid putting an accent*:
   - Make sure you speak in a simple and straight forward manner.
   - Putting an accent and using slangs like "gonna", "wanna", "ya", etc. is an absolute no. You must use proper and formal english and be your natural self to get the best results.

  iv. *Good mannerism helps*:
   - Your conduct must display that you are well-mannered.
   - Despite your good achievements, displaying humility and politeness is important.

   v. *Displaying over-confidence is not desirable*:
   - Over-confidence is far more damaging than displaying a bit of under-confidence.
   - Interviewers often take over-confidence as arrogance.
   - Since, experience has shown that, it is very difficult to train over-confident people, interviewers often don't prefer to select over-confident candidates. But, you must be adequately confident of your self.

vi. *Watch your body language*:
   - You must maintain normal eye contact with the interviewer or interviewers.
   - Sit in an erect posture and consciously avoid excessive head/hand movements or gestures.
   - Slight lean forward depicts your keen interest in the interview proceedings.

vii. *Prepare in a planned and systematic manner*:
   - Interviewer may grill you for your academic achievements. Make sure, you can apply your theoretical knowledge in dealing with practical situations.
   - Do brush up your general awareness and take a stock of things that are happening around you.
   - Update your data and display that, you are inquisitive about what goes around you and also keep yourself abreast with the latest happenings.

viii. *Honesty is the best policy*:
   - It is never advantageous to tell half-truths or lies during an interview.
   - Remember, if you get caught in your own web, it could be the end of the road for you.
   - We all commit mistakes. Accept your mistakes gracefully and show a positive attitude while doing so.

ix. *Display enthusiasm*:
   - Maintain a cheerful disposition and display youthful enthusiasm by your words and actions. This would show that you are really keen to get your dream job or admission in your chosen MBA institute.

x. *Throwing humour*:
   - To display pleasant side of your personality, you may throw some humour during the interview.
   - But, if it does not come to you naturally, don't attempt it. In any case, never tell a joke to interviewers.

It would be interesting to note that, the word '**INTERVIEW**' itself contains the points one should keep in mind while facing an interview. Each alphabet is so meaningful as given:

I	*Identify weak areas of your personality*
N	*Notice correct dress code*
T	*Truthful and trustworthy answers*
E	*Eye to eye contact with the interviewer*
R	*Result oriented outlook and self-confidence*
V	*Verify and update data and info on current topics*
I	*In-depth knowledge of your subjects and hobbies*
E	*Ensure logical and convincing responses*
W	*Working towards adapting a positive body language.*

Frequently Asked Questions (FAQs) during an Interview

Depending upon the abilities needed for a job, or to undergo a course of instruction, interviewers often frame questions to assess these abilities in the candidates. A good number of questions asked during an interview are, however, common and largely based upon the information provided by the candidate in his/her CV or Personal Information Questionnaire (PIQ). These questions relate to areas such as personal, family details, educational background and work experience, hobbies, extra-curricular activities, general awareness, self-awareness, depth of knowledge and other probing questions to assess personality traits of the candidate. It is strongly recommended that candidates read a large number of FAQs during their preparatory phase to familiarise themselves with these questions to reduce the element of surprise during an interview. In view of this, some FAQs for handy reference of candidates are appended below under a few common headings.

Questions which are 'Personal' in nature:

1. Tell us about yourself?
2. How would you introduce yourself to us?
3. Describe yourself in 8 words.
4. What is your guiding principle in life?
5. How are you different from others around you?
6. What values do you cherish in your life?
7. Tell us something about yourself, which is not there in your CV.
8. What are your strengths and your weaknesses?
9. Apprise us about your family background.
10. How do you plan to overcome your weaknesses?
11. Between your father and mother, whom do you love more and why?
12. Tell us about your home town and what do you admire or dislike about your home town?
13. What is the meaning of your name and how may people of the same name you know who are famous?
14. List three achievements and three failures of your life.
15. What has been your saddest moment of life?
16. Do you think God exists? If yes, explain!

17. If you are asked to sell yourself, how would you do so?
18. Tell us an incident which has great impact on you.
19. Whom do you consider as your role model and why?
20. How do you spend your spare time?
21. Tell us about the person who has influenced you the most.
22. Why should we select you?
23. Tell us a situation, where you have displayed your managerial skills.
24. Do you feel corruption can be removed from our lives?
25. As per you, what is success in life?
26. Would you offer bribe to get your job done in a Government office?
27. Would you use unfair means to achieve your goal or not?
28. Why do you think, you can become a good manager?
29. Do you think, a business man can also be honest and a man of ethics?
30. What are your alternative plans, if we do not select you?
31. How many close friends do you have? And why do you like them so such?
32. Who was your best teacher and why do you think so?
33. Explain significant qualities of a good leader.
34. How would you manage a job and a family at the same time? (For girl candidates).
35. Do you feel that, menace of dowry can be fully removed from our society?
36. Why do you want to leave your present job?
37. What do you think is the key to success?
38. How do you think, have you performed in this interview?
39. Tell us five points against joint family system?
40. Tell us five points in favour of ragging.
41. Why do you think, you are the fittest person for this job?
42. Why have you decided to join this company or join this institute?
43. Till date, what has been the most difficult moment of your life?
44. What is the cherished dream of your life?
45. What qualities you should have in you to lead a team?
46. Describe the functions of a manager.
47. Why do you want to enter into such a competitive world of business as a manager?
48. Tell us five points in favour of a vegetarian.
49. What is your greatest moment of life and why do you consider it so?
50. What do you think are your obligations towards society?

Questions based on 'General Awareness':

1. Tell us something about your state, its political situation and economy, etc.

Unit I Interviews

2. What are the problems of industry in your state?
3. Tell us major problems, which are a hindrance in the development of your state.
4. Name four important places for tourist in your state and do they have any historical significance?
5. Your state has how many districts?
6. Name all coastal states of India.
7. Do you think, we have neglected north eastern states of India for a considerable time?
8. Tell us about Babri Masjid demolition issue?
9. Name four wild life sanctuaries, which are located close to your state.
10. Are you of the opinion that Income Tax should be abolished? If so, why?
11. Which sector is performing better, private sector or public sector and why is it so?
12. What are the major problems faced by public sectors of India?
13. Which are the Maharatna PSUs?
14. Describe ways and means to reduce corruption in India.
15. Name the politician you admire in India and why?
16. Tell us about the Narmada Valley Project.
17. Do you think that after the success of Commonwealth Games in Delhi, India should hold Olympic games?
18. Explain the controversy over the Women's Reservation Bill.
19. What are the latest advances made by India in Space Research?
20. What is the core issue involved in the Kashmir Problem and how should it be addressed?
21. What are the social issues that trouble you the most?
22. Tell us your views on the Afghanistan situation.
23. Name five foreign banks which are operating in India.
24. Which are the major exports and imports of India?
25. Explain to us India – Nepal relations of today.
26. What is the difference between science and art?
27. How do you define management?
28. Which rivers flow through India and Bangladesh?
29. What are the main reasons of victory of Nitish Kumar in elections held in Bihar in November, 2010?
30. Which are the states through which Narmada river flows?
31. Name India's top-5 IT companies and their CEOs.
32. What are the reasons of declining performance of Australian Cricket Team?
33. What are the major problems faced by Sri Lankan Government after elimination of LTTE?

34. Can India become a permanent member of UN Security Council? What are the problems in this regard?

35. Name India's top-5 advertising agencies.

36. What were the significant reasons that were responsible for the disintegration of USSR?

37. Most people believe that India's major problem is population. How can India successfully implement a family planning programme?

38. Are you in favour of film stars becoming politicians? If yes, why?

39. In the recent past, China has become increasingly dominating? Why is it so and what should India do in this regard?

40. What do you know about Chipko Movement?

41. Do you feel judiciary needs immediate reforms?

42. What do you plan to do for your country?

43. What should we do to stop honour killings?

44. Do you think honesty has become a drawback these days?

45. What is the role of newly formed Niti Aayog?

46. Tell us 5 national and 5 international news of significance during the past three months?

47. Explain greenhouse effect?

48. If you wish to start an industry today, where and why will you start?

49. Name all Prime Ministers and Presidents of India.

50. What is the percentage of Indians below the poverty line?

51. How can status of women be improved in India?

52. What is SAARC? It has how many members?

53. What are your views on unification of Germany?

54. Should agricultural income be taxed?

55. Which are India's poorest and richest states?

56. Is right of service the next step after implementation of RTI?

57. Name India's neighbouring countries and their currencies.

58. What is the literacy rate in India? Which state has the highest literacy and which one has the lowest?

59. What is European Union? What is its significance for India?

60. Where are headquarters of IMF, World Bank, WTO, UNICEF, WHO, etc. located?

61. What is motivation? How does it benefit an organisation?

62. India Railways has been divided into how many zones?

63. How many countries are members of ASEAN? Name three countries who are members of ASEAN.

64. Do you think reservation of jobs is desirable in private sectors?

65. How are RSS and Shivsena different?

Unit I Interviews

66. It is believed that, Japanese industry is more successful than US industry, yet, Japan does not have any business schools? Why is it so?

67. How many countries are members of WTO at present? As of now, what are the controversial issues before WTO?

68. Are we doing enough to check global warming? Briefly, tell us the outcome of various international meets in this regard.

69. Consequent to Indo–US Nuclear Treaty, what are the impediments for India to join the club of NSG?

70. What is a Joint Parliamentary Committee? What are its powers? How does it differ from PAC?

FAQs on Matters concerning 'Economy':

1. What do you understand by BPL (Below Poverty Line)? What is our government doing for the people of this category?

2. In your opinion, what all our government should do to improve the lot of people who are poor in India?

3. Tell us how, our government makes and implements 5-Year Plans? Which agency finally approves these plans?

4. When was the first 5-Year Plan launched and which 5-Year Plan is currently running?

5. What do you understand by an Open-economy?

6. Can you tell us, what are the major problems affecting Indian economy?

7. Tell us major reasons for the economic success of countries like Japan, China and Germany?

8. When and why was WTO (World Trade Organization) established? What is its present role?

9. What do you think, are the trade barriers between countries?

10. Do you feel, arrival of MNCs in India has adversely affected Indian companies?

11. What are the major exports and imports of India?

12. What do you understand by 'balance of trade'?

13. How do you think, can we improve the productivity of our workforce?

14. What do you understand by GDP and how do you calculate it? What are the major factors affecting it? How does it differ from GNP?

15. What is inflation and what is the current rate of inflation these days?

16. What are 'Sensex' and 'Nifty'?

17. What is FDI and how do you think, India can increase its quantum?

18. What is black money and how do you think, can we stop its circulation?

19. What do you think are the main sources of income of the government?

20. What are the major functions of RBI?

21. Do you feel that, India can become a developed country by 2020?

22. What were the economic issues which led to breaking up of erstwhile USSR?
23. What do you think are India's foreign exchange reserves presently?
24. Who was the first Finance Minister of India?
25. Government has proposed to hike 100% FDI in single brand retails and 51% FDI in multi-brand retails. What do such hikes mean for consumers, companies and politics?

Questions on Hobbies/Interests and Extra-curricular Activities:

General

1. What hobbies and extra activities do you pursue?
2. Why did you select this hobby and what was your motivation to pursue it?
3. How do you balance your time between studies and these activities?
4. How do you think these hobbies have benefitted you?
5. Do you think you have achieved anything due to these activities?
6. Do you feel, such activities assist you in your personality development? If yes, how?
7. As you get on with your life, how do you plan to continue pursuing such activities?
8. Can you name some persons who have achieved much by pursuing these hobbies?
9. Do you feel, participating in extra activities helps one become a better team person and take more initiatives?
10. Do you feel every person must have some hobbies/interests?

Sports

Cricket

1. Why did you choose cricket as your favourite game?
2. Are you a bowler or a batsman?
3. Who do you think is more important in the game of cricket, a batsman or a bowler and why?
4. Which is your favourite cricket team, give reasons?
5. Do you think, cricket is being played in our country at the cost of other games?
6. When will be the next Cricket World Cup and where will it be organized? Do you think, India can win the Cup again?
7. What do you think are the reasons for the sudden decline in the performance of Australian cricket team?
8. What is a googly ball? What is a Chinaman ball?
9. Who do you think should be the next Captain of the Indian cricket team?

10. Tell us, in how many ways can a batsman get out?
11. What do you understand by 'power play'?
12. Do you think, introducing technology like 'Third Umpire' is good for the game of cricket?
13. How do you think can we prevent match-fixing?
14. What are the areas in which you think Indian cricket team is weak?
15. Do you think, selection of players in India is merit-based?

Badminton

1. What are the dimensions of a badminton court?
2. What is the height of the net?
3. Name a few best known badminton players of India?
4. Which country is presently dominating the game of badminton?
5. Looking at our population, why India has not been able to produce players of international standard?
6. Which badminton player do you admire and why?
7. Do you think badminton is a power game or of skill and art?
8. What do you think are the reasons for good performance of Saina Nehwal?
9. In your opinion, what should India do to produce more players like Saina Nehwal?
10. Do you feel that, administration of badminton in our country is responsible for the poor show of our players? Do you think, Badminton Association of India is managing the show well?
11. What are the major achievements of Prakash Padukone?
12. What should we do to make badminton a more popular game in India?

Football

1. In spite of so many tournaments that we organize, why Indians fail badly at the international level of football?
2. Which football player do you admire and why?
3. It is said that football is the most popular game in the World. Is it so in India also?
4. European football clubs offer so much money to players, but why the same does not happen in India?
5. Do you feel that, popularity of cricket in India has hampered the development of football?
6. What are the dimensions of a standard football ground? How far apart are the two goal poles?
7. Which position is considered critical in the game and why?
8. Name a few well known football players of India?
9. Under what circumstances does a team is given a penalty kick?
10. Which state is well known for the game of football in India?

Hockey

1. India has been one of the best teams in the world, but in the recent years, we are not playing that good, why?
2. Do you feel that, India's Hockey Federation is mainly responsible for the decline in India's performance?
3. Do you feel that, style of playing hockey has changed and India has not been able to adopt these changes?
4. What are the advantages and disadvantages of playing hockey on the astro-turf?
5. Which Indian and International hockey players do you admire and why?
6. Can you name some major hockey tournaments being organized in India?
7. What are the major achievements of hockey wizard of India, i.e., Dhyan Chand?
8. When is a penalty-stroke awarded in the game of hockey?
9. Do you feel hockey has become a power game these days?
10. Which team won the gold medal(s) in the last Olympic games/ Commonwealth games/Asian games?

Lawn Tennis

1. Which are "Grand Slam" tournaments?
2. Who provides ATP ratings and how are they calculated?
3. Which Indian and International tennis players do you admire and why?
4. Do you think, India can win the Davis Cup in 2011/2012/2013?
5. Do you think, Indian players need international coaches to improve their game?
6. Tell us what are the requirements is terms of infrastructure that India needs to excel in the game of tennis?
7. Even though Leander Peas and Mahesh Bhupati are very good players, yet they do not play together in doubles. Why is it so?
8. What are the different kinds of surfaces on which tennis is played? What kind of surface is there at Wimbledon?
9. Whom do you think is the best player of tennis ever? What are his/her achievements?
10. Name some significant tennis tournaments organized in India?

Swimming

1. Tell us the main reasons, due to which India has not been able to produce swimmers of international standard?
2. Which swimmer has won the maximum number of gold medals in an Olympic game?
3. Who is the best swimmer India has produced so far?

Unit I Interviews

4. Which are the different styles/strokes of swimming and why did you select a particular stroke?
5. What are the attributes required in a person to become a good swimmer?
6. Name a few good swimmers of India.

Chess

1. What is the criteria to become a 'Grand Master' in Chess?
2. Who is the current Chess Champion of the World? Whom did he defeat to become the champion?
3. How do you describe a 'stale-mate' situation?
4. In which country did the game of chess originate?
5. Do you feel, computers can play a better game of chess than human beings?
6. In your opinion, what are the personality traits needed to become a Chess-Champion?
7. Who is the current national champion in chess?
8. Name five top players of chess, past or present.

'Reading' as a Hobby/Interest:

1. What kind of books or magazines do you read and what is your area of interest?
2. How many books have you read so far? What was the title of the book you read recently and what did you learn from it?
3. Who is your favourite author and why do you like his/her style of writing?
4. Name four Indians or Indian origin authors who have been awarded Bookers' prize.
5. How many Indians or Indian origin authors have been awarded Nobel Prize for literature?
6. What kind of news attracts you in the newspaper, such as political, social, science and technology, sports/games or concerning economy, etc.?
7. Who is your favourite Indian author and how do you compare him/her with foreign authors?
8. Which is your favourite newspaper/journals and why do you like it/them?
9. Which permanent column of the newspaper do you read and who is the author of the column?
10. In your opinion, what is the significance of the Editorial Column of the newspaper?
11. Do you feel, newspapers in India are playing a responsible role or they highlight negative aspects of life only?
12. What do you know about Vikram Seth or Kiran Desai? Name any two books of these well known authors.

Questions on 'Music' as a Hobby/Interest:

1. Are you interested only in listening music or can you play some musical instruments or sing?
2. What type of music are you interested in? Can you classify the type of the music you are interested in?
3. Can you tell us, what is Indian classical music? What do you understand by SPIC-MACAY?
4. What type of music is more popular in India? Classical, Rock, Pop or Jazz?
5. Why do you think, classical music is not so popular in India these days?
6. How do you differentiate between Indian classical music and western music?
7. Can you explain the concept of Gharanas in Indian classical music?
8. What do you understand by a 'Raga'?
9. What do you think about 'Remixing' of music? Do you feel it helps in development of music?
10. What do you think is the impact of music on culture and society?
11. Can you suggest some effective methods to check music piracy in India?
12. Can you name your favourite singer and composer? Name the singer you can not listen to? Why is it so?
13. Can you name some pop groups you admire?
14. India's highest award 'Bharat Ratna' has been awarded for music to a few Indians. Who are these?
15. Which musical instruments do you play and why did you prefer this instrument?

Questions on 'Dance' as a Hobby/Interest:

1. Which form of dance are you interested in?
2. Can you tell us, what are the various benefits of dancing?
3. Can you name various folk dances of India and which state they originate from?
4. Have you ever performed on stage?
5. Can you name two personalities who are famous for Bharatnatyam form of dance.
6. Kuchipudi dance form originated from which state of India?
7. Name a few organizations, which are engaged in popularizing Indian classical dance and music?
8. Name the states from which Kathak, Mohiniattam, Bharatnatyam and Kathakali dance forms had originated.
9. Can you name two popular dance competition shows on Indian TV?
10. Name three well known choreographers of India?

Questions on 'Painting' as a Hobby/Interest

1. How did you get interested in painting and what kind of painting do you do?
2. What pleasure do you get out it?
3. How do you describe a modern painting?
4. Do you often visit painting exhibitions and who is your favourite painter?
5. Name five well known painters of India.
6. What is Madhubani painting and why is it so famous?
7. Do you feel that painting as an art has somewhat declined in modern world?
8. MF Hussain who is a famous painter, has left India and settled abroad, why did he do so? In which country has he settled now?
9. Do you think, use of computers has adversely affected the art of painting?
10. Tell us, how fabric painting and canvas painting are different?

Questions on 'Travelling/Touring' as a Hobby/Interest

1. How did you get interested in this hobby?
2. Which are the various destinations you have visited?
3. Which is the best place you have visited so far and why did you like it so much?
4. What mode of travel do you prefer and why?
5. Don't you think that travelling is expensive and, therefore, how do you manage your expenses?
6. Tell us, what all should we do to promote tourism in India?
7. A large number of tourists from abroad do not come to India due to security reasons? Is it true? What should we do about it?
8. Please tell us, what is 'Incredible India' campaign and how far has it been successful?
9. Some people say that, India has not fully developed its potential to present various tourist spots? Do you agree?
10. Who is India's Minister of Tourism and what is her/his contribution to develop tourism in India so far?

Questions on 'Watching TV/Movies' as a Hobby/Interest

1. What type of programmes do you watch on TV?
2. Do you consider, TV as a source of entertainment or information on current affairs?
3. What kind of news do you watch on TV, political, social, concerning economy or financial matters, etc.?
4. Do you think, various TV channels mainly focus on negative aspects of news these days, or not?
5. What are TRP ratings?

6. With so many channels on TV, do you feel quality of programmes has been compromised?
7. Do you feel, there should be censoring of TV programmes also?
8. Name five well known TV personalities and why do you like them?
9. Name a few TV programmes which are known for their high TRPs?
10. Do you feel, advertisements on the TV are productive, or are they sheer waste of money?
11. Do you think, TV viewing has spoilt the popularity of cinema?
12. Some people feel, that TV viewing keeps our children indoors and they do not take part in outdoor sports and games. Do you agree?
13. Do you feel, vulgar and sub-standard programmes on TV are wasting our children's time?
14. What kind of movies do you watch? Do you like art or commercial cinema?
15. Do you feel, western influence on our cinema has been quite damaging?
16. Some people say, it is embarrassing to watch today's commercial movie with your son and daughter. Do you agree?
17. Who is your favourite actor or actress and why do you like him/her so much?
18. Some people feel that, a large number of crimes committed these days have been inspired by movies. Do you agree?
19. Do you feel, Censor Board has been rather lenient, of late?
20. Who is heading our Censor Board these days?
21. How do you compare old movies with cinema of today? Do you feel, creativity has suffered in the modern era?
22. Do you feel, hero-worship of our film actors is justified?

Unit I Interviews

Trends of Interview Methods of Premier MBA Institutes

After the written stage, a number of institutes including IIMs send a form to be filled-up by the candidates and this form is required to be sent back for perusal and retention of the institute. The details required to be filled-up in this form include:

1. Personal information about you and your family.
2. Details of work experience, if any.
3. Typical questions such as:
   a. Why do you want to join a particular institute like IIM, XLRI, IIFT, etc.?
   b. Description of your job responsibilities.
   c. What is your purpose or aim to join this MBA programme?
   d. Why do you prefer a career in management etc.?

- Even though, it may not be mandatory, yet, most interview panels at IIMs and other premier MBA institutes will closely scrutinize this form filled by you and generally ask you questions around it. Of course, they will not restrict their questions to the content of information available in the form alone.
- Most premier MBA institutes conduct their interviews through panels of experts and experienced people and it is best to be honest and straight forward while writing answers to the questions in these pre-interview forms.
- There would be questions on activity/activities you have been involved in so far. If it is only academics, they would probe the depth of your knowledge in your subjects/specialities.
- If you possess work experience then, they will be probing about your previous assignments and companies/organizations you have worked for.
- There would be questions on your long-term goals in professional and personal life.
- How do you plan to transform your dreams into a reality? You must display clarity of thoughts here.
- How does the MBA programme you intend undergoing fits into the larger picture of your above-stated long-term goals?
- You must plan your answers to these questions logically and in a practical manner.
- Your answers must be coherent and convincing. Of course, you must appear genuine and sincere to the interviewers.

- Even though broad aspects of interviews remain unchanged, i.e., all institutes do ask questions on academics, work experience (if any), current affairs, extra-curricular activities/sports, etc. and the overall thought process that goes to do the MBA, experience indicates the following trends with regard to premier MBA institutes:

IIM(C) and IIM(L)

IIM(C) and IIM(L) ask more questions on academic achievements and they probe the candidate's depth of knowledge in the preferred field of study. Depending upon the background of the candidate, i.e., engineering, commence, science and economics, etc., there is an emphasis on details/fundamentals of the subjects and important topics. In between, there are questions on general awareness of the candidates too. Questions on hobbies and reading habits of the candidates have been asked often. On a number of occasions, political situation of the country and benefits of doing an MBA course have been discussed during interview sessions.

Some other questions asked by interviewers of IIM (C) and IIM (L) are:

1. Who is your role model?
2. How much do you know about finance?
3. How did you prepare for CAT?
4. What else are you good at besides academics?
5. What is the greenhouse effect?
6. What are your alternative career plan, if we do not select you?
7. What are the rules of snooker?
8. Questions on work experiences and job profile.
9. Questions on music and movies.
10. Are psychological tests reliable?
11. Why should you wear a tie?
12. How will you market liquor?
13. What are your salary expectations after finishing MBA?
14. Questions on hobbies and games played by candidates.
15. What is socialism?
16. What was the headline of Economic Times day before yesterday?
17. What types of books do you read and further questions on book mentioned?
18. Comment on current education system in India.
19. What are the major problems faced by people of North-eastern States of India?
20. What were the major upsets at Oscar awards this year?
21. How many states have woman Chief Ministers? Name them?
22. What would be your preference in case you get calls from other IIMs too?

23. What are the qualities of a world class manufacturer?
24. What measures would you adopt to enhance profile of your company?
25. What is the present literacy rate in India?
26. Why should we select you?

IIM(A)

IIM(A) puts sufficient stress on extra-curricular activities. A number of candidates have been asked to solve practical puzzles also. Social issues have been discussed during interviews at this institute. Some actual questions that have been asked from candidates in the past during interviews at IIM(A) are listed below:

1. What is the positive impact of corruption and need for privatization?
2. Questions on work experience.
3. Why did you leave your first job?
4. What chemical is used in perfumes and shampoo products?
5. Questions on hobbies and extra-curricular activities.
6. What does success mean to you?
7. Name some management gurus.
8. Should doctors be governed by an ethical code of conduct?
9. How will you define failure?
10. What is the difference between an ellipse, hyperbola and parabola?
11. What questions do you expect from us?
12. Questions on Sensex.
13. What is GDP, fiscal deficit, excise duty, sales tax and octroi tax?
14. What is the difference between a manager and an entrepreneur?
15. Mention salient features of this year's budget.
16. What is the difference between preference and normal shares?
17. What are your career goals?
18. Is the division of districts into smaller parts desirable?
19. What is your opinion on Woman Reservation Bill?
20. What are deep interest bonds?

IIM(B)

At IIM(B) work experience is often discussed in detail besides other aspects. Some real questions that have been put to the candidates at interviews in IIM(B) are enumerated below:

1. What would you like to achieve?
2. Comments on the performance of Infosys.
3. Why should we select you?
4. What programmes do you watch on TV?
5. What events have you organized so far?

6. In which direction is Indian industry heading?
7. Who is a Venture Capitalist?
8. What rivers merge at Sunderbans river basin?
9. Who were the last two Governors of RBI?
10. Speak for two minutes on Akshay Kumar?
11. What are the various forms of dances? Which one do you know?
12. Where do you see yourself five years down the line?
13. What you don't like in yourself?
14. Which is the most recent book that you have read? What have your learnt form it?
15. What is a PSU?

IIM(K)

At IIM(K), questions based on candidate's background and hobbies/extra-curricular activities are normally asked. Some actual questions asked in the past are given below for candidates' reference:

1. Mention five sentences about yourself.
2. What is elasticity of demand?
3. Mention some applications of statistics?
4. What is the most significant achievement of your life?
5. Many successful IITians have opened firms without doing an MBA. So why do not you follow that route to entrepreneurship?
6. Questions on the home state of the candidate.
7. Talk about your father's business.
8. What other calls have you got? Which one will you prefer?
9. What are your favourite subjects?
10. What was your project in the final year?

IIM(I)

At IIM(I), there is an emphasis on questions based on academics as well as general awareness of the candidate. Some real questions asked during interviews at IIM(I) are listed below:

1. What are mutual funds?
2. What are your long term goals?
3. Prove that MBA is suitable to expand your skills?
4. Define caste system.
5. What are your views on Hindi as a national language?
6. In your opinion, who has been the best Prime Minister of India?
7. Who is the best cricket test player ever?
8. In depth questions on candidate's subjects have been asked.
9. What are Bulls and Bears?

10. Two minutes extempore on "Do women make better managers"?
11. Do you agree that Indians are not great at science?
12. How will you disapprove that maths people make bad managers?
13. What kind of activities were you involved in your school?
14. Who is your role model?
15. Is the media in India acting responsibly?

FMS, Delhi

At FMS, there is stress on general awareness besides academics. A few questions which have been asked in FMS, Delhi interviews in recent years are listed below:

1. When was Planning Commission formed? Which five years plan is being followed now?
2. Mention ten uses of this pen?
3. Fresh candidates are grilled on academics.
4. Which is the most recent book have you read?
5. What are the applications of linear algebra?
6. What are the various types of marketing strategies?
7. Questions on extra-curricular activities were asked.
8. What are public limited and private limited companies?
9. Comment on India's performance in cricket?
10. What are the applications of standard deviations?
11. How will you establish your product in the market?
12. Differentiate between aggression and assertiveness.
13. Questions based on work experience and projects undertaken were asked.
14. How will you spend money in shares?
15. What is the difference between a 'mentor' and a 'coach'?

IIFT, XLRI and Symbiosis Institutes

At IIFT, XLRI and Symbiosis Institutes there is an emphasis on questions on economic issues and business news.

TISS and JNU

At TISS and JNU, interviewers often ask a number of questions on current affairs and possible solutions to a number of burning social problems.

- Interview questions being asked by different MBA institutes have also been discussed sufficiently in details in other chapters of this book.

10 Tips on Body Language for an Effective Performance in an Interview

It is commonly known that gestures mirror one's state of mind. Everyday, we unconsciously send out many signals through our body. Research suggests that 70% to 80% of the meaning in a message is communicated nonverbally. Bodily movements and gestures contribute almost 55% of the total exchange of meaningful conversation between persons. Thus, our body language speaks louder

> Remember that your body conveys much more than your words. Correct body language is significant for displaying your attitude.

than our words and can have huge impact on your interactions with others, indicating your level of engagement, or distraction/boredom. The way you carry yourself, sit, stand, talk, look, behave and move your hands or feet convey a lot and reflect your state of mind. Thus, body language is far more eloquent than spoken words. During an interview situation, since the candidate is being observed by the interviewer due to his close proximity, the candidate must adopt suitable and positive body language while facing an interview. In this context, the following body language tips are noteworthy:

(i) *Pleasant facial expression*: Charles Gordy had appropriately said, "A smile is an inexpensive way to improve your looks". A smiling face conveys a relaxed state of mind and also demonstrates your self-confidence, friendliness and a positive attitude. It also conveys that you are able to present yourself in

> A smiling face conveys a relaxed mind and good stress management.

a good mood after getting over the anxiety of facing the interview. Prior to appearing before the interview, do share some pleasant and lighter moments with your friends or family members to relax your mind. Any activity which makes the candidate cheerful could be undertaken by him/her before one proceeds to appear before an interviewer. Remember, a genuine smile expresses interest and happiness. But a nervous smile or one that lacks authenticity can undermine your interactions with interviewers. Flushed cheeks could convey nervousness or limited self-confidence.

(ii) *Walking and sitting posture*: Your body posture says a lot. Sitting and standing upright and in a relaxed manner projects self-confidence. You must stand and sit erect and display reasonable enthusiasm and energy while you walk. A slight lean forward

> Sit and stand erect to display self-confidence.

indicates your keenness to communicate with the interviewer. However, leaning forward excessively would display your lack of self-confidence and anxiety.

Leaning back would indicate your disinterest in the proceedings of the interview. Similarly, controlling "close body postures" while sitting is very important during an interview. It means avoid crossing your arms in front of you or holding an object, may be a file, to create a barrier between you and the interviewer.

(iii) *Eye contact*: Maintaining good eye contact helps you connect with people and is important during interviews or when networking with recruiters. Limited eye contact, shifting eyes, smirks, rapid blinking and squinting might convey that you're being dishonest or phony. While replying to questions the candidate should positively establish eye-contact with the interviewer. Generally, the interview panel consists of two panelists. The candidate should look towards the interviewer who had asked the question but in-between should look towards the other interviewer also to indicate that he/she is also part of this discussion. Direct eye-contact displays your self-confidence. But make sure that you do not stare, as this indicates aggression. Certainly avoid looking around or outside the room while you are talking, as this conveys a lack of confidence or discomfort and disinterest with what is being discussed.

> Direct eye contact with the interviewer displays self-confidence and a positive attitude.

(iv) *Avoid fidgeting*: There is nothing worse than playing with your hair, tapping your foot, clicking a pen top, touching your body parts, fiddling with your ring or jewellery or spectacles during an interview. Constant fidgeting and yawning create a negative impact on the formal setting of an interview and displays your disinterest and distraction to the interviewer.

> Fidgeting and yawning are certainly distracting and must be avoided.

(v) *Head and hand movements*: You can emphasize your speech and key points with hand gestures. Some gestures, such as touching your fingertips together like a steeple, can convey confidence, thoughtfulness and focus. Interlaced hands with thumbs up also says confidence. However, too many gestures can be distracting and will definitely turn off recruiters. Rubbing your hands together or fiddling with your pen or jewellery can convey insecurity or discomfort. Candidates should not stand with their thumbs hooked in their pockets because that can signal insecurity. You should not move your hands excessively as this indicates lack of communication skills. However, slight movement of hands once in a while is quite acceptable. Also anxiety makes one move his/her head frequently. Not moving one's head at all may sometimes indicate disinterest in the ongoing discussion. Thus, nodding of head should be done in a subtle manner, but not vigorously.

> Check those excessive and avoidable hand and body movements.

It goes without saying that, if a candidate will keep the above tips on body language in mind, it will make a big difference in terms of flow of information between the candidate and the interviewer. It will also go a long way in creating a positive impact on the interviewer.

Chapter
11

Ten Smart Tips for Managing Interview Stress

Perhaps one cannot remove all the apprehensions that go with a selection interview, but definitely one can minimize the stress involved. As time for interview draws nearer, situation becomes stressful for the candidate. We all know that, some amount of anxiety is normal and perhaps essential before a selection interview during an entrance test or job interview. Even though, we need a certain degree of stress in our lives to spur us to action and achieve higher results, we need to beat

> Over-emphasizing the significance of interview may lead to avoidable stress.

the stress and not get beaten by it. It is common that a variety of symptoms of stress are experienced by candidates. Some of these include, lack of sleep, crying spells, changes in appetite, complaints of body pain or headache, dizziness, loose motions, self-neglect, negative thoughts and feeling of helplessness, etc.

Even though one cannot eliminate the stress of modern day life, candidates get stressed before the interview mainly because of high expectations from themselves or parents/peer group. Over emphasizing the significance of clearing an interview at a particular point of time to join a prestigious job or MBA institute makes things worse. One should take the situation of appearing in an interview on its face value and remember that in the final scheme of things in life, it is just a passing phase and nothing more. Therefore, there is no need to become panicky or allow extra pressure or tension to build-up.

In this regard, the following time tested 10 smart tips to manage interview stress are enumerated for the benefit of candidates:

1. *Breathe easy*: It does not matter, if you do not know *yoga*, take frequent deep breathing breaks. Intake of oxygen relaxes your mind and prevents stress build-up. Take short breaks, preferably outdoors.

2. *Don't alter routine drastically*: One shouldn't neglect his/her routine while preparing for an interview. Do find time to play your favourite game or watch TV. However, due to paucity of time, you may allot much less time to these activities.

3. *Sleep adequately*: Don't compromise on your sleep of at least 6–7 hours during the night just before the interview day. Sleep is essential to relax you and keep your mind alert during the interview session.

41

4. *Find time to relax:* Do find time to relax yourself during the preparation phase by listening to music or using techniques like meditation, etc. These activities rejuvenate you and relax your mind a great deal. Talking to your friends or family members is also very relaxing.

5. *Consolidate efforts:* Remember, it may not be humanly possible to prepare everything which includes vast topics like current affairs and general awareness, etc., for an interview. Certain amount of uncertainty always lingers in an interview situation. Therefore, recognize the difference between things you can and things you cannot control. You should stop getting stressed for those things, which are well beyond your control and you should consolidate on topics, which you have prepared well and also feel confident about.

6. *Remain positive:* Under any circumstances do not let negativity upset your time schedules and always look at positive aspects of the situation in hand. After all, most candidates appearing in the interviews are in a similar situation. Thus, there is no reason for you to become pessimistic about yourself. Recall your past achievements to remain positive and feel encouraged by them.

7. *Be organized:* Planning your preparation well in advance and sticking to a set time schedule will make you organized and ward off considerable stress. People with good organizing abilities always achieve higher results. Be rest assured that, if you manage your time effectively, you will most likely achieve your target.

8. *Physical exercises help:* Moderate physical exercises are a big help to check stress. Exercises also guarantee instant relaxation and make you feel fresh and positive.

9. *Avoid anti-anxiety medicines:* Anti-anxiety medicines could have some side effects which could disturb your preparation schedule just before the interview. It could even affect your mental alertness at a crucial time.

10. *Balance your diet:* Don't over-eat. Consume food that is rich in proteins and vitamins. These nutrients assist in keeping your brain alert and sharp. Make sure you eat a balanced diet. Fruit juices are considered good.

Remember, you are not expected to answer each and every question during the interview, but a logical approach to answer questions is of crucial importance. Always keep in mind, that tough situations do not last, but tough people last.

Have faith in God and yourself and everything will fall in place for you during the interview.

12

Services Selection Board (SSB) Interviews

Pattern of Testing in Services Selection Boards (SSBs)

For selection of officers in the Armed Forces candidates are subjected to fairly comprehensive testing in SSBs. This testing lasts for 5–6 days and candidates are assessed with the help of three techniques, namely:

1. Interview technique
2. Group testing technique
3. Tests of psychology

Interview technique involves a face to face conversation between the candidate and one interviewing officer for a period of about 20–30 minutes. Interview technique will be discussed in this chapter subsequently. Group testing involves assessing the candidates while they are part of a group comprising 8–10 candidates. This testing may last for 2–3 days in SSB. Candidates are given various practical situations on ground and their performance is observed as a team member and also a leader. Tests of psychology involve subjecting the candidates to a number of psychological tests such as WAT (Word Association Test), TAT (Thematic Apperception Test), SRT (Situation Reaction Test) and SD (Self Description), etc.

Assessing Criteria in SSBs

Based on the job requirement of defence officers, fifteen OLQs (Officer like Qualities) have been identified. To assess these OLQs, the three techniques mentioned above are applied on the candidates independently and on the final day, assessments of the three techniques are compared and a consensus reached with regard to selection or rejection of a candidate.

As mentioned earlier, assessment of personality traits of a candidate is quite comprehensive in SSBs unlike selection of candidates in MNCs or jobs in private sector or Government organizations, etc. Fifteen OLQs cover a wide spectrum of qualities of the candidate. These OLQs broadly pertain to planning and organizing abilities and practical intelligence of the candidates including his ability to express his ideas in an effective and concise manner. OLQs also cover social adjustment and ability to work as an active member of a team and behave in a responsible manner. OLQs encompass leadership qualities of a candidate including his ability to arrive at decisions correctly and quickly and have adequate self confidence. Finally, OLQs include a candidate's ability to cope with stressful situations in a cheerful manner and have sufficient determination, mental and physical courage and stamina.

Peculiar Aspects of Interviews in SSBs

Broadly speaking, interviews in SSBs are more probing in nature and the questions are asked in such a fashion that all fifteen OLQs emerge rather clearly. The candidates are encouraged to speak spontaneously and share their ideas with the Interviewing Officers in a frank and forth right manner. To achieve this objective and to create an atmosphere, which is free from stress, only one IO interviews the candidate. This is unlike most interviews, which are conducted in Private/Public sector or UPSC for high level jobs, and where a panel of experts grill the candidate. The SSB interviews do not confine to assessing mental ability of the candidate, but probe a number of personality aspects, which are quite relevant for effective functioning in the defence services.

Preparing for Interview in the SSB

Most guidelines enumerated in this book for candidates appearing in selection interviews are by and large relevant for SSB candidates as well. Therefore, SSB candidates must also read these guidelines. However, candidates must bear in mind that SSB interviews, besides assessing mental abilities, lay increased emphasis on probing behavioural aspects of the candidate. While preparing for SSB interview, candidates should get familiar with defence related matters such as various defence deals, acquisition of defence equipment and other such developments. Besides, they must be aware of essential information in respect of their village/town, state and India in general. Candidates are also expected to have basic information regarding general awareness, which a well informed citizen ought to have. As mentioned earlier, to collect requisite information and data, the candidate must read a national newspaper besides journals on current affairs to update their knowledge about various developments in the country and elsewhere. A list of Frequently Asked Questions (FAQs) is given in the end of this chapter for easy reference of candidates, who are going to face interviews in the SSBs.

As you might be aware, defence services lay specific emphasis on discipline, team work, physical/mental stamina and courage, besides other qualities of the candidate. Therefore, candidates must pay pointed attention to these aspects during their stay in the SSB.

Dress Code for SSB Interviews

SSB interviews are conducted in a formal setting though in an informal fashion to put the candidate at ease. Accordingly, a candidate is expected to dress up in a formal manner for the interview. Formal dress involves a light coloured shirt (full sleeves) and a dark coloured pant with leather shoes which have laces. Candidates should also put on a tie to make the dress appear formal. During winters, candidates may put on a coat or sweater, as required. Candidates must shave their beard and have a haircut, as these aspects are considered a part of discipline in the armed forces. Girl candidates should put on sober clothes and use minimum jewellery and only essential make-up. Wearing of casual clothes like jeans, T-shirts and sports shoes must essentially be avoided. Make sure, mobile phone is not carried during the interview, even if the phone is switched off.

Appearing before the Interviewing Officer

The candidates are made to sit at some distance from the IO, so that, the IO can clearly observe the body language of the candidate. The interview in the SSBs lasts for about 20–25 minutes in a cordial atmosphere where IO merely guides the direction of the conversation to ensure that candidate provides the relevant and sufficient data for assessment.

1. On being called to the IOs room, the candidate must seek permission before entering the room of the IO.
2. On entering of the room, the candidate must appropriately wish the IO, i.e., Good morning, Good afternoon or Good evening.
3. The IO may stretch his hand to shake hand with the candidate and if he does so, the candidate should smile and shake hand with the IO with a firm grip indicating confidence and warmth. The candidate should not take the initiative of shaking hand with the IO.
4. The candidate should occupy his chair after the IO offers his/her a seat. It would be appropriate if the candidate thanks the IO while occupying his/her seat.
5. While sitting in his/her seat the candidate should adopt an upright posture taking the help of the back of the chair and must not bend forward or backward.
6. While talking to IO, the candidate must look towards the IO and not else where.
7. Candidates should not attempt to manipulate his answers or tell lies to the IO and answer in a frank and forth right manner.

Pattern of Questions asked in a SSB Interview

As is well known, past behaviour pattern of a person usually guides his present and future behaviour pattern. Therefore, IO makes an attempt to comprehensively assess the past behaviour of the candidate, and based on this, IO will try and forecast a candidate's future behavioural pattern consequent to his/her selection and training in the armed forces. Towards this aim, the IO would generally ask certain broad based questions, which will be discussed in details in this chapter.

Significance of PIQ during SSB Interview

A large number of questions asked during the interview are primarily based on the information provided by the candidate in his/her PIQ. Information given in the PIQ includes socioeconomic and educational background, family details and the extent of participation in extra-curricular activities including games/sports, NCC, etc. PIQ also contains information on interests/hobbies pursued and position(s) of responsibility held by the candidate. Possession of above information equips the IO to frame a large number of questions. Therefore, the candidates should be fully prepared to answer all questions related to the information provided in the PIQ. Candidate should ensure that, answers given during the interview must match the information provided in the PIQ.

Introductory Questions to Establish Rapport

As soon as the candidate settles down in his chair, the IO normally establishes a good rapport with the candidate by asking him/her certain routine questions for which the candidate need not make much effort to answer. Answering these questions would make the candidate somewhat relaxed. These questions may relate to:

- Journey to the SSB
- Details regarding home-town or place of present stay
- Stay at the SSB
- Weather and adjustment with new climatic conditions
- Routine and evening schedule at the SSB

Broad-based Questions

Consequent to building a rapport with the candidate, the IO gradually switches over to ask a number of broad-based questions to assess OLQs of the candidate. Towards this aim, the IO may probe the following broad areas:

a. Questions based to collect details regarding education, training and extra-curricular activities of the candidate.

These questions may relate to:

- Performance of the candidate in various exams or training programs undergone
- Wide variation in performance or there are gaps in completing courses of instruction
- Change in subjects or stream
- Change in school/college
- Strong likes or dislikes for a subject, why?
- Problems of adjustments, if there is change in school/college
- Most/least favourite teacher and why?
- Advantages/disadvantages of being a boarder/Day scholar
- Reasons for not clearing SSB/Competitive exam in the past
- Participation in extra-curricular activities and any achievements
- Problems/difficulties faced in handling positions of responsibility in school/college like house captain/class monitor/school captain/class representative, etc.

- Questions based on examination pattern/system
- Efforts put into clear various exams. Were they adequate?

b. Questions aimed to assess social adjustment of the candidate with his/ her friends and teachers, etc.

These questions may relate to:

- How many close friends?
- How does the candidate spend time with his/her friends?
- Any problems with friends and teachers?
- If some person he/she does not like, how does the candidate react?
- If some teacher constantly troubles the candidate, his/her reaction?
- Does he/she keep in touch with friends on moving to another place?
- Was the candidate frequently punished by teachers? If yes, why?
- What all qualities does he/she admire in a friend/teacher?

c. Questions based to know the family background of the candidate and his cooperative/responsible attitude.

These questions may cover:

- Family details of father, mother, sisters/brothers and neighborhood friends?
- Extent of interaction with family members.
- His/her relations with brothers/sisters. Are there any problems?
- Sharing of facilities/resources in the family.
- Details of daily routine of the candidate.
- Comparison between father and mother or other family members.
- Responsibilities discharged in the family.
- Help extended to other family members?
- Does he/she prefer a joint/nuclear family. Why?

d. Questions aimed to know spare time hobbies, interests, participation in games/sports and achievements in these areas.

These questions may relate to:

- Essential knowledge of games and hobbies/interests pursued.
- Basic rules/specifications/terminology of games/hobbies.
- Famous personalities in the fields of hobbies/interests and well known players of the games played by the candidate.
- Awareness of latest developments in the areas of hobbies/games, etc.
- Knowledge of major tournaments, size of grounds and other details of various games, etc.
- Details of achievements, if any, in the field of hobbies and games.
- Critical analysis of achievements of Indian players vis-à-vis players of other countries, what do we lack?
- What all needs to be done to improve the standards of sports in India?

e. IO may pose one or two synthetic situations to assess the planning and organizing abilities and stress management of the candidate. These

situations may also give a pointer towards courage and determination of the candidates.

- The exercise helps to assess reactions of the candidate while facing a stressful situation on ground.
- Candidate must remain positive and logical and boldly face the situation.
- Attempt should be made to cover as many details as possible in the given circumstances.
- While facing such situations, body language of the candidate is of special significance.
- It is important 'what you are saying', but equally important is 'how you are saying' your answers.
- Synthetic situations posed may include organizing some sporting event such as hockey/football/cricket match or facing a situation of stress, like meeting with an accident or facing similar adverse circumstances.
- Attempts should be made to remain calm, composed and practical/focused. Must display a good presence of mind.

f. **Questions to know candidates' reading habits, followed by one or two questions on general awareness.**

These questions may relate to:

- What kind of books/magazines/newspaper does the candidate read?
- Does he/she watch TV programmes to update his awareness about current happenings?
- Candidate must brush up basic information about his home town/home, state and India as a whole. These should include population, location, industry, business, etc.
- Requisite information about India's neighbours and India's relations with her neighbours.
- Major current happenings – both national and international.
- Special emphasis should be given to defence-related news.
- Information related to India's development and infrastructure.
- Brushing up current affairs for the past 4–6 months should be considered adequate.

g. **Candidate may be asked to bring out his/her strengths and weaknesses to assess self awareness and what efforts are being made by the candidate to improve the weak areas of personality.**

- These questions relate to self-awareness of the candidate. Aim of such questions is to assess whether the candidate is aware of his weak areas and what steps she/he is taking or have taken to eliminate such weak areas.
- Candidate should highlight 3–4 good points (strengths) and one or 1–2 bad points (weaknesses).
- Efforts made by the candidate to get over these negative areas must also be brought out.

h. Questions to assess the motivational level of the candidate to join the armed force.

These questions relate to:

- Priority allotted by the candidate to a defence services job.
- Why does the candidate want to join armed forces?
- What all aspects of defence services does the candidate admire and why is it so?

i. Questions for candidates who are already employed.

Such questions may cover:

- Contents of present job.
- What does the candidate admire in his/her job and are there any dislikes?
- Why does he/she want a job change?
- Relations with seniors and juniors in the present job.
- Over all job conditions or working environment of the place of work.
- How does he/she compare his present job conditions with those of defence services?

j. Questions to assess a candidate's alternative plans, in case he/she is not selected in the armed forces.

- These questions are asked to assess a candidate's planning for his future life, incase he/she fails to join armed forces.
- It would be appropriate if the candidate tells the IO his alternative career plans. However, the candidate should tell the IO that he would try his best to join the defence services before taking any steps to join an alternative career.

Questions on the above broad areas are generally asked by most IOs in SSBs, and based on the answers provided by the candidates, the IO may ask a number of other probing questions to clarify or elaborate on certain aspects to assess Officer Like Qualities in a candidate.

Once the IO indicates that he has finished the interview, the candidate should thank the IO and leave.

Some FAQs on matters of Defence Services are appended below:

FAQs on Matters Concerning Defence Services

1. Tell us, all ranks of officer cadres of Army/Navy/Air Force.
2. Why do you find a career in defence services so attractive?
3. How do you compare the jobs in civil services or MNCs with defence services?
4. What is the role of DRDO?
5. Tell us, which are the transport and fighter aircrafts used by Indian Air Force?
6. After the Bombay terrorists attack, what all measures have been initiated by our government to increase security of our coastal areas?

7. Differentiate the roles of Indian Navy and Coast Guard.
8. Why do you prefer a particular Defence Service in comparison to other two services?
9. In case you are not able to become a Defence Services Officer, what are your alternative plans?
10. Who is the present Chief of Army/Navy/Air Force?
11. How many Field Marshals did the Indian Army have? Name them.
12. Name the missiles presently used by the Indian Army? What do you know about Brahmos missiles?
13. Indian Air Force has recently acquired a trainer aircraft. Why was this aircraft required by the IAF?
14. How do you compare the Indian Army/IAF with Pakistan/Chinese Army/ Air Force?
15. How many commands are there in the Indian Air Force/Army/Navy?
16. Indian Navy flies which all types of aircraft?
17. There are how many commands in the Indian Navy and where are they located?
18. Which country has supplied 'Aerostat' Radar systems to the Indian Air Force?
19. What do you think are the major advantages and disadvantages of working in the defence services?
20. What is the equivalent rank of a Col in the Navy? etc.
21. What are AWACS and what is their role?

Unit II

Group Discussions

Part I

Concept of a Group Discussion and How to Effectively Participate in a Group Discussion

Introduction to
Small Group Interactions

Need for Group Interactions

1. In our social life or as a member of a modern organization, we spend a considerable amount of our time in groups. We must, therefore, communicate effectively as a member of a group, which could either be a small or large group. A group assumes significance, since one person alone does not possess the requisite knowledge, skill or talent to achieve a complex task. However, through working together in a group, one can achieve far higher goals than an individual who is functioning all by himself. This is so because we need material as well as intellectual inputs from others to attain difficult targets. A group can markedly help us to ensure that our chances of success are improved significantly. The fact remains that small groups are the basic building blocks of a modern society and to positively contribute in the group functioning, one must interact and communicate meaningfully within the group.

2. Interestingly, a recent study in the United States has brought out that most executives spend about half their working time in business meetings. These business meetings are generally called at a very short notice, giving little opportunity or time to the executives to make preparations for these interactions. During such type of interactions, a number of personality traits assume significance. These include the skill of an individual to discuss an issue combined with having an open mind to resolve an issue. During such discussions, while on one hand, one may gain something, on the other, one may also have to give up something for the sake of others. As a good team member, one must have explicit faith in the spirit of give and take, keeping the overall benefit of the organization in view.

3. Academic achievements notwithstanding, in the recent past, quality of an individual to become an effective team member has been attached increased importance. In a recent survey of 750 leading American Companies, 71.4 percent of respondents mentioned "ability to work in teams" as an essential skill for MBA graduates, more important than knowledge of quantitative and statistical techniques. Knowledge without adequate team spirit and responsibility could easily become a liability for any organization.

Unit II Group Discussions

Defining a Group Discussion

1. By definition, a discussion implies the process of examining or considering something in detail, generally in a conversation. It may also connote a kind of debate or an argument about a contentious issue. The primary aim of a discussion is to arrive at some point of agreement or a valid decision, and its purpose is to obtain various shades of opinions and ideas on the subject or topic, which is under consideration. In this regard, it is important to note that the process of discussion is as significant as the final decision arrived at. It has to be ensured that in an effective discussion, many different aspects of a subject are brought out fairly in detail so that the process of deciding becomes somewhat simpler. In an office scenario, the members of a group while discussing a subject must necessarily complement each other and avoid becoming competitive. On the other hand, in a test situation, candidates taking part in a group discussion, in their zeal to score over others, do become more competitive rather than remaining complementary to each other. It, therefore, stands to reason that an exchange of opinions during a discussion should generate more light than heat to make sure that rationality and logical thinking are never lost sight of. In case, due to whatever reason, more heat does get generated, the very purpose of holding a discussion stands defeated and the whole effort becomes a futile exercise.

2. When a group of candidates is subjected to a group discussion, its focus immediately shifts to assessing various attitudes of participating candidates. Today, most organizations have adopted the group discussion methodology as a tool, which is an essential part of their process of selection. This approach is quite logical since job contents of a modern professional demand that not only should he/she possess the ability to express his/her ideas in a convincing and logical manner, but also provide a fair opportunity to others to convey their thoughts in a congenial atmosphere. Today, ability of an executive to convince others, and also get convinced by others, has emerged as a pivotal personality trait, which has become almost indispensable for a team leader. This significant quality also goes a long way in keeping a group of professionals together as a team and something that all members of a group really look up to in their leader. Recent researches show that this quality also helps a manager to lead from the front, especially in stressful situations.

3. Having explained the necessity to acquire the skill to discuss problems or situations in a group, by conducting a group discussion, one creates a real situation where group members are given an opportunity to display these skills in a given time frame. The time constraint is deliberately introduced to impel group members to give out their best performance in the shortest time possible. It is evident that a more skilled person can substantially influence other persons' decision-making process, make better options available, and eventually help reach a more sound solution of a problem. How to acquire such specialized skills will be discussed sufficiently in detail in this book in subsequent pages.

Why are Group Discussions Conducted?

By exposing a certain number of candidates to a group discussion situation, selectors are able to observe a number of personality traits or attitudes of the participants. Of course, selectors do require a lot of experience and specialized training to conduct this task efficiently. Conducting a group discussion makes a lot of sense in view of the following reasons:

a. A group discussion reveals the real intellectual capability and general awareness of the participants, as group members are allowed a very limited time to prepare the subject under discussion.

b. It clearly brings out the communication skills of the candidates in the language used in the discussion.

c. Members clearly display their logical reasoning as well as ability to realign their thoughts with those of others.

d. Candidates are given an opportunity to adjust themselves in the presence of others and assess themselves in relation to others.

e. The ability of a person to discard irrelevant ideas and adopt new ideas and concepts is easily revealed.

f. Team spirit displayed by the group members emerges rather clearly. Also, cooperative attitude of the individual becomes apparent.

g. Candidates' obligation and sense of responsibility towards a cause or society get exposed.

h. Self-confidence of the individual is comprehensively tested in a group discussion by observing his persistence in making known and holding on to his arguments.

i. Knack of a candidate to initiate and sustain a discussion becomes visible.

j. Ability to reach a logical decision, consequent to listening to various arguments in favour and against the topic, can be observed.

k. Often some group members emerge as leaders by virtue of displaying certain leadership qualities. Leadership qualities are a combination of traits such as tact, self-confidence, empathy for others, higher intellectual level and initiative, etc.

l. Display of courage and levels of mental and physical stamina also emerge rather clearly.

Consequences of a Group Interaction

Being an independent personality, each member of a group has his/her own perceptions, emotions and a set pattern of behaviour. During a group discussion, these three aspects are subjected to sustained interaction with perceptions, emotions and behaviour of other members of the group. This situation may lead to constructive or negative repercussions, in certain situations, or a mixture of both.

Part I Concepts

On the positive side, the following could be highlighted:

a. ***Increased motivation of members***: Discussing a topic in the presence of others increases the motivation levels of members substantially. Spirit of competition among members gives further impetus to this aspect.

b. ***Enhanced understanding of issues***: A group discussion leads to more varied understanding of the subject from different angles. Members present their own point of view and perspectives of the problem, which gives each member a chance to get exposed to a number of new ideas. This obviously leads to better understanding of the subject by all the participants in a group discussion.

c. ***Better understanding among members***: Since group discussions are generally conducted as a tool for screening or selecting candidates, prior to this exposure, the participants do not know each other. Exchanging ideas on a topic helps to build improved understanding among the participants. Agreements or disagreements apart, members of a group do get to know each other better by taking part in a group discussion.

d. ***Reaching better decisions***: While discussing a topic, one often discovers mistakes in reasoning, fallacy of an argument and how one ignores a valid point of view or an implication. A group discussion effectively deals with all such obstacles. Such constructive measures definitely help in reaching a more logical and reasonable solution of a problem.

Negative consequences of a group discussion also need a mention, as this awareness helps in preparing ourselves to prevent such consequences to the extent feasible.

a. ***Creation of ill feelings among candidates***: We all love a situation where everyone agrees with what we say. Disagreements may sometimes lead to bad feelings and bitter experiences. Many a times, discussions do become acrimonious and even insulting. This may happen when group members start focusing on persons, rather than on issues.

b. ***Splitting of a group***: Some candidates bring the discussion to a point where arguments and counter arguments take the shape of personal attacks. This negative situation, if allowed to prolong, may even tear the group into splinter groups.

Classification of GDs

It has been observed that usually group discussions are classified, into three broad categories by the selectors. This classification is based on the type of participation or roles played by the members of the group during a group discussion. These three categories are:

1. Leaderless group discussions
2. Leader nominated group discussions
3. Role play type group discussions

1. **Leaderless group discussions:** In this classification of GD, members start on equal position and are not assigned any specific role by the moderator. By virtue of their participation and display of leadership qualities during the discussion itself, group member or group members become natural leader(s) of the group. Selectors thus get adequate opportunity to observe certain abilities and personality traits of the candidate during the course of the discussions. This type of group discussions are conducted most commonly by the selectors these days. We will be mainly focussing on this classification of GDs in this book.

2. **Leader nominated group discussions:** Unlike leaderless type of GDs, in this category one group member is asked to assume the position of a leader of the group or become the Chairperson of the group. Either the moderator appoints the leader or the group members are asked to appoint their leader. In this way, moderator sets an opportunity to observe the ability of group members as a leader as well as member of the team. However, this category of GDs are not usually conducted, and therefore not discussed in this book.

3. **Role play type group discussions:** During a role play type of group discussion, each member of the group is assigned a specific roles in order to resolve a problem or tackle a given situation. Usually, roles allotted to various members may need varying skills or abilities. This type of GDs reveal as to how a group member can swiftly adapt himself to a new situation to eventually resolve a problem. Since use of this category of GDs is not quite common for selection purposes, we have also not discussed this category of GDs in this book.

Types of Topics

As explained earlier, leaderless GDs are normally conducted by selectors as a part of selection process for entry level jobs or admissions to a course of study, etc. These GDs are structured and a wide variety of topics are given to the candidates for discussion. These topics are generally divided into three types. These are:

1. Reality – based topics
2. Imaginary or abstract topics
3. Case study group discussions

1. *Reality–based topics*: This type of topics are most commonly used for selection purposes. These are usually topics on current or contemporary issues. Most of these topics are somewhat controversial and members of a group can present a variety of views on the subject. These are topical issues and need preparation by the candidates. The knowledge base of the candidates is clearly visible when they discuss this type of topics. These topics are most commonly discussed during selection GDs, and, therefore, they are discussed sufficiently in detail in this book.

2. *Imaginary or abstract group discussion topics*: Discussion on this type of topics is left to the imagination of the candidate or left open to interpretation. Such topics involve lateral thinking and unconventional perspectives. Here, the most difficult task of the candidate is to understand the topic and interpret it. If given this kind of topic, one should focus on what the topic could mean. Candidates may mean different things to the topic, but the main task of the candidate is to justify his interpretation and the group should also agree with the justification and logic. It is seen that no body wants to initiate a discussion on such topics and there is silence intermittently. Under these circumstances, it is significant to give direction to the discussion by a new and creative interpretation. These topics do not have a certain format or structure. Some examples of such topics are, Zero; A is to Z, what Z is to A; Here, there and everywhere; The world is a stage; Does God exist?, etc.

3. *Case study group discussion topics*: Here, a corporate situation or person/ organization-based situation is presented and group members have to arrive at the best solution by mutual discussion. Some business institutes, including IIM Ahmedabad conduct GDs with this type of topics given to the candidates. Usually a brief situation, covered in less than a page is given and the group is required to arrive at a decision as asked for in the situation. Advantage of this type of topic is the fact that all members of the group have an equal input to resolve the issue and nobody possesses any advantage over others in terms of information about the topic. The participants display their ability to process the information, analyse a problem and group skills are visible rather clearly. Participants need to reach a consenus and solve problems, unlike other types of GDs.

To effectively participate in such GDs, the participants should first analyse the situation critically and look at various alternatives quickly. Thereafter, logic and practical approach should guide the candidate to arrive at the most appropriate solution of the problem. In other words, first, find the cause of the problem. Then, find alternative solutions by giving various choices. Thirdly, weigh the pros and cons of the alternatives. Giving a suggestion is not very difficult, but understanding the solution is significant. Finally, participants should give both long and short term solutions after brain-stroming with the group.

As brought out earlier in this Chapter, we will be mainly discussing in detail GD topics which are based on Reality and most commonly used in selection group discussions.

Some Significant Aspects of a Group Discussion

1. **Importance of group discussion as a selection tool:** Group discussions are now being used as a selection tool for screening as well as selecting candidates for pursuing higher education and performing a variety of jobs. Like selection interviews, the exercise of group discussion primarily aims at assessing personality aspects of a candidate. During a group discussion, a candidate's logical ability, behavioural skills, communication skills, innovativeness, knowledge-base and leadership attributes emerge quite clearly.

2. A group discussion takes place among the candidates themselves. More often than not, candidates taking part in a group discussion have similar educational qualifications and age, etc. It is also preferred that candidates with similar backgrounds are clubbed in one group, so that there is not much dissimilarity among the members of one group in terms of their capabilities and potential. This ensures that a group remains a homogeneous entity. Typically, a group has 8–10 candidates. However, some groups have accommodated 12–14 candidates also. This number is considered just about adequate from the examiner's point of view, as he/she is able to observe each candidate individually as well as, the entire group as a whole. To facilitate this facet, candidates are normally made to sit in a semi-circle, with the examiner at a place from where he/she can observe all candidates conveniently. While discussing the details of a group discussion, the following significant aspects deserve our attention.

3. **Informal exchange of ideas**: Since group discussions are being widely utilized as an exercise to provide significant inputs for personality evaluation, the examiner deliberately gives a free hand to candidates to exchange their ideas. To achieve this purpose, the examiner briefs the candidates to emphasize the fact that his/her role in the whole exercise would be minimal–at best only that of a facilitator and the candidates would themselves have to decide as to who would initiate the discussion and who would come forward to conclude the interaction. As the discussion is normally conducted in an informal manner, candidates are encouraged to speak in any order and no time limit is set for each candidate to speak at one time. Also, a candidate is at liberty to speak as many times as may be feasible for him/her during the period of discussion. Time duration

normally prescribed for the entire interaction is approximately 15–25 minutes.

4. It would be observed that restrictions as applicable in a formal debate or speech are not imposed in a group discussion. Unlike a formal debate, a candidate may speak for or against the topic or may even decide to remain silent. A candidate is also at a liberty to present both advantages and disadvantages or merits and demerits of a situation. However, one does expect a candidate to firm up his/her ideas and speak on a certain line of thought and not get totally swayed by ideas presented by others. To ensure that the atmosphere of a group discussion remains informal, candidates are not expected to stand up and should remain seated while presenting their ideas.

5. *Concept of a leaderless group*: Formation of an informal group is also planned as a leaderless entity. As explained earlier, the examiner or the moderator of a group discussion, usually withdraws to the background and may not be even visible to all the candidates. He/she certainly does not act as the leader of the group nor does he/she designate any candidate as the leader. Hence, the group when it is formed, has no designated leader of its own. This situation is purposely designed to develop as such, since the group is expected to identify its own leader. It is quite obvious that overall superior performance of a candidate would project him/her as the leader of the group. Secondly, to achieve any objective or task, a leader is essentially needed to guide the members of a group. So, a member who possesses certain leadership personality traits would automatically emerge as the leader of the group. The situation makes the task of the examiner rather simple, as the member, who has the requisite potential to become a leader, would get himself/herself identified rather easily.

6. The process of this identification could be explained without much difficulty. With the intention of scoring over other members of the group, each member tries his best to grab the opportunity to speak. However, even while everybody is speaking, the group listens to the person who is making a vital point or revealing something new about the topic for everyone's benefit. In this regard, the behavioural pattern of the candidate also becomes relevant. If a member is liked or preferred by the group and he/she also speaks effectively, the possibility of him/her becoming the leader is fairly high. Another development observed during group discussions is the natural formation of sub-groups within a group. These sub-groups may have their own leaders and one sub-group may ascribe to one school of thought, while the other sub-group may hold a view that is diametrically opposite to the view of the other sub-group. The fact remains that formation of such sub-groups also helps in identifying leadership qualities of the candidates. Due to this reason, a number of institutes/organizations conduct more than one group discussion to screen

candidates in stages. Candidates thus screened are put to further and more exhaustive testing before final selection.

7. *Choice of topic*: The language used for most discussions, during screening tests or admission tests or for selections for various government and private jobs including defence services etc., is English. Usually, to prepare the stage for a discussion, the examiner offers the candidates a set of two or three topics to choose from. Candidates are given the option to select one topic out of these topics for discussion. Thereafter, candidates discuss among themselves to collectively reach a decision about the topic for group discussion. It may so happen that the set of topics offered have some subjects that require a higher level of intellectual ability or general awareness for interpretation and discussion. Therefore, in the process of reaching a decision, each member of the group would display his/her preference based on his/her own level of intellectual ability or awareness. Obviously, a candidate with higher capabilities may go for a more difficult topic, while a candidate having average capabilities may like to discuss an easy topic. The examiner carefully watches the preferences of all candidates in this regard, and may keep this input at the back of his/her mind while finally assessing a candidate towards the end of the exercise.

8. *Analysing the topic*: Once a topic has been chosen by the group, the candidate must try to carefully define the topic in his/her mind and then analyse various components of the topic. If the topic has several components, each component should be analysed separately to recapitulate sufficient material on all aspects of the topic. It would be appreciated that defining the topic would certainly help its understanding substantially. Since emphasis in a group discussion is primarily on the analytical approach of the candidate, this exercise assumes increased importance. For example, if the topic is "Democracy in India has failed," the candidate should analyse important terms in the topic. Analysing the topic would entail defining as to what is democracy. What all it takes to ensure that a democracy runs smoothly? What are the factors that favour its efficient functioning and what are the factors that are considered an impediment? Once you have considered these aspects sufficiently in detail, you should think about the next term, i.e., what is the ground situation in India for running of democracy? Where do we stand in this regard? It would involve various factors such as conduct of elections in India. What kind of candidates take part in elections? Are the elections conducted in a fair and free manner, etc.? Further, what all it takes to mould public opinion in India? What are the factors that affect pattern of voting? You should also consider influences such as religion, language, caste and other regional biases. Then, how critical factors such as illiteracy, poverty and unemployment affect our elections? Thereafter, you may think about the factors that have made democracy function in an efficient manner in

Part I Concepts

countries like USA, etc. In this regard, a comparison between conditions prevailing in India and certain other countries would be quite appropriate at this juncture. You may also like to reflect on various aspects pertaining to democracy that have undergone some changes in India during the past 60+ years, since India attained her freedom.

By the above example, an attempt has been made to show as to how analysis of the topic helps in gathering sufficient material on the topic. If the candidate deliberates upon various terms of the topic in such a manner, it is expected that he/she will be able to accumulate enough talking points to effectively participate in a group discussion. It is quite apparent that this approach to analyse the topic would provide an opportunity to the candidate to tackle the problem from different angles. Thus, you will have enough points on which you can positively speak on. So relax!

9. ***Grabbing the opportunity to give the topic a format:*** Consequent to analyzing the topic as discussed above, if you are adequately confident of yourself, it would be advisable to initiate the discussion. While doing so, it is recommended that one should give the topic a format, i.e., showing the path on which the discussion should proceed. This means defining the contours of the topic; what the discussion should aim at; examining various implications, and finally, reaching a willing consensus on the decision. Doing so helps in giving a much needed direction to the discussion, displays a systematic approach and, of course, saves a lot of time and energy, which would have been wasted on discussing not-so-relevant aspects of the topic. Remember, the person who initiates the discussion does get the individual attention of the examiners. In case you initiate well, you definitely score over others, but if you do not have sufficient material in your kitty, it could, rather work against you as well. So, be doubly sure and act accordingly. If you fail to initiate, do not despair, as there is ample time still. Similarly, if you also lose the opportunity to give the topic a format, still you have enough time with you to prove your mettle. So, look ahead and plan your interjection in a logical manner and grab the opportunity to speak at the earliest.

10. ***Dealing with an aggressive candidate:*** It is accepted that group discussion is a stressful situation and matters tend to become worse due to the imposed time crunch. Under such conditions, some participants show aggression to have their way. Most well-meaning candidates find-dealing with such participants rather difficult and feel even somewhat helpless. One would realize that ignoring such people does not really help and thus these aggressive candidates tend to eat away a large chunk of time. Similarly, it is also not correct to show aggression, as this approach may make things worse and vitiate an atmosphere of a healthy discussion. Under such circumstances, it has been experienced that diverting attention of the group to another person or another aspect of the discussion usually works. Since,

the focus shifts to a new situation, the aggressive person normally gets sorted out in this fashion.

11. ***Landing up in a difficult situation***: In case you happen to face a situation, when, despite your best efforts, you do not have anything new with you to effectively participate in the discussion, you just cannot keep quiet and only watch others. On such occasions, you can still make a positive contribution by adding a few more facts or some data to the ongoing argument. By doing so, you would make some value addition to the argument and that will go in your favour. However, meanwhile keep applying your mind to somehow hit upon an original idea which you could then add. In case you land up in an unfortunate situation when you are not able to speak at all, in that case, you should start by supporting the participant who seems or is behaving like a leader thus far.

12. ***Do not open your cards in the beginning***: It has been seen that some candidates, without due consideration, tend to take a stand in the beginning of the discussion, which they later find difficult to defend. On the other hand, in case the candidate changes his stance during the course of discussion, evaluators may conclude that he/she is not able to make up his/her mind and this may go against his/her interest. In view of this, it is recommended that candidates must put up his/her justification first and towards the end of the discussion, come out with their considered stance on the issue. This will certainly obviate considerable embarrassment for the candidate. Moreover, this approach would broadly indicate that the candidate has a logical way of reaching a decision and he/she does not decide before considering all aspects of the problem. Yet another difficulty that arises when the candidate declares his/her decision prematurely is the fact that all those candidates who may not agree with the candidate, would start opposing to whatever he/she may put across. This would, obviously, make the going tough for the candidate. Therefore, do not make the mistake of opening all your cards in the very beginning of the discussion.

13. ***Forming an opinion about the topic***: In a number of group discussions, members are tested for their team skills and ability to arrive at a consensus after the completion of the discussion. In such situations, candidates may be asked to discuss a topic and subsequently also put forth the collective opinion and thoughts of the group on the subject after a consensus is reached. This task requires maturity on part of all the members, as diverse and conflicting opinions need to be blended into a cohesive whole. Here, mutual respect and spirit of cooperation plays an important role in achieving the desired result. Members must possess the spirit of give and take and willingly cooperate to make the task of reaching a consensus rather easy.

Part I Concepts

Criteria of Assessment in a Group Discussion

As we have discussed earlier, "Group Discussion" is now being increasingly utilized as a selection tool to assess the personality characteristics of a candidate and assess his /her suitability for the job in hand. Towards this aim, candidates are left to themselves to initiate as well as conclude a discussion on a controversial topic. The process and modalities of conducting a group discussion are deliberately planned in such a fashion that candidates participating in a discussion themselves display a number of personality traits during the course of this interaction. In this regard, the selectors evaluate candidates on certain parameters or against a set of predefined assessing criteria. Some general assessing criteria are listed below and it is felt that their awareness will substantially assist candidates in their preparation for participating in a group discussion.

a. ***Depth of knowledge/awareness***: Academic knowledge of the candidate about the subject being discussed in terms of range and depth gets assessed. Additionally, candidates' general awareness and its updation get fully exposed.

b. ***Ability to express ideas***: The ability of the aspirant to communicate his/her thoughts fluently and put across his/her arguments in a rational, planned and systematic manner gets evaluated.

c. ***Flexibility***: The fact whether a candidate is accommodative to ideas expressed by others or remains rigid about what he/she thinks, can be easily judged by the examiner. It is better to be assertive, but not rigid in your approach.

d. ***Adjustment with new people and new ideas***: Since one gets exposed to unfamiliar persons in a group discussion situation, time consumed in adjusting and acclimatizing oneself to an alien and new situation becomes evident. Similarly, a person's adaptability and receptivity to new ideas also comes to light in a very short span of time.

e. ***Display of self-confidence***: Ability of a person to have faith in oneself and face a group of people while expressing one's opinions, often in the face of disagreement, comes to the fore. A shy and under-confident person will not be in a position to display this quality in this strenuous situation.

f. ***Courage of conviction***: Capability to defend one's own position and holding on to one's convictions becomes clearly visible in a group discussion.

g. *Leadership attributes*: The fact that a candidate is able to generate a following and leave a mark of his/her presence on the group can be easily discernible. The skill of being able to convince other members about one's convictions and motivating them in this regard also becomes evident.

h. *Reactions under stressful situations*: Owing to the very purpose of testing participants' reactions under stressful situations, the element of time constraint has been introduced in a group discussion. A group discussion pressurizes the participants to give their best within a predetermined time frame. Of course, the level of stress experienced under the circumstances would differ from one person to the other. Under these conditions, the ability of an individual to remain cheerful and also keep other members in good humour would clearly indicate the stress management capability of the participant.

i. *Willingness to learn*: The only constant theory in the world is change. Situations around us and business scenario keeps changing on a regular basis mainly due to availability of new and better products and matching demands. One needs to constantly update his awarness about happenings around, and also update his knowledge about new technological developments. Selectors keenly look for this quality in candidates.

j. *Eye for detail*: A good manager must be a good organiser and should also be a meticulous person. He/she must not miss out minor details of any job or project to ensure an effective output. Assessors look for this quality in a candidate during a group discussion by watching his tendency to care for minor details of a situation.

k. *Logical thinking*: This includes correct understanding of the topic and balanced point of view, avoiding jumping to conclusion. Logical person will take an objective view of both sides of the arguments before arriving at a conclusion. Also, a logical person would carefully avoid an emotional way of looking at things and will give adequate justifications for his stand.

Part I Concepts

Basic Elements of Group Discussions

If one intends to perform fairly well in a group discussion, it is significant to understand as to what are the basic elements of a group discussion. Awareness of these rudiments would provide a definite edge to the participants and at the same time help in preparing for a group discussion. Some of these essential elements are enumerated below:

a. *Initiating a discussion*: Most candidates are under the impression that initiating a discussion is crucial in putting up a good performance and thereby emerging a winner. However, the answer to this question is neither an emphatic yes nor no, and it is recommended that one should adopt a careful approach in this regard. In case, the candidate is familiar with the topic under discussion, it would be positively worthwhile to initiate the interaction and display one's confidence and knowledge of the subject. Introducing the topic would then be comparatively easy.

> If familiar with the topic, do initiate the discussion, otherwise, listen to others and then speak at the earliest.

But, if the candidate is not familiar with the topic, then lack of knowledge would pose a serious impediment in initiating the discussion and the thoughtless move of trying to set off the discussion may even go against the candidate. Infact, it would be worthwhile to listen to a few others before jumping into the fray. In such cases, speaking after two or three candidates would be a safe bet and is strongly recommended. This wait would provide a good opportunity to the candidate to collect some more information about the topic and organize one's own ideas on the issue.

Generally, the candidate who initiates the discussion is expected to define the topic in detail and subsequently put across his/her own views. Candidates would do well to remember that the key to success is their knowledge and confidence and not necessarily the order of speaking in a group discussion.

b. *Possessing requisite knowledge*: As explained earlier, a group discussion chiefly aims at assessing various personality qualities of the candidates. In this regard, a candidate's depth of knowledge of the topic is an essential element that helps him/her put up a spirited performance in this test. Candidates are

> Do make positive efforts to acquire knowledge about a wide variety of topics. Quality counts, not quantity.

understandably expected to possess adequate knowledge on a wide variety of subjects of general interest. Possessing requisite knowledge, preferably with essential data and statistics, would provide them opportunities to be capitalized. Unfortunately, some candidates, who are blessed with the gift of the gab, feel that by virtue of their fluency in the language, they can easily cross the hurdle of clearing the test of group discussion. This, if truth be told, is a myth that needs to be treated as such. It needs to be emphasized that in the absence of fundamental knowledge of the subject, one cannot communicate one's ideas and have the required impact on others. Additionally, lack of knowledge would also hamper the display of self confidence of the candidate. Thus, candidates must make concerted efforts to read exhaustively and remain well-informed to equip themselves for participating in a group discussion. Remember, by merely speaking more you may not be able to impress the evaluators. What really counts is quality and not quantity. Your knowledge base counts here immensely.

c. ***Communicating effectively***: A large number of candidates do possess the required knowledge on the subject under discussion, but somehow fall short of the crucial ability to convey their thoughts to others in a systematic, logical and convincing manner. Want of this ability seriously hampers the impact they could otherwise make on the group. This ability pertains to arranging all relevant and significant information in an organized and logically structured manner, so as to make a desirable impression on others. These skills are largely acquired consequent to extensive training and effort and also contribute positively towards display of leadership qualities in the candidates.

> Good communication skills are certainly required to make the right impression.

d. ***Role of body language***: Gestures mirror one's state of mind. In a group interaction, body language must send the right signals to have the desired effect of what one conveys verbally. The study of body movements, which is called 'Kinesics', asserts that 40–50% of information on character, impact and credibility of a person is conveyed via body language. Body language signals include one's facial expressions, movements and gestures, movement of eyes, sitting posture and voice modulation, etc. These signals make a far greater impact on others than spoken words of the candidate. Body language signals aid considerably in establishing and maintaining a congenial atmosphere throughout the discussion. To illustrate, even if you disagree with someone, a soft smile will go a long way to guarantee that friendly atmosphere is not disturbed. Similarly, a slight lean forward indicates that you are keen for the discussion, whereas eye contact with the person who is talking will show that you have requisite interest in the discussion. Your alert body posture, appropriate facial expression and nodding of head would also give out appropriate body signals, which contribute positively towards

> Adopt correct Body language to make the lasting impact.

Part I Concepts

a healthy group discussion. Further, eyes are the most expressive part of our body and a person expresses various sentiments through his/her eyes and eyebrows. Lastly, a candidate expresses himself/herself by suitable voice modulation. Subtle changes in pitch, volume and rhythm also indicate how one feels about something. The above details clearly indicate the significance of adopting appropriate body language during a group discussion and would noticeably help carry out the group interaction in the right manner. Details in this regard have been discussed in the chapter on 'Impact of Non-verbal Communication in Group Discussions'.

e. *Maturity and mutual respect*: As pointed out earlier, the very purpose of group discussion is to generate more light than heat. It is, for that reason, important to build and keep up an atmosphere of cooperation throughout this interaction. Candidates are expected

> If you respect others, they will respect you, accommodating others, shows your leadership skills.

to demonstrate maturity by way of showing mutual respect for others and remaining reasonable and fair to views of the other candidates. One may even agree to politely disagree with a point of view and avoid creating any bad blood among participants. You may contradict others in the group, but make sure that you remain polite. For example, you may say, "I have an alternate point", instead of saying. "I disagree or I do not agree". In this regard, being reasonable with others would ensure that a conflict situation is most certainly evaded. It should be kept in mind that caring for others and acknowledging their standpoints would eventually win you their praise and respect. Encouraging others to talk while accommodating their perspectives would make you a favourite, and that would help you surfacing as the leader of the group.

f. *Making an impact*: A candidate should not only possess knowledge on a subject, but also utilize this advantage to make a lasting impact on others. There is a general belief that if you talk more, you create a positive impression. This may not

> Speak briefly, but convincingly to influence others.

be so, as even if you speak for a lesser time, but present new and valid ideas, your interaction would create the right kind of impact. Thus, even a brief presentation of ideas would be valuable and become convincing, if something substantial is put across. However, one must present one's ideas in an informal manner and should not make a group discussion an occasion to deliver a speech or a formal address. You must speak 4–6 times during a GD which lasts for about 15–20 minutes. In case, you find that others do not allow you to speak and often interrupt you, tell them politely, but a bit firmly, that you should also get a chance to present your ideas.

g. *Technique of interruption*: In a group discussion scenario, due to the time crunch, all participants want to, by some means, grab the opportunity to speak. This urge induces them to interrupt when others are voicing their

> Interrupt tactfully and at the right time to ensure that others are not annoyed.

views. When interruption does become unavoidable, one should wait for the right moment, i.e., till the person who is speaking, has "completed the sentence or has paused". When you interrupt some one, make sure that, he/she has made most of his arguments/points. In this situation, that person may not out-rightly object to your interjection. Otherwise, your interruption may even become counter productive. However, at the same time, waiting for too long is also not advisable, as you may thus lose the opportunity altogether. So, be quick and tactful before you interrupt.

Yet another thing which is important while you interrupt is that, if you add "I tend to agree with you, but...", in all probability, he/she might allow you to speak. While, on the contrary, if you start after interruption by saying that you did not agree with him/her, the person would mostly interrupt you back. Thus, making your job that much more difficult. In addition, one should remember that interrupting somebody prematurely is considered to be bad manners and should be avoided, as far as possible. All participants should try and speak as briefly as possible, so as to allow others also to have their say.

h. ***Reaching a consensus***: All group members should make certain that all members get a chance, at least once, to put forward their views. Subsequent chance-taking would depend upon each member's initiative and the quantum of knowledge one possesses about the subject. Once all members have got their rightful opportunity and the prescribed time is about to get over, effort should be made by all group members to reach a consensus on the issue. Customarily, the moderator or the examiner would himself/herself issue instructions in this regard. If a candidate is fairly confident about himself/herself, he/she should take the initiative and step forward to persuade others to find a consensus. While reaching a consensus, members should jointly deliberate on the core issue in trying to find a solution to the problem and consciously avoid getting caught up in the trivial and inconsequential aspects of the issue. Some candidates may suggest taking a vote to reach a consensus. Such action is not recommended as seeking a vote tantamounts to merely counting numbers and lacks the desired approach of logical reasoning and analysis. Effort should be made to reach a willing consensus consequent to a healthy discussion, where rationality should be the driving force, and short cuts like voting, must take a back seat.

> Be confident and go ahead to reach a willing consensus. Rationality must be the driving force.

Part I Concepts

Essential Preparation Required for a Group Discussion

Preparation is the key to success. One should always bear in mind the old adage, which ascribes, "If you fail to prepare, be prepared to fail". Group Discussion is used as a mirror to reflect the educational, cultural and psychological background of the candidate. As past background of the candidate cannot be changed overnight, a well planned strategy of preparation can help the candidate perform better in a GD. A candidate is recommended to focus his/her attention on the following aspects to get sufficiently equipped to face a group discussion situation. In this regard, a candidate must cultivate reading habits which should include going through various magazines and a national newspaper in detail. This would undoubtedly provide the basic grounding to the candidate on an assortment of current issues.

a. *Acquiring relevant information:* These days, to a candidate's delight, there is a profusion of easily-accessible information in the market and elsewhere via internet, which can be picked-up for use by a candidate. Reading a regional or local newspaper does not provide satisfactory coverage and desired exposure that a candidate requires to discuss a wide spectrum of topics in a group discussion. Reading a national newspaper, therefore, becomes essential. This information needs to be supplemented by regularly reading a number of magazines such as Frontline, Yojana, Outlook, India Today, etc. and a number of business related magazines that are available in the

> Must read one national newspaper and magazines to acquire needed information. Knowledge is the key to success in a GD.

market. One financial newspaper and one economic survey should also be referred to as they provide handy data and information that is considered necessary to update studies on economic aspects. Yet another way of keeping abreast of present-day developments is watching TV News Channels and analytical TV programmes, wherein, current affairs are discussed by eminent personalities. To sum up, the candidate should read and collect relevant knowledge on matters of politics, economy, social science, technological developments, cultural activities, sports, etc. to ensure his superior performance in a group discussion. Candidates should constantly train their minds to analyse topics on a wide variety of subjects, including current affairs. It must be clarified that being aware of these issues is not good enough, one must have thorough knowledge of these issues to form an opinion and argue about them.

Sometimes, candidates are given a topic which does not require much of a preparation to participate, e.g., topic such as 'Joint family system has failed in India' etc. On the other hand, some topics can't be discussed unless adequate preparation has been made, e.g., 'Will India and China become global giants'. Therefore, acquiring information on a wide variety of topics is considered extremely essential.

b. ***Creating a data bank of important information:*** In case you are seeking an entry level job or admission to a B-School, you must get into the habit of looking at any topic from business perspective. Start reading business news regularly, and join on-line groups of people preparing for GDs and interviews.

> Must read important news of the past one year and prepare short notes for handy recall just before the GD.

In addition, you must keep abreast of major business related developments, especially from the past one year. For example, be aware of which important mergers and acquisitions took place in the last six months or an year. Subsequent to identifying the sources of information, one needs to select the more important information in the form of a data bank for easy reference and improved comprehension. The candidate should revise these short notes or data bank repeatedly so that he is in a position to reproduce the data during the time of taking part in a group discussion. Quoting specific information and data helps a candidate in getting an edge over others and come out a winner.

c. ***Improving communication skills:*** Most certainly, merely collecting information on a wide variety of topics would not suffice for a winning performance in a group discussion. To improve communication skills (both written and verbal), it is strongly

> Read, assimilate and regularly practice speaking to improve your communication skills.

recommended in the first place, that the candidates should read about a topic and after assimilation, must write the information gained in their own language and also practice speaking on the topic. Speaking could be practiced at home or in front of friends. After a few days of this exercise, the candidates should start practicing making an extempore speech in front of a mirror or in front of brothers/sisters or family members or friends. These sessions would assist in assimilation of ideas and then developing the skill to put across ideas in a logical sequence.

Remember that communication is not about fluency in english or command over language, but assessors look for sincerity, honesty, reliability, willingness to learn and an eye for detail. Be clear in what you say and be honest in your communication. Clarity of thought reveals a significant part of your personality. Moderator is keen to observe your thought process and how well you are able to express ideas. Essentially, avoid using slangs or any type of non-parliamentary language during a GD.

d. ***Participating in mock group discussions***: Once an aspirant finds himself fairly confident in presenting his thoughts before others without much preparation, he should plan to take part in a mock group discussion. It would be now worthwhile to organize a group of students, and conduct mock group discussions on a variety of subjects, where

> After acquiring good amount of information and communication skills, organizing mock GDs will give you the required confidence.

topics of progressively increasing difficulty could be chosen. The above steps would substantially help the candidates in acquiring more confidence to face a group discussion in reality. During such exercises, effort should be made by the candidate to try and put across his ideas in a convincing and logical manner in a short time, quoting precise information and adequate data. It is good to be assertive, but also allow others to speak and remain reasonable with other group members in order to win their confidence. Winning the confidence of other members of the group by keeping your cool and displaying tact would help in making you the leader of the group.

e. ***Displaying leadership qualities:*** Having taken adequate measures to prepare himself for a group discussion, a candidate must mentally prepare himself to display leadership qualities. These pertain to displaying good mental abilities and over all conduct and good behaviour of the candidate. While a candidate must

> Have a good knowledge base, remain focussed and confident. Your over all good conduct will make you a leader of the group.

remember that he has to 'sell' himself to the moderator of the GD, he must show compassion for others, but at the same time, remain focussed, self confident and tactful while dealing with tricky situations during the course of the discussion. Possessing a reasonably good knowledge base and fluency in expression would come handy here as well. Candidate must possess the art of convincing others, using logic and supporting data and must display the ability to withstand pressure. These abilities will assist the candidate in displaying leadership qualities.

A Dozen Smart Hints for Excelling in Group Discussions

Subsequent to making preparations for participating in a group discussion as stated earlier, candidates should carefully take a note of the following practical hints to put up an impressive performance.

Build Rapport

Prior to commencement of the group discussion, while waiting in the waiting room, try to build a rapport with other candidates by making a mental note of their names, etc. Make friends with them. This helps a great deal in establishing contact and building an understanding with other members of the group and to consolidate your position when the discussion commences. Carry a pen and notebook with you so that you can jot down the topic and important points as they strike you while the group discussion is in progress.

Initiate Only if Sure

When the group discussion starts, unless you are fairly confident that you are adequately prepared to discuss the topic, do not attempt to initiate the discussion. In case you feel you are not quite confident of initiating the discussion, it is prudent to carefully listen to one or two participants before taking your turn to speak, since this gives you some time to arrange your thoughts and present them in a planned and cohesive manner. Jot down all relevant points pertaining to the topic. There will definitely be some aspects on which you can express your ideas. Focus quickly on these aspects and then speak.

Be Heard

If others are not giving you an opportunity to speak, you may not have an option but to intervene and grab an opportunity to speak. Be tactful while doing so and carefully avoid being abrasive. If needed, raise your voice as required to draw attention and thereafter speak normally so that you are heard by all concerned. If you are being interrupted repeatedly, tell the group members politely but firmly that they should let you continue.

Adopt Correct Body Language

Maintain eye contact with other members of the group and adopt a receptive body language. Eye contact helps you to know who is on your side and who is not. Do not look at only one person, but maintain eye contact with as many members as possible. Do not raise your hands or point fingers at others and avoid adopting aggressive body posture. Sit straight with a comfortable body posture. Pay due attention to others when they speak.

Support Arguments with Data

Make a positive contribution by adding up-to-the-minute information and putting across your thoughts in a logical and convincing manner along with facts and figures to support your arguments.

Make Adequate Contribution

Be a good listener and try and logically reply to arguments put across by others. Take a special note of points which you think you can reply. Wait for the right opportunity to interject and, then put-across your ideas. Interject your thoughts into the GD at least 4 to 6 times during the 15–20 minutes period over which a group discussion normally stretches.

Remain Composed

Remain firm and assertive without being arrogant. Whatever the case may be, do not antagonize others. Try to maintain a cordial atmosphere and remain calm and receptive when others are presenting their ideas. Remember, if you help others, they would also help you when you start speaking.

Quality Matters

It is true that the content of your ideas presented is more significant than the time you take to present them. Be brief and to the point and avoid digressing from the topic at any cost. Remain constantly focused on the issues involved despite all provocations. Speak in english and avoid changing your language to hindi or other languages. Do not use slangs during a GD. It is essential to keep a check on your language.

Remain Unbiased

It is indeed desirable to present your ideas in a balanced and unbiased manner. Rationality and logic must prevail and positive effort should be made to avoid any bias for or against any religion, nation, caste or creed.

Be Rational

Emotions should largely take a back seat and a reasonable and practical approach must be adopted while handling complex problems and tricky situations. Expression of extreme ideas clearly indicates lack of adjustment with situations and individuals and should be scrupulously avoided. Generally, sweeping statements are neither factual nor fair to any person or a situation.

Take Control

In the unfortunate eventuality of the discussion getting out of control and not leading to any fruitful conclusion, it may become essential to intervene and display your leadership skills. While doing so, remember to be assertive but not aggressive at any cost. Being aggressive amounts to forcing your way and brushing aside others, much to their annoyance. While being assertive implies putting across your point of view in a forceful manner, but at the same time, not annoying others. Remain calm and collected and focused on the core issue of the discussion. Avoid being emotional about your point of view.

Group Consensus Matters

Having made adequate positive contribution, during the course of discussion, take initiative to conclude the discussion by reaching a willing consensus. Giving due respect to the thoughts presented by others and displaying a broad outlook towards things would help in this effort and eventually place you in a winning situation. Do not forget that forcing a consensus would invariably go against you and would show that you have a tendency to push things rather prematurely. Therefore, make positive efforts to ensure that others appreciate your views.

Part I Concepts

Conduct of Group Discussions in Services Selection Boards

Services Selection Boards (SSBs) are responsible for selecting officers for the three armed forces. SSBs have a fairly elaborate procedure for screening and selecting candidates. This procedure entails three techniques—Interviewing, group testing and conducting tests of psychology. Group discussions are conducted as an important part of group testing technique in SSBs. The format and procedure of conduct of GD in the SSBs is slightly different due to their specific testing requirements. Though the general guidelines discussed in earlier chapters are equally relevant for SSBs too, certain aspects, specific to SSBs, deserve a mention here. GDs are conducted by examiners called the GTOs (Group Testing Officers)–generally a major or at times a Lieutenant Colonel rank officer of the Army/his equivalent in the Air Force and Navy.

Preparation for Conduct of GD

GD is the first of the 'Group Tasks' conducted at the SSBs. Candidates are carefully divided into small groups of 8 to 9 — but not exceeding 10 in any case. For easy identification, the candidates wear an allotted chest number. To facilitate quick reference of the Group Testing Officer (GTO), the candidates are required to sit with their chest numbers in an increasing order in a clockwise direction. The group, after a small informal talk/rapport building by the GTO, is thus readied for the conduct of a GD.

Holding the Group Discussion

Before commencing the GD–the GTO briefs the candidates that he would conduct the GD in two phases. In the first phase, he would announce two topics and leave the choice to the group to decide one of the topics for discussion. He asks the candidates to remain seated during the discussion, speak anytime, any number of times and as long as they want to speak. They need not speak in turns. They may speak 'for' or 'against' the topic or may alter their options as and when any ideas strike their mind. He cautions them not to shout and fight during the course of discussion, but speak one at a time so that every one is heard. He then announces the two topics and gives about 30 seconds to the group for deciding on their option. The GTO will generally introduce topics which are interesting as well as current, so that all members of the group can actively take part in the proceedings. Topics are also selected in such a way that these could be debated from different angles or perspectives. The topics are so chosen that they match the age, qualifications and interests of the group. Once the topic is decided by the group, he announces the topic so that it is clearly heard by all. He, then starts the discussion and sits slightly away from the group to observe them, giving them enough freedom to talk. When almost all have expressed their views or about 12–15 minutes have passed; he comes in and stops the discussion and encourages the group to carry on into the second phase.

In the second phase, usually only one topic is given to the candidates and they are asked to discuss the same. Topics given in the first phase are generally of average difficulty, while difficulty level of topic in second phase would largely depend upon the performance put up by the group during the first phase. Again, after about 12–15 minutes the GTO takes charge and stops the discussion making some pleasant remarks about the proceedings thus far.

Assessment during GDs by the GTO

Due to the reason that Group Discussion is normally the first task allotted to a group, inputs obtained by the Group Testing Officer (GTO) during the discussion are relevant, but certainly not conclusive.

A GTO may look for the following additional attributes/approaches of a candidate during the two rounds of GDs:

a. Logic and soundness of ideas expressed.
b. Are the ideas practical/not-so practical?
c. Are the ideas repetitive or original/on new lines?
d. Receptivity to others.
e. Candidate's impression on others.
f. Others reaction to the ideas expressed.
g. Empathy for others.
h. Encouragement given to others.
i. Firmness and tact displayed by the candidate.
j. Knowledge base of the candidate.
k. Raising/lowering the level of discussion.
l. Level of confidence.
m. Whether candidate's approach has been critical, optimistic, involved, etc.

Some Do's and Don'ts for GDs Conducted at SSBs

Do's

a. Listen and understand the briefing by the GTO without interrupting and asking unnecessary questions–till he finishes his briefing.
b. Help the group in deciding the topic for discussion in the first phase.
c. Mediate, if the discussion is going haywire.
d. Give opportunity to others who are not able to speak.

Part I Concepts

e. Bring new/original ideas and give new dimension to the discussion of the topic.

f. Add liveliness, if the group becomes tense during the discussion.

g. Display a positive attitude to resolve an issue.

Don'ts

a. Speaking louder than others–merely to prove your point.

b. Not listening to others, carrying on speaking whether some body listens to you or not.

c. Making wild gestures/displaying poor body language during a heated discussion.

d. Use of unparliamentary language or slangs even to your friends in the group.

e. Calling the candidate by name and not by the chest number.

f. Indulging in side talks, while some one is talking.

g. Bluffing, by quoting anonymous or secret sources/giving incorrect data/ figures.

Role of Non-verbal Communication in Group Discussions

We have discussed various aspects that are considered relevant for putting up an impressive performance in group discussions. Whereas, communication skills of a candidate come to the fore in a group discussion, non-verbal communication skills also have a major role to play. As a matter of fact, it is now common knowledge that much more than words, it is our body language that speaks volumes. In this regard, the way you place or use your hands, carry yourself and use your eyes, etc., assume critical importance. It is felt that the following handy tips would help candidates a great deal to adopt suitable and positive body language while participating in group discussions.

- *Facial expressions*: A pleasant look on your face goes a long way to convey that you are a relaxed as well as a confident person. In this respect, furrowed brows, tense jaw and nervous twitches should be scrupulously avoided. Although, a certain amount of anxiety cannot be kept away, a relaxed look does go in your favour and indicates that you can take a substantial amount of stress in stride. In this regard, reading some light material and having a good sleep during the previous night would generally help. Prior to taking part in the GD, do share some lighter moments with your friends or family members to keep stress at bay. Otherwise, any activity that makes you cheerful could be undertaken to ensure a pleasant look on your face.

- *Movement of hands*: While expressing yourself verbally, keep a deliberate check on excessive movements of both your hands. Vigorous and frequent movement of hands reflects your limitations in verbally expressing yourself. Slight movement of hands once in a while may be acceptable, but pointing fingers towards other candidates would undeniably amount to bad manners on the part of the candidate. A palm-closed finger gesture reveals aggression and should be avoided at all costs.

- *Body posture:* The posture of sitting with your head erect and shoulders back, generally reflects your alertness. A slight lean forward would also indicate that you are keen for the discussion. On the contrary, an extended lean backwards would reflect your disinterest in the proceedings and should, therefore, be avoided under all circumstances.

- *Head movements:* It has been experienced that anxiety makes a candidate nod his head rather excessively. On the other hand, not moving one's head at all may sometimes indicate disinterest in the ongoing discussion. It is, therefore, recommended that nodding of head should be done in a subtle manner, but never excessively or vigorously.

- *Eye contact:* Our eyes reflect the general state of our mind. A good eye contact with the other person indicates your attention and interest in that person. Consequently, during a group discussion, it would be prudent to keep an eye contact with the person who is presenting his/her ideas. However, it must be clarified that keeping an eye contact with the person, who is talking does not imply staring at him. Of course, breaking the eye contact occasionally would be in order to ensure an occasional glance away. On the other hand, when you are talking, address the group members and not the moderator. Try and maintain eye-contact with as many members as may be possible, when you are talking. This helps in getting a positive response from these members.

- *Voice modulation*: While conveying ideas in a group discussion, the candidate should appropriately modulate his/her voice. Speaking loudly does not bring about the desired impact. Moreover, subtle changes in pitch, volume and rhythm also indicate how one feels about something. A candidate having a mature and balanced outlook would maintain the required modulation to convey and lay emphasis on certain significant aspects.

- *Movements and gestures*: Our gestures reveal a lot about our state of mind. Constant fidgeting and yawning create a negative impact on the formal set up of a group discussion. Never get up in your enthusiasm while discussing any point or physically restrain other candidates from speaking. A candidate should consciously avoid certain unnecessary movements and gestures such as tapping of feet, repeated touching of hair, fiddling with the ring, jewellery or spectacles, lip-biting, etc. These movements are distracting and indicate that a candidate is either bored or nervous or has become impatient. Consulting one's watch frequently or looking outside the window should also be avoided as these gestures suggest a lack of interest on the part of the candidate. Narrowing of the eyes is a particularly strong negative gesture that is indicative of disagreement and even resentment. Similarly, raised eyebrows convey disbelief and communicate that you do not trust what the other person is saying.

The above discussion clearly indicates that small changes in one's body language make a big difference in terms of flow of information between the candidates and create a substantial impact on the proceedings of a group discussion.

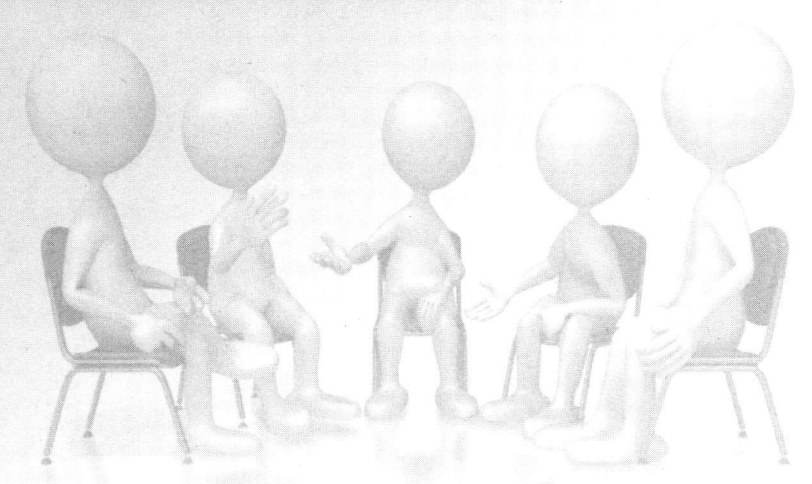

Part II

Mock Group Discussions

Will e-Commerce Dominate the Indian Retail Business?

Eight Candidates are Taking Part in this Group Discussion

Candidate No. 7

I think we have been given a topic which has surprisingly engaged the attention of young India in modern times. With so many technological advancements in the recent past, internet became a household name in India and it was inevitable that e-commerce acquired tremendous popularity. While we talk of e-commerce, 'e' stands for electronic and 'commerce' implies selling/buying items or services as a business activity.

Candidate No. 4

It is rather interesting to note that while our politicians were trying their best to stop the entry of large western retail chains to save *Kirana* stores, e-commerce has rapidly acquired the centre-stage. It is now obvious that the era of great big retail chains has effectively come to an end. Much to our astonishment, Indian e-commerce sites have grown extremely rapidly. The explosive growth in mobile internet is fundamentally shaping the Indian classified internet market.

Candidate No. 1

I think we all know that e-commerce is growing rather quickly, but can someone tell us why is this happening?

Candidate No. 3

I feel it allows the customer to buy items sitting in the comfort of his house, which saves precious time and effort. Secondly, one can shop anytime during the day or night as the e-shop never shuts.

Candidate No. 7

The best thing is that goods are much cheaper on the net and quick home delivery adds up to the charm of e-commerce. Items can be returned or replaced at an extremely fast pace. Not only that, the availability of items is so large without any boundaries that the customer has an extremely unlimited choice. By just moving your mouse, you can compare the quality and cost of an item at different sites and finally exercise your best option. Isn't that great? That's technology for you!

Candidate No. 2

No, but what you are saying may be right. But apparently you cannot buy everything on the net. So, how can it replace the retail market? Am I right?

Candidate No. 4

Yes, but as of now, items which are currently available include mobile phones, clothes, laptops, books, kitchenware, shoes, toys, furniture, watches, hardware and sanitary fittings, items of home décor, home furnishings and numerous other home and utility products.

Candidate No. 3

The list of items available on different sites varies. But, today Amazon, Flipkart, Snapdeal, Myntra, Infibeam, e-bay and Jabong, etc. are considered major players in this game. By the way, recently Myntra was acquired by Flipkart. In addition, Quikr and OLX are dealing with jobs, automobiles, used goods, electronics and services.

Candidate No. 7

Presently, there is terrible neck-to-neck competition between these sites. They all offer cash on delivery, 100% money back guarantee, easy returns and 100% original products with applicable warranty. In addition, discounts and savings and everyday new deals are offered to lure customers. For instance, Flipkart launched 'Big Billion Day' sale and Amazon is on track to touch $1 billion in gross sales. Finally, after a few years the winner among them will become India's top retailer and also one of India's most valuable companies.

Candidate No. 4

I think e-commerce will bring out the lowest price for the ultimate benefit of the customer since brands will be forced to reduce prices to remain in the fray. Currently, people are loyal to their favourite brands, but certainly e-commerce will change this scenario. Moreover, people may not remain loyal to any e-commerce site even, but buy items from wherever they get the best deal. This may change the face of retail business in India gradually but surely.

Candidate No. 2

Yes, I agree with No. 4. I would like to add that in the recent past, looking at the growing popularity of e-commerce, some brands are launching their new products only on specific e-commerce sites offering substantial discounts and benefits. Currently, we see new books and mobile phones fall into this category already. Also, some well-known companies like Raymond, Bombay Dyeing and Arvind Mills etc. have also entered e-retailing to drive more profits.

Candidate No. 4

Another interesting development in this area is that top fashion designers are now jumping online to fashion a new growth story since online business of clothes has already become a craze in India. Today, top fashion designers are now coming up with a special collection at a special price for online retail to tap into the segment. They now mean big business for the fashion crazy. Fashion retailer Myntra has got designers like Sabyasachi and Ritu Kumar to bring out affordable products for the not-so-rich customers. Rohit Bal is working for Jabong and has been doing well recently.

Candidate No. 7

Not only that, certain websites have taken the initiative to employ stylists to advise customers. If a customer has bought a few dresses from the site, the stylist would help the client to choose what clothes should she/he wear on a particular day or occasion. Companies like Myntra and Jabong have already lined-up stylists to offer personalized advice to customers via phone or chat. According to these sites, this initiative will democratize fashion in India.

Candidate No. 5

Looking at the fantabulous growth rate of e-commerce, a steady stream of investor money is now pouring in from Indian as well as foreign investors. Ratan Tata and Azim Premji have invested in Snapdeal and Ratan Tata has also invested in e-jeweller 'Bluestone'. Chinese e-commerce giant 'Alibaba' and Japan's Soft Bank Corp. etc. have enabled Snapdeal to raise funds up to $650 million. This clearly indicates the trust e-commerce is generating rather steadily among all investors.

Candidate No. 4

A new trend is that a large number of customers are from smaller towns as well. During festive seasons, size and price are no bar for buyers and sales are up by more than 20 times during this period. E-commerce was built on discounts, but now people wait for sales because of selection of products available online.

Candidate No. 1

Excuse me! What I am hearing from all of you, it appears that e-commerce has no disadvantages at all. I don't agree with this kind of an analysis. Could somebody point out what major problems one faces while buying items online?

Candidate No. 5

Yes, we have a number of disadvantages. I will tell you about them. For example, there are a number of items which one wants to feel before buying, such as furniture and quality/texture of clothes, etc. Some items such as clothes and shoes, etc. require a comfortable fit and need a trial. All this is not possible online. Moreover, colours of fabric shown on the website may be a shade different than what you get in your hand finally. Further, as online transactions are duly recorded, e-commerce sites often bombard the customers with business calls and messages to buy their latest products. This is a nuisance and is totally avoided while doing retail shopping. Some top electronic companies are also considering withdrawing their sales through e-commerce sites as rock-bottom prices erode their brand values. Online retailing also operates in grey areas when it comes to taxation depriving the government of a major source of tax revenue.

Candidate No. 3

I hope you remember the problems 26 million users of Flipkart faced during the 'Big Billion Day' sale held. Due to overload, they ran out of stock within minutes and their site crashed.

Candidate No. 8

I may add that a large number of cases of e-commerce frauds have been reported of late. This is very alarming and we must take concrete steps to check these frauds, if e-commerce needs to be promoted. As of now, I understand that jewelry items are not on the hit list of e-shoppers because of the above reasons.

Candidate No. 4

But I understand jewelry is poised to be one of the fastest growing segments in India's e-commerce market, which is now projected to become an $8 billion industry in the next two years. As you know, Indians are damn crazy to buy jewelry online or offline.

Candidate No. 8

Gentlemen, I think we have discussed almost all aspects of e-commerce and would somebody now like to conclude this discussion?

Candidate No. 7

Friends, I think Candidate No. 6 has not spoken at all and we must give him a chance to at least conclude the discussion.

Candidate No. 6

I liked the discussion very much, but let Candidate No. 4 conclude the discussion.

Candidate No. 4

Yes, we may conclude this discussion by saying that the fast growing popularity of e-commerce would eventually hugely benefit the lower middle class of India and they would be able to buy the 'so called' branded products at reasonable rates. E-commerce in India is a $25 billion dollar market right now, but as per current estimates, it will become $300 billion by 2025. I am sure e-commerce is here to stay and stay for a good time. Thank you.

Critical Analysis of Candidates' Performance

Good: *Candidate Nos. 4, 5 and 7*

Candidate No. 7 has initiated the discussion and has displayed his knowledge about the topic. He has made a fair impression on other candidates due to his preparation and effort. Candidate No. 4 and No. 5 have also expressed their views for furtherance of the GD. All these three candidates have brought out the latest developments in the field of e-commerce, which is commendable. Candidate No. 5 has spoken only twice, but has made valuable and quality arguments. Candidate No.7 has encouraged candidate No.6 to take part since he did not take part in the GD at all and this approach will go in his favour.

Average: *Candidate Nos. 2, 3*

These candidates have shown their limited knowledge of the subject. They have taken part in the discussion but did not make adequate contribution in the GD. Obviously, they need to improve their knowledge-base on the subject and display increased confidence.

Below Average: *Candidate Nos. 1, 6 and 8*

Candidate No.6 has remained a mute spectator during the entire GD. Candidate No.8 has been taking part in a very limited fashion and has been asking only others to speak. Therefore, his contribution to the GD is not considered adequate. Similarly, Candidate No.1 has only asked others to speak, while he himself did not make any contribution in the GD.

Can BRICS Pose a Formidable Challenge to the West?

Eight Candidates are Taking Part in this Group Discussion

Candidate No. 4

As we all know, BRICS represents a group of nations comprising Brazil, Russia, India, China and South Africa. This is comparatively a new assembly of countries and we are discussing whether this could become a game-changer in the years to come, both in terms of world economy and strategic alliances. Western countries have already described this union as a complicated venture which will have a hard time getting off the ground and it can never match the expertise of World Bank. I think we need to know its historical background to understand its aims and intentions.

Candidate No. 2

Yes, I recall BRICS countries have been meeting and talking for the past almost ten years, they realized their power only in 2008, when the economy of some Western countries began shaking. During this financial crisis, the BRICS countries played a vital role as drivers of growth which helped the global economy substantially. BRICS did not pose as a threat to world economy but as an opportunity for global growth. BRICS countries realized that they must interact more closely to finance and help each other.

Candidate No. 4

Let me elaborate by saying that BRICS countries realized that it was essential for their future for the members to finance each other's infrastructure projects, inter-nationalize their currencies, provide trade credit to each other, ease visa norms and encourage investment in each other's country. During the meeting of BRICS countries in Delhi in 2012, all these vital issues were discussed and agreed upon by the big five emerging economies of the world. They realized that today's emerging economies may become tomorrow's global powers, if they also create a new global bank, which will hold the group together in future.

Candidate No. 2

All these developments are fine, but the West is quite worried about this grouping and there is tremendous negativity about this development. They are worried, since for the first time, a global architecture is emerging, which does not involve them. The West is considering BRICS a global rival that could not be controlled from Washington. So far, the West could integrate the world probably because they exclusively controlled capital flows and technology. They point out that it is the fundamental incompatibility of the BRICS nations, not their lack of organization, which prevents this collection of emerging economies from acting as a meaningful force on the world stage.

Candidate No. 5

But, things have now changed. The BRICS nations have gradually re-taken control of their vast resources and markets and are also creating surplus capital. They are also quickly learning to innovate, since they have skilled manpower and vast resources. All these developments make BRICS nations confident that they can also integrate the world, and then role of western countries would automatically reduce over a period of time. That is why the west is nervous.

Candidate No. 6

No, I am sorry, I do not think BRICS can do this kind of a wonder. They can do no magic to compete with the developed world, that too in a short period of time.

Candidate No. 2

But, the western countries have not realized that BRICS is no more an idea, but already a reality. How can you ignore that BRICS represents nearly half of the world's population and a quarter of its land mass and GDP. During the year 2011-12, trade between BRICS countries stood at $230 billion and by 2015, it was $500 billion. China, India and Brazil are world's first, second and fifth most populated nations and they present tremendous business opportunities to the world. Today, the BRICS contribution to global economic growth has now reached almost 50%, making this group the principal driver of global economic development. How can you ignore these facts?

Candidate No. 8

May be what you are saying is true, but I still feel that west will not allow BRICS nations to dominate the global economy.

Candidate No. 3

But let us not forget that west has not done much for the quota and governance reforms in the IMF, which also disappointed the emerging economies. Secondly, the BRICS nations are in favour of abiding by UN sanctions and not unilateral ones imposed by US and European countries on Iran, Syria and even Russia.

Candidate No. 4

That is why, BRICS nations have now moved much ahead to consolidate their mutual cooperation during their significant meeting in Brazil in July 2014 after the World Cup Football matches in that country. During this meeting, it announced the decision to establish the New Development Bank (NDB) and the Contingency Reserve Arrangement (CRA). These are considered modest

Part II Mock GDs

counters to the World Bank and International Monetary Fund respectively. In view of this development, BRICS summit in Fortaleza (Brazil), which was 6th BRICS summit, is considered the most successful of BRICS meetings so far.

Candidate No. 7

But, I heard there was much wrangling over location of the bank's headquarters during this summit. Is it not?

Candidate No. 2

Yes, that is true, but finally all agreed that headquarters of BRICS bank will be located in Shanghai and India secured its first presidency. There was also noted compromise on the size of capital, with all members contributing $50 billion now and $100 billion eventually. This bank would mobilize resources for development work in developing economies, while CRA would assist nations who require economic support from time to time. These developments would reduce dependence of BRICS nations on IMF and World Bank.

Candidate No. 1

Do you think all this is adequate to counter World Bank and IMF? I don't think so.

Candidate No. 8

It may not be adequate now, but it is a great beginning, that we should be proud of.

Candidate No. 3

It is noteworthy that BRICS leaders are now discussing challenges and threats facing the world today. These include cyber crimes, climate change and conflicts in Africa, Syria, Iraq, Afghanistan and the Iran nuclear issue. However, I must add that there was a bit of disappointment, as BRICS did not decide significantly on the issues of reforming UN Security Council and democratizing it. New areas have been identified for exploring cooperation in the future.

Candidate No. 5

I am quite sure that BRICS is a rising geopolitical power and the world cannot ignore this fact in today's multi-polar world. In the recent past, BRICS leaders also interacted fruitfully with leaders of South America. We have also noticed steady progress in intra-BRICS cooperation and this is a very positive development.

Candidate No. 1

Let us not forget that India will host the 2017 summit and can include leaders of South Asia to interact with BRICS.

Candidate No. 4

But, I think the political weight of the group will largely depend upon the internal coherence which the members need to display, especially since China,

India and Russia have complex bilateral relations. Secondly, the BRICS economy must grow at a fast pace to make an impact on world economy. Significantly in the recent years, BRICS agenda has witnessed a steady expansion. During the BRICS conference in June 2017, member countries displayed an understanding to enhance cooperation in the areas of security and counter-terrorism. India highlighted Pakistan's state sponsored terror activities and the urgent need to curb this global menace during this conference.

Candidate No. 7

I think we have discussed almost all aspects of BRICS and let us conclude this discussion now.

Candidate No. 2

Let us conclude by saying that by setting up a bank, BRICS is all set to become a serious global player. In March 2017, China has come up with a new idea of 'BRICS Plus', which involves inviting other developing countries to this group. India thinks it is a move by China to dilute the role of India and expand Chinese influence and seek support from countries like Pakistan, Sri Lanka, Mexico etc to further Chinese interests. In the recent past, Chinese leaders have been talking that they love peace. I think if China rises in a peaceful manner, BRICS has a significant role to play in global politics.

Critical Analysis of Candidates' Performance

Good: Candidate Nos. 4 and 2

Candidate No.4 has initiated the discussion and subsequently has displayed his above average knowledge of the topic. Other candidates have listened to him carefully and appreciated his point of view. Similarly, Candidate No.2 has made adequate preparation and has spoken with confidence quoting lot of data and information on the subject and finally has also concluded the discussion. Therefore, performance of these candidates has been assessed as 'Good'.

Average: Candidate Nos. 3 and 5

These two candidates have interjected during the discussion a few times, but did not highlight any specific points and their knowledge-base of the subject is clearly quite limited. They need to gather more facts and prepare in a focused manner. Obviously, their level of confidence is also rather low. Therefore, their performance is adjudged as 'Average' only.

Below Average: Candidate Nos. 1, 6, 7 and 8

These candidates have been only disagreeing with other candidates, but did not express their views by bringing some additional points. Obviously, their knowledge of the topic is quite low. They have shown their casual attitude towards the progress of the group discussion and have hardly made any contribution. Therefore, their performance is considered as 'Below Average'.

Should We Allow Indians to Die with Dignity?

Eight Candidates are Taking Part in this Group Discussion

Candidate No. 3

Well, I think we have been given a very significant topic to discuss. Euthanasia deals with the practice of killing a person without causing any pain. While some nations have allowed this practice, others have opposed this idea.

Candidate No. 7

I think the term "euthanasia" speaks volumes about itself. The literal meaning of the term euthanasia is 'good death' *(eu* = good, *thanatos* = death). "Euthanasia is deliberate bringing about a gentle and easy death, making the last days of the patient as comfortable as possible." It is generally resorted to as the last option for ensuring a peaceful death to allay the misery of a patient suffering from a terminal illness or disability. Euthanasia is known to be of three types: active–by administering a lethal injection, passive–by withdrawing life support systems and death by double effect–by giving heavy doses of pain killers to speed up the patient's end. Passive and double effect euthanasia is common in European countries.

Candidate No. 1

To me, euthanasia is nothing short of murder. It goes against one's conscience to kill a person when one cannot bear to hurt even an animal. When we as humans do not have the capacity to give life to anyone, we do not have the right to snatch it from anyone. Every inhabitant of the planet is important and Nature's will must be respected. "Survival of the fittest" may be true in some cases but one cannot allow murder, simply because one is not recovering from an illness. The society cannot allow people to kill themselves.

Candidate No. 6

Yes, I agree with Candidate No. 1 when he says that Euthanasia is nothing short of a murder.

Candidate No. 2

I feel that incurably diseased people should have a say in their destiny. In fact, the moment we use the word 'allowed', we try and gain control as decision-makers for someone else's life. The fact remains that each one of us has a right to live with dignity and consequently the right to die with dignity, if life gets excruciatingly painful, as is the case with terminally ill patients.

Candidate No. 4

I would support Candidate No. 1 in opposing legalization of euthanasia. If we are talking about survivors then any critically ill person who has continued to struggle so far, is automatically a survivor because nature willed so. It is unethical to kill a fellow human being just because a group of people decides that it is pointless for the person to keep alive. What is even more gruesome is that doctors perform it or at least support it as is the case in passive euthanasia or assisted suicide. Does not it go against the Hippocratic oath of saving human lives?

Candidate No. 2

But I think, that is one way of looking at things. Is it ethical to let a fellow human being suffer pain and indignity? Mercy killing is not new. In our national heritage, concepts like *Samadhi, Nirvana* and opting for death at a certain age of life have been well-accepted, much before western jurisprudence incorporated them. Gandhiji also favoured dying with dignity for all human beings. Have not we heard of putting injured animals to rest. It is doctors' duty to give patients a dignified death, if there is no hope. There is an inherent kindness in this act. The very act of killing is aimed at providing relief to the sufferer.

Candidate No. 3

How can you even compare animals with humans?

Candidate No. 5

We are not comparing other species with humans. We are comparing the guiding emotion of mercy and the act of taking moral responsibility of relieving somebody's pain. There is nothing inhuman about it and it should have been legalized in India. In fact, the Dutch Parliament legalized it in April 2002 through a thumping majority of 104 to 40 votes.

Candidate No. 2

In fact, in the Netherlands, Belgium and Oregon (US), laws permit euthanasia. In Denmark, kin of terminally ill patients can withdraw treatment. In Australia's Northern Territory, a euthanasia Bill was approved in '95 but overturned in '97. But in India the proponents of euthanasia have met with little success. In the year 2001, two cases in Patna and Kerala High Courts came in the public eye where euthanasia was not permitted by the courts. Subsequently, in the case of Hyderabadi youth, K Venkatesh, also Andhra Pradesh High Court did not allow mercy killing. Presently, in India doctors could be charged for murder if they kill a patient, and in addition, attempt to commit suicide is also a crime. However, in 2006, after some public debate Law Commission had recommended permitting mercy killing in some form.

Candidate No. 8

Yes, I fully agree with Candidate No. 2.

Candidate No. 4

Exactly, if we legalize euthanasia we will transform what is currently a crime into 'medical treatment' and then we would be giving everyone a license to kill. Do you realize that, it would give a free hand to some opportunistic parties related to critically ill patients who want to grab their property and could easily resort to misusing the law if it is enacted? Also, it could be a case of faulty diagnosis and the patient would have to pay with her/his death. Furthermore, an appeal for euthanasia by a patient may be an outcome of depression resulting in the feeling of worthlessness.

Candidate No. 7

You have raised some valid concerns regarding the issue. One may say that, there is a very fine dividing line between what is a justifiable cause for euthanasia and what is not, and a set of guidelines to help one out of this dilemma, does help. In most cases, it is the patient who makes it known as to whether her/ his present state of being is acceptable to her/him or not. In other situations, where the patient is unconscious and therefore unable to decide, the team of supervising doctors and the family members of the patient may decide on her/his behalf. We must build safeguards to avoid its misuse.

Candidate No. 1

I still think that, people's decisions can be manipulated and in some cases bought. Any attempt to prepone someone's death is unethical and should be avoided. Only kindness and compassionate care should be promoted. Take the example of Mother Teresa's Missionaries of Charity. The organization takes in people who are sick and dying and have no hope and takes care of them till their last breath. If euthanasia is the best answer to deal with human suffering, then probably all the effort that these people are putting in, is useless.

Candidate No. 5

Euthanasia is not about supporting mass murder at one's whim and fancy. It is the quality of life that is more important than the actual length of one's life. Incurably diseased people endure an exceedingly arduous and painful period in waiting for an equally or more painful death. Life becomes a slow anguish for them. Recently, Hindi movie 'Guzarish' also pleads in favour of mercy killing

Candidate No. 8

We do not have the right to deliberately prolong someone's life, if it means prolonging one's agony.

If a person is suffering from a progressive disease, e.g., cancer in its last stage, and the only cure that can rid her/him of unbearable pain and trauma is death, and the person wishes to end her/his life, then probably one should not think twice about opting for euthanasia or mercy-killing as it is commonly known.

Candidate No.7

It is an irony of sorts that, sometimes the cure lies in death and not life. Prolonging one's vegetative existence even when it means torment and pain—borders at inhumanity and not ethics. World-renowned Cardiac Surgeon, Dr. Christian Barnard who did the world's first human heart transplant in December 1967 said, "*It's the quality of survival that's important. The goal of medicine should not be to prolong life but to improve its quality*". In fact, it is argued by some that after the point when all possible medical interventions have been tried and nothing humanly possible has been left un-attempted, one becomes duty-bound as a fellow human to put an end to the torment of the patient by opting for euthanasia. Death is the ultimate truth of life. A good death is what everyone deserves and in the case of a terminally ill patient, it is the duty of a doctor to do everything possible–even if it translates into the last resort of relying on euthanasia. Dr. Barnard gives the instance of a terminally ill elderly patient who disconnected his respirator to end his life. The patient left a note for the doctor saying, "The real enemy is not death, the real enemy is inhumanity".

Candidate No. 2

If the patient strongly felt that since his life was effectively over as merely breathing could not be called living–it was simply a vegetative existence and it was 'inhuman' for those around him to extend her/his ordeal. In 2007, Supreme Court asked the government to consider whether, 'Right to die with dignity' should not be included in 'Right to live with dignity' guaranteed under Article 21 of the Indian Constitution. However, government opposed it quoting it could be misused in India.

In effect, euthanasia has been illegal in India but there have been contradictory judgements by courts in this regard. It will happen only in extreme situations when there is no other option left. Also, if legal safeguards are put in place, and the decision to go ahead comes after much careful thought and deliberations, it would actually be a boon and not a curse.

Candidate No. 7

Recently, commenting on the mercy killing, well is known lyricist Javed Akhtar said, "If Capital Punishment is morally right, why not euthanasia? Are we to believe that revenge killing is right but mercy killing is worng?" Finally, in the case of Aruna Shanbaug in March, 2011 Supreme Court rejected the appeal for mercy killing of Aruna. But it allowed passive euthanasia–or withdrawal of life-support systems–in case a person is being kept alive only mechanically,

Part II Mock GDs

through life support systems and has been in that condition for some years, and there is no plausible possibility of recovery. Active euthanasia–injecting a lethal drug to induce such a patient death– remains illegal. Supreme Court said that only High Court can give nod for passive euthanasia, after consent from patient's relatives coupled with report of court-appointed expert panel, comprising a neurologist, psychiatrist and a physician.

Procedure laid down by court will hold good till Parliament enacted a law on the issue. Court also asked Parliament to delete Section 309 of IPC, which makes attempt to suicide a criminal act. Supreme Court also mentioned that, "A person attempts a suicide in depression, and hence needs help, rather than punishment".

Thus, passive euthanasia is now a reality in India as well. Subsequently in July 2014, while examining legality of active and passive euthanasia, Supreme Court recommended a nationwide debate on the topic and a law on euthanasia to be enacted by the parliament. As of now, passive euthanasia is allowed in most states in U.S.A., Germany, Japan, Switzerland and Albania. If we are a caring country, we should not delay making a law that will reduce the pain and agony of prolonging an artificial life.

Critical Analysis of Candidates' Performance
Good: Candidate Nos. 2 and 7

Candidates, Nos. 2 and 7 have dealt with a number of significant aspects of the problem. They have displayed their superior knowledge base. Other members of the group accepted their views and they could put up convincing arguments in support of their views. Due to these reasons, performance of these two candidates has been assessed as 'Good'.

Average: Candidate Nos. 1 and 4

Candidates Nos. 1 and 4 have also contributed towards the progression of the discussion in a positive way. However, they have displayed that their knowledge about the subject is a bit restricted. With a bit of more initiative, they could have made a more meaningful contribution towards the discussion. Therefore, performance of these candidates has been assessed as 'Average'.

Below Average: Candidate Nos. 3, 5, 6 and 8

These candidates have clearly displayed their inadequate knowledge about the subject. These four candidates have mostly agreed or disagreed with other candidates and made hardly any contribution from their side during the discussion. They clearly lacked initiative and ability to convey their ideas. Hence, performance of these candidates has been assessed as 'Below Average'.

Indo-Russian Relations in Present Times

Nine Candidates are Taking Part in this Group Discussion

Candidate No. 3

"Hindi-Roosi–Bhai-Bhai". Dear friends, India and Russia were always close friends and will always remain so. I feel, we cannot afford to live without each other. What do you say friends?

Candidate No. 5

I am sorry, but I do not agree with you. There are no permanent friends or permanent enemies in diplomacy.

Candidate No. 1

Both Russia and India are among the top ten countries in terms of economic growth, and both have set goals to double their GNPs within a decade. India has valued its friendly relations with Russia for quite sometime now. This relationship, which is more than 70 years old, has closely witnessed the rivalry of Cold War as well as the sudden disintegration of the powerful USSR. Despite many ups and downs in the international politics, Russia has always extended its unqualified support to Indian concerns. Therefore, I have no hesitation in saying that if India is asked to name one really good and durable friend, she will name no other nation, but Russia. It is of course a different matter, that Russia is no more a superpower. But, it is still the most important military power in the world after the US.

Candidate No. 7

It was really sad that USSR disintegrated into several segments and it lost its halo of a super power of the cold war era.

Candidate No. 2

Yes, let us have a close look at the Indo-Russia relations during the cold war days. After gaining our independence from the British rule, India had joined the club of Non-Aligned Nations. Subsequently, Pakistan sought military alliance with USA and also became a member of CEATO and CENTO. This compelled India to worry about her security aspects, and in this regard, Russia provided the requisite support to India. Russia preferred to look into military, political and economic concerns of India.

At present, Russia's trade and economic ties with India are well below the capabilities of both countries.

Candidate No. 6

Russia has always supported us since the times of Nehru, Shastri and Indira Gandhi. They supported us in handling various political issues even till recently, when Russia was not a superpower anymore.

Candidate No. 4

Nowadays, when globalisation is the key word in polity and diplomacy, can we still afford to stick to Russia alone ? We will have to, of course, maintain good working relations with Russia, but at the same time, keep reaching for long term partnerships with European nations also.

Candidate No. 5

It was okay in the past, but now our relations are having a different dimension. In the recent past, due to disintegration of USSR things have changed substantially.

Candidate No. 7

Friends, let's not forget that when Kashmir issue was taken to the international forum for a discussion, Russia unequivocally supported India's stand in every international forum. At the same time, Russia supplied modern defence equipment, including military aircraft, to India in a bid to strengthen our armed forces. Trade relations between the two countries also improved markedly. In 1962, when Indo-China relations worsened and India also had to fight a one-sided war with China, once again Russia supported India's stand and denounced China for its unprovoked armed attack on India.

Candidate No. 5

Earlier, we followed, 'Hindi-Chini–Bhai-Bhai' and we were stabbed in the back. I only hope, Russia will not ditch us in a similar fashion.

Candidate No. 8

But, I will like to remind you that in 1971 during Indo-Pak war, Russia assisted India by providing crucial military equipment. Not only this, it supported India's stand in the Security Council by not allowing any action that could have been taken against India. It is, therefore, apparent that Russia provided the much-needed support to India during the armed conflicts it had against its two neighbours. During this time, since Pakistan received full support from USA, it was only due to Russian support that India could manage to maintain its stance as a non-aligned nation. Even today, Russia and India are strong advocates of reviewing the centrality of the UN in managing challenges to international peace and stability, and resolution of conflicts.

Candidate No. 4

I think, we have been mainly talking about political and military aids that Russia has offered to us. I feel, we should also be talking more about the economic help that Russia gave us, including the help to develop our heavy industry set ups. Russia had also encouraged export of Indian goods to Russian markets. I think the hallmark of this good relationship was the 20 years treaty of peace, friendship and cooperation that was signed in 1971 between the two countries.

Candidate No. 2

Yes, let us not forget Russia's technical and financial assistance. Metallurgical complexes in Bhillai, Vishakhapatanam and Bokaro, the mining equipment plant in Durgapur, the thermal power station in Neyveli and the construction of Kundankulam Nuclear Power Plant etc were all built with Russia's help. India's first satellite, Aryabhata was launched in 1975 with Russia's help and Rakesh Sharma travelled into space in 1984 as a crew member of Russian Soyuz T-11.

Part II Mock GDs

Candidate No. 1

Well, I think we have now adequately discussed the Indo-Russian relations during the Cold War period. Let us now focus on the period after the collapse of USSR. It is a fact that relations between India and Russia showed a downward trend after the down fall of USSR, due to a number of political as well as economic factors. There was considerable political uncertainty prevailing at that time, and therefore, trade links also suffered a great deal. Obviously, unless such a fluid situation settled down, tradesmen of one country would not have liked to opt for commercial dealings with the tradesmen of the other country. It is also a fact that, Russia then no more remained a strategic partner of India due to its changed status. Owing to disintegration of USSR, military supplies to India were considerably hampered and India started to look for other suppliers of military equipment.

Candidate No. 6

Yes, I fully agree with Candidate No. 1 but this trend started reversing during late 1990s. Subsequently, the visit of then President Putin of Russia in October 2000, also played an important role in the resumption of Indo-Soviet relations. During this visit, a declaration of strategic partnership was signed, which specified the structure of bilateral relations between the two countries in the immediate future. This agreement covers relations between the two countries encompassing a large spectrum of activities, especially in the field of defence procurements and Research and Development.

Candidate No. 2

In this context, I would like to add that the visit of our former Prime Minister Shri Vajpayee to Russia in November 2001 further cemented our relations with Russia. During this visit, an agreement was also signed for supply of submarines, which can also carry nuclear weapons. Indo-Russian relations got a boost when Mr. Putin visited India yet again in December 2002. During this visit also, a number of outstanding issues, including strategic cooperation between the two partners, were discussed by a team of officials of both the countries. Our former Prime Minister, Shri Vajpayee again paid a visit to Russia in November 2003, and discussions were held on matters of mutual interests.

Candidate No. 7

I feel, India should keep good relations with Russia to maintain the balance of power in SE Asian region. Our relations with Russia are fairly warm and we must keep allotting Russia a high priority.

Candidate No. 8

I think, yet another issue that we need to discuss is the new power equations that have emerged in Central Asia after the collapse of USSR. USA wants to keep Pakistan as a strategic partner to keep a check on activities in Central Asia. Russia is also trying to re-establish its military presence in this region. Towards this aim, in the recent past, Russia has entered into military alliances with Kyrgyzstan and also Tajikistan.

Candidate No. 9

Yes, I agree with No. 8

Candidate No. 2

Let us not forget that even in the recent past, Russia has endorsed our stand on terrorism, of having a uniform attitude against all kinds of terrorist attacks and not being selective in our reactions to these acts. Similarly, Russia has repeatedly agreed with our serious concern against terrorist activities in J&K region and especially over cross-border terrorism. In reciprocation, India has also given its support to the Russian stand on Chechnya. Finally, during all these years, Russia has fully supported India's candidature for a permanent seat in the UN Security Council.

Candidate No. 3

Yes, we only hope and pray that India will get this seat this time around.

Candidate No. 8

But, I feel that economic relations between the two countries need consolidation and further improvement. Consequent to the collapse of the USSR, our trade relations have really suffered and this needs our urgent attention. In this connection, a large number of businessmen had visited Russia with the former Primer Minister Shri Atal Behari Vajpayee in November 2003. Both Indian and Russian Governments are taking several steps to strengthen trade ties on priority. It is sincerely hoped that the construction of North-South corridor between India, Iran and the Russian Federation will appropriately promote trade ties between India and Russia. Already, Russian companies are now participating in the construction of our nuclear and hydel power plants, highways, modernisation and construction of steel plants, mining, oil and gas exploration in the Arabian Sea and Bay of Bengal as also in north-eastern states.

In 2003, India accounted for about 42% of Russian arms exports, which compared to China's share of 38%, made it the leading importer from Russia. In the year 2004–05, Indian-Russian trade was worth $1.95 bn, while it increased to $2.72 bn in 2005–06. The trade turn-over target for 2010 was $10 bn.

Russia has also launched joint weapons development programmes, for example, Brahmos antiship missiles and India-Russia MTA (Multi-role Transport Aircraft). Russia not only delivered ready to use products, but has been selling licences for the production of a number of state-of-the-art weapons (SU-30 MKI or T 90s MBTs), etc.

Candidate No. 2

But, I must painfully bring out that in 2007, defence services have informed that some of the equipment supplied by the Russians were not of the desired quality, and there were also delays in supplies. All these developments mark a new low in India's arms transfer ties with Russia. Russia has also demanded doubling the cost of refitting the Gorshkov aircraft career for India. In this regard there are problems of quality in respect of Krasnopal Laser-guided artillery shells, Klub class missiles, RVV–AE air-to-air missiles, Akula class sub-marines and T-90S Tanks supplied by Russia. Similarly, there are delays in development of IJT engines and modifying delays of Phalcon AWACS. There are also allegations in respect of escalating costs of Sukhoi-30 MK-I aircraft to India. As per deals signed between India and Russia in March and December 2010, India could only get Gorshkov in 2013–instead of earlier 2008–by paying $ 2.33 billion, instead of $ 974 million as contracted in 2004. Also, India is in the process of getting 45 more MIG–29k maritime fighters, Sukhoi-30 MKI-s, Brahmos missiles, T-905 tanks, Multirole transport aircraft, MI-17 helicopters and Frigates, etc. But currently, Russia is delaying a number of defence projects/supplies.

Candidate No. 8

Due to these reasons, presently India is buying more military equipment from other countries. However, in 2017, India has invited Russia to partner with Indian companies to produce military equipment under 'Make in India' framework. Being India's oldest partner in defence hardware and equipment, Russia would have a comparative advantage in partnering with Indian firms. Finally, India needs to consider that, should she strengthen ties with U.S.A. at the cost of impairing relations with Russia.

Candidate No. 1

I think, we have discussed the topic fairly well. Let us now conclude by saying that Indian and Russian friendship has been very durable, though it received a setback due to the sudden collapse of the USSR. There is tremendous scope for cooperation between the two countries in the fields of IT, electronics, biotechnology and pharmaceuticals, etc. Yet another area where there is much scope for collaboration is building of satellites by Indians and utilizing the growing Russian Space Technology. Besides, there is an urgent need to resume timely supply of military equipment of appropriate quality to India by the Russians. Most importantly, since Russia gives a higher priority to India in its foreign policy and strategic calculations than the US or other power centres of the world, India should decide its equation with Russia depending upon what is in our best national interest. During his visit to India in March 2010, Russian PM V. Putin expressed concern over terror groups in Pakistan and current situation in Afghanistan. During the visit, to strengthen India – Russia relations, a number of agreements, to construct Russian designed nuclear power plants, cooperation on the use of atomic energy for peaceful purposes, production of satellite navigation equipment and supply of military aviation and equipment, were also signed. These developments show the huge potential to develop better ties between India and Russia in the times to come. Russia continues to be a major defence partner for India along with US and Israel.

Critical Analysis of Candidates' Performance

Good: Candidate Nos. 1, 2 and 8

These candidates entered early into the discussion and brought out a number of significant aspects of the topic. They made a fair impression on the group due to their sound knowledge base. They have brought out latest developments on Indo-Russian relations. The group did accept their points of view. Thus, they have contributed significantly to the discussion and their assessment is 'Good'.

Average: Candidate Nos. 4, 6 and 7

These candidates did take opportunities as they came their way and managed to speak two or three times. It is apparent that they did not make adequate preparations for participating in the group discussion. Their views were for furtherence of the group discussion. However, their contribution to the discussion remained just about 'Average'.

Below Average: Candidate Nos. 9, 3 and 5

Candidate No. 9 generally remained aloof and withdrawn, while candidate No. 3 could only put across some not-so practical ideas with not much logic to support his arguments. Candidate No. 5 put up some impolite statements, which were not accepted by the group. Thus, he made hardly any contribution to the group discussion. Therefore, performance of these candidates is accordingly assessed as 'Below Average'.

Are Slums Urban Eye Sores and Must be Removed?

A group of 8 candidates choose this topic for discussion. This GD is conducted as a part of selection process for entry into a premier management institute. After all the candidates have occupied their seats, the GD proceeds in the following manner.

Candidate No. 7

Good Morning friends, what a beautiful topic we have today to discuss. All our major cities face this scar; but we have found no permanent solution to it. What do you say No.1?

Candidate No. 1

We all know that slums are a very visible and an ugly mark on the cities. They symbolize dirt, serve no gainful purpose and breed crime. The government should not allow them to grow and thrive. There must be laws to ban these slums in our cities. In 2011, 93 million people lived in slums in India, but by 2017, the population will rise to 104 million. Maharashtra, U.P., A.P. and M.P. will host largest chunks of this population.

Candidate No. 4

Yes, I agree. We must put a stop to these slums at any cost.

Candidate No. 2

What you just expressed is clearly the popular and dominant view regarding slums. But there is more than what meets the eye. The muck and unhygienic surroundings may not match the glamour and glimmer of the city's prosperous areas, but they are home to workers and labourers who are the real developers of any city. They form the foundations of our economy and contribute immensely to its growth. We all want servants and other workers to work for us. But, once they have finished the work, they should vanish in thin air and appear again the next day. After all, we have to make some provision for these poor workers and should not just wish them away. We have to change our attitude towards this problem and should not consider slums as a burden, but part of our society.

Candidate No. 8

I beg to differ with you on this. Slums are a nuisance and a problem that should be done away with. Slums are illegal occupation of government land by people who cannot afford to pay the requisite rent. Also, there is widespread theft of electricity by the slum dwellers. The slum population continues to grow in magnitude with more and more migrants joining it regularly. In any case, family sizes are bigger in slums. This will take a toll on the city's resources and load bearing capacity.

Candidate No. 5

What you just said is replete with misconceptions about life in slums. I would build further on what Candidate No. 2 said about slums. Although slums are largely inhabited by the city's poor, they actually represent a large cross-section of the city.

Candidate No. 7

Well said No. 5, but what is the solution of this problem?

Candidate No. 4

There is no solution to it. They will grow along with the cities and I don't think we can do much about it. We have to live with this problem.

Candidate No. 2

But let us first analyse as to why are they growing ? Even when they are evicted, they reappear after a short while. Let me try and explain as to who all live in slums. A typical occupational profile of a slum would range anywhere from daily wage labourers to taxi drivers, hawkers to housemaids to small business owners to teachers and even to government employees. A slum signifies hetero-geneity at its best and it is visible even in the occupational variety in slums.

Candidate No. 3

Let us not forget that 75% of nation's urban GDP is contributed by slum dwellers alone. Substantial manufacturing work is outsourced to slums and then nicely packaged in big industries and sold in posh markets.

Candidate No. 2

Let us not forget that, the leather industry of Agra and the famous embroidery units of Varanasi are mainly located in slums. Slums, essentially are the hub of hidden manufacturing activity which contribute to the overall resources of a city and get back hardly any share of the available resources.

As per UN- Habitat Report 2004–2005, Delhi will be one of the five largest urban agglomerations of the world soon. Obviously, it will attract a large number of migrant labour giving rise to considerable problem of slums. As of now, more than 30 lakh people are living in slums and rehabilitation colonies in Delhi. In the recent past, some slums have been shifted to outskirts of Delhi metro, but it has led to other related problems. It is often ignored that first priority of migrant labour is their livelihood and not their houses. If migrant labour is shifted to a far off place from where commuting for jobs is either cumbersome or costly, then again this does not resolve the problem of their rehabilitation. The problem needs to be tackled depending upon the area specific, and not on a macro level.

Candidate No. 8

In addition to what has been said, the myth of slum dwellers being disrespectful to the laws of the land should be broken. Most slum dwellers spend about 50% of their incomes on food, but, one-fourth of the slum dwellers do pay rent. Almost all slum dwellers face several risks and threats. These include the constant threat of being ousted from slums—their home by municipal authorities. Quite a few of them are a part of the unorganized sector and sweat it out in hazardous industries. My friend mentioned about slums acting as centres of crime and homes to criminals. I would only say that nothing is black and white. Criminals live everywhere and it could be a simplistic explanation of things to conclude that slums are crime breeding zones of cities. In fact, the brunt of most crimes is felt in slums by slum dwellers. This risk is compounded by the fact that unlike the more privileged areas of cities, slum dwellers enjoy little protection against criminal onslaughts and violence. Law enforcers tend to focus more on the wealthier areas of the city and ignore slums. The irony is that there have been reports of Law enforcers harassing slum dwellers on a constant basis.

Candidate No. 6

Even if one accepts parts of what has been earlier mentioned about slum dwellers, it is true that slum dwellers are not interested in helping themselves or bringing about a positive change in their condition. This does have an undesirable effect on the health of a city.

Candidate No. 2

A significant section of slum dwellers suffers from voicelessness. The situation may be changing in some metros, where slum dwellers have grouped themselves to be able to voice their concerns better. Also, I think that all the dirt, congestion and miserable living conditions associated with slums are not so much linked to the lack of willingness to change on the part of slum dwellers, but due to a larger systemic failure.

Candidate No. 7

Yes, I agree with you. What do you say No. 4?

Candidate No. 4

Yes, yes, very well said. I agree.

Candidate No. 1

We need today people like Shabana Azmi and other NGOs to bring in awareness amongst the masses for the rights and rightful relocation of hutments from the towns—still keeping the dwellers connected with their employment.

Candidate No. 5

See, whenever the government relocates them, it is found that they sell off the newly allotted flats at a premium and then again come back to their old places of residence.

Candidate No. 7

That means there are loopholes in the system. Isn't it ?

Candidate No. 4

Yes, I agree. We should devise better plans to relocate these slum dwellers.

Candidate No. 6

Let me explain the loopholes. See, it is a direct outcome of either loopholes in existing laws and housing policies or in their sound implementation. The fact remains that slums make city run. They provide industries and households extremely cheap labour. According to a recent report, in several cities around 60% of the employment is in the informal sector of the urban population. Also, the share of jobs held by slum dwellers is expected to increase significantly with rise in the number of small scale enterprises.

Candidate No. 8

We are supporting the growth of slums to the extent that we have stopped seeing the damage slums are doing to our culture. These pockets mar the cultural richness of our cities, especially our metros.

Candidate No. 6

Slums have a heritage of their own. They are no "social coastlands", but centers of cooperation and mutual coexistence. Slum dwellers too have a sense of community participation and they do have a heritage, a system of beliefs and practices, something that they bring with members. When they migrate to cities this gets changed over time with influence of their fellow slum inhabitants. Slum is here to stay and there is no doubt about that. If we view them as a problem or an eyesore, they will remain that to us. But if the society and all concerned perceive them as a contributing and valuable section of the society, and work collectively towards dealing with the real issue of improving living conditions in a slum, we would succeed in making the right start.

Candidate No. 8

In million-plus cities, merely 40% households are in slums. Mumbai, Delhi, Chennai, Hyderabad and Kolkata, account for over 50% of India's slum households. Concerns naturally arise over tardy progress in streamlining slum development and rehabilitation policies across the country as well as in implementing them to reduce migration-related pressure on overstretched urban infrastructure. But housing construction as envisaged under the Rajiv Awas Yojana hasn't quite taken off. Authorities need to free up land so that artificial scarcity doesn't push up land costs, disincentivising the private sector from partnering the effort to build low-cost housing. All states need to see that inclusive city development means legalizing the urban poor's informally held assets, so that the economic energies of slums can be harnessed.

Candidate No. 2

Let us now conclude by saying that we should make adequate provision for rehabilitation of our slum dwellers. For example, Delhi Metro is in the process of making a Master Plan to handle this problem within the next five years. This Master Plan would lay the "road map" for relocation and rehabilitation of slum-dwellers in Delhi. We need to initiate similar steps in other big towns as well. Earlier we deal with this situation, better it is.

In June 2017, Delhi CM said that his government was committed to making all slum areas free of open defecation by March 2018. He said that AAP government has constructed 10,583 toilets in the last 2 years and made provision for supply of free water in slum areas.

In some countries including Mexico, people being rehabilitated were helped to set up micro-enterprises and self-help groups. In India, perhaps influx of migrant labour into metros in search of work could be curbed considerably, if sufficient employment opportunities are created in rural areas to arrest this influx.

Critical Analysis of Candidates' Performance

Good: Candidate Nos. 2, 6 and 8

The contributions of Candidate numbers 2, 6 and 8 have been noteworthy with their logical exposition of thought process. They have analysed the problem and put up arguments that were accepted by other members of the group. They have shown their awareness about the real issue and offered practical solution of the problem. Therefore, their performance has been graded as 'Good'.

Average: Candidate Nos. 1, 3 and 5

These candidates have put up just about Average performance with their few short bursts. They certainly propelled the discussion further by their arguments. However, their contribution has been somewhat limited. They lacked depth of knowledge on the subject. Due to these reasons, their performance has been assessed as 'Average'.

Below Average: Candidate Nos. 4 and 7

Candidate No. 4 was merely a yes man to every one. He had nothing much to contribute. Candidate No. 7 was prompt enough to initiate the discussion but thereafter mostly remained a mediator—contributing no original ideas from his side. These two candidates did not prepare the topic and, therefore, did not possess much information on the subject. Thus, their performance has been assessed as 'Below Average'.

He/She Works, He Comes Back, She Comes Back and Cooks

Seven Candidates are Taking Part in this Group Discussion

Candidate No. 7

I think, we have been given a very interesting topic to discuss. I am sure all of us are familiar with this subject. In brief, issue before us is whether a working woman should continue to look after her house-hold affairs also.

Candidate No. 1

In today's world, when the cost of living has gone up considerably, women have joined the workforce in large numbers to support their families. But with little support from family members, they find it difficult to skillfully manage work and home with equal ease.

Candidate No. 2

But, before we deliberate any further, I want to ask a basic question. What is the need for women to work outside their homes? They should stay at home and take care of the family.

I think, all these problems emanate only because women are becoming more and more ambitious even when they lack the capacity and ability to compete in the tumultuous world. The true place where women belong is home. They should stay at home. It is important for women to care for the family.

Candidate No. 6

That is the problem. Effort made by women as a homemaker is overlooked time and again; it is not treated as productive or contributing to growth. I think, we are blind to the fact that even in home-based businesses, one sees that, though the actual selling may be done by men, women are actively involved in manufacturing or allied activities apart from their other home-keeping duties. But, unfortunately, their indirect contribution remains hidden.

Candidate No. 1

I think, we are digressing from the topic.

Candidate No. 6

I don't think so. Probably I was unable to put my views across succinctly. Taking on from where I left, I would like to drive home the point that, if women can take on the so-called responsibilities of men out of necessity or otherwise, why can't men actively render their support to women in homemaking activities, taking care of the child, etc.

After all, at the end of the day both of them have worked equally hard and are equally tired. Why is it then that only women are expected to balance both fronts, even when they are overburdened?

Candidate No. 1

I agree with Candidate 6. I think one has to change with times. And changing one's attitude to empathize with others and in this case with one's spouse, is crucial for a stress-free living. Managing house and work can be a tight-rope walk for everyone without exception. But, successful management depends largely on willing support from family members.

Candidate No. 2

Men, who have succeeded in life, give credit to the women of their family who nurtured them to their current status/ position. It is not a question of equality. It is a question of division of work for proper sustaining of society. Men are good at income-generation activities while women perform tasks of home-keeping better. And in any case, women enjoy cooking and caring for the family. They themselves do not perceive it as a demanding task. For them, it is a way to relax.

Candidate No. 4

I think, even if men try to help women in cooking or allied tasks, it would be disastrous and would make the process more complicated. The satisfaction that women derive out of caring for their family after returning from office is incomparable to any other thing. Staying at home is not work.

Candidate No. 5

Yes, I fully agree with Candidate No. 2 in this regard.

Candidate No. 6

It is really disappointing to know that a woman's nurturing role in the family is viewed as nothing more than 'staying at home'. Household work is a demanding task and can be exhausting. A woman has to single-handedly keep the home running–handling everything from cleaning to cooking.

If she is working outside, then she has to do all this without expecting any help from her 'liberal and considerate' (having given his permission to his wife to work) husband. It would then be prudent to say that what we are dealing with is a highly efficient robot, who is not supposed to feel tired. What is more, she actually gets money home instead of charging for her services. In return she fails to even secure a pat on her back for her incessant efforts. Let us not forget that working women feel that new technology coupled with a demanding career and house hold work has made their lives more hectic than ever. As a

Part II Mock GDs

matter of fact, in America, 30% of working females had regularly been driven to exhaustion and burnout by work and home commitments.

Candidate No. 4

I would support Candidate No. 2 in saying that women do not need to indulge in income generating activities as earning is primarily the task of the man. Everyone should perform the tasks they are best at. A woman's physical constitution does not make her suitable for rigorous physical exertion, something that is increasingly required in the world of cut-throat competition. Similarly, men are meant to rough it out in the outside world. They have never expressed a desire to stay at home and interfere in what is essentially a woman's role. Women are in a better position to take on the nurturing and caring role, as they are by nature more sensitive. In an attempt to do everything, we risk losing the art of maintaining a fine balance that has long been our traditional strength.

Candidate No. 2

Nothing could be farther from the truth. Men are sensitive and caring too. It is another matter that social norms do not allow them to display their emotions publicly. I think, the argument about women's constitution being suitable only for domestic duties and for the care taking role is nothing but a way to slot them into what the society thinks they do best, or rather they should do best. Also, 'roughing it out in the outside world' does not necessarily indicate a regular display of one's physical prowess. We live in the knowledge age and mental faculties are gradually scoring over physical might. With lesser gender segregation at the workplace, and not very starkly visible divides, men and women shoud begin to cooperate at the home front too. Why do we forget that some of the best cooks in the hospitality industry are men?

Candidate No. 1

I think that, the argument regarding each other's work as valuable contribution and helping women manage home and office work, is not so much about 'role reversal', as argued by some, but about complementing each other's strengths for better life management and personal growth.

Candidate No. 3

I feel women are equally capable of discharging all kinds of duties. They should be given appropriate opportunities. Is it not?

Candidate No. 7

Let us sum up the discussion by saying that men and women should work together and share responsibilities of home and office in a judicious manner. Mature outlook and ability to adjust would pave the way to achieve the desired results.

Critical Analysis of Candidates' Performance

Good: Candidate Nos. 2 and 6

These candidates made noticeable contribution towards the Group Discussion. They brought out a number of relevant issues and their ideas were accepted and even appreciated by the other group members. They displayed their adequate knowledge base of the topic.

Average: Candidate Nos. 1 and 4

These candidates helped in continuation of the discussion and made just about average contribution. They had some idea about the topic and managed to contribute their bit to remain in limelight. Due to these reasons their performance has been assessed as 'Average'.

Below Average: Candidate Nos. 3, 5 and 7

Candidate Nos. 3 and 5 hardly took part in the discussion. They merely kept listening to others. Their knowledge base of the topic was pretty low. Candidate No. 7 did initiate and conclude the group discussion. However, his own contribution was nothing much to mention. He had very limited knowledge of the subject and was under the wrong impression that by initiating and concluding the discussion, he would have done his bit. Due to these reasons, performance of Candidate Nos. 3, 5 and 7 has been assessed as 'Below Average'.

Importance of Marketing

Eight Candidates are Taking Part in this Group Discussion

Candidate No. 6

Friends, I assume we have chosen a very lively topic for discussion. While we all know that almost all organisations cannot do without marketing their products or services, presently issue before us is to examine whether these organisations are laying over emphasis on this aspect.

Candidate No. 4

I feel very strongly that most companies lay over emphasis on marketing and if I may say so, this activity has now almost become a public nuisance. Media is cashing on this essential need of companies and they are making a fast buck in the process, much to the discomfiture of the people.

Candidate No. 3

Yes, I completely agree with Candidate No. 4 in this regard.

Candidate No. 1

I am afraid, we are proceeding too fast with the discussion. Even before understanding and appreciating the meaning of this topic, we are already passing judgements. To my mind, marketing is an important managerial activity, and our topic is to carefully evaluate whether this activity has become more significant than other managerial functions. Thus, the issue before us is to examine the significance of marketing compared to other managerial activities.

Candidate No. 5

Let us talk in specific terms. If I may quote Oxford Dictionary, marketing is an activity of showing and advertising a company's products in the best possible way. And obviously, effective marketing will lead to increased sales. Over a period of time, art of marketing has markedly developed due to technological advancements during the past five decades. As a result, attracting peoples' attention has become increasingly feasible, and even fashionable. The amount of expenditure that companies incur on marketing is really colossal and mind boggling.

Candidate No. 6

If I may add, American Marketing Association defines marketing as the performance of business activities that direct the flow of goods and services from producer to consumer or user. It is apparent that marketing as a management process strives to ensure that the right product is positioned in the right place, at the right time and also at the right price. Marketing demands tremendous coordination, planning and successful implementation of campaigns to achieve good results. In today's competitive world, the success of any commercial venture largely depends upon its marketing team. Marketing acts as a bridge between an organisation, its markets and its customers.

Candidate No. 5

I would like to clarify that often people tend to think that selling and marketing are one and the same thing. Basically, one needs to first identify customer needs, then evaluate what your competitors are offering and then develop a strategy to deliver those offerings at a reasonable rate. I must make it clear that selling is only confined to delivery of the offering, while marketing is a very broad concept, which entails a number of other activities as well.

Candidate No. 7

Yes, I agree with No. 5. Of course, marketing is a much wider activity than selling. But, presently companies are obsessed with marketing, and more emphasis is laid on this aspect than product quality or good service.

Candidate No. 4

Let me bring out that marketing activities encompass a large number of functions which may include activities starting with even production. Main objective of marketing activities is to meet aspirations and expectations of consumers and all efforts of any organisation must focus on this objective. Thus, marketing includes product and brand management, and even market research.

Candidate No. 6

While selling activity may be satisfied with the existing technology and reducing the cost of production, marketing activity emphasises on new technology and innovation in all spheres. This is so, since marketing seeks to focus on customer satisfying process and nothing else. Marketing thus is a typical function of business, which largely satisfies the goals of an organisation. No. 3 what do you say about this aspect?

Candidate No. 3

If we agree with Candidate No. 6, then it emerges that marketing does become the most significant function of managerial activities. So, why are we so surprised if all companies are focusing their attention on marketing. I think, it is quite natural and we must accept this fact. That is how I take it. What do you say Candidate No. 5?

Part II Mock GDs

Candidate No. 5

Quite correct, I agree with you No. 3.

Candidate No. 1

Yes, as it emerges that marketing essentially marshals the efforts of an organisation, so that it can meet the ever increasing requirements of the customers on whom the organisation depends. So, the fact remains that marketing is the unique and most important activity of business. Let me also tell you that experience has shown that marketing is by far the most difficult activity to perform, especially in this age of intense competition and innovations. Let us give a chance to No. 2 also.

Candidate No. 2

Yes, I agree with candidate No. 1. It is not so difficult to produce some items or provide a service, but it is really very cumbersome to sell it to customers and that too at a competitive price. Nowadays, marketing job does not finish with customer satisfaction, but now 'Customer delight' is the buzzword. This calls for new strategies of marketing and increased effort by the marketing teams of all organisations.

Candidate No. 4

I would like to divert your attention to another aspect of the issue. As we are appreciating that marketing function is fairly unique and significant, yet selling or marketing people in an organisation hardly take pride in their jobs and do not hold their profession in a high esteem. People often look towards sales persons with suspicion, and there is clearly a lack of trust when we talk of a Salesperson.

Candidate No. 8

Gentlemen, let me also participate in this discussion.

If I may intervene and point out that this suspicion is not totally unfounded. Many marketing people do sell substandard products and do not fulfill their promises and even misguide people and fleece their money. More often than not, their knowledge about the products they are selling is rather inadequate, and they are not able to convince the customers. All these factors are the basis of this mistrust and suspicion.

Candidate No. 1

But I feel, these days the focus has somehow shifted from the salesmen to the persons who are involved in Direct Marketing. It involves approaching the customer directly to sell a product or service in either a person-to-person or party-plan method. As we know Direct Marketing creates its share of market by various methods. It is essentially a strategy and not a tactic. Direct Marketing uses media as a contact strategy and does not focus on creating favourable impressions and brand awareness or brand recall. More and more companies are now using direct marketing as their sales strategy. This is becoming popular, since it is essentially an information based discipline, as we are living in the information age. Hence its popularity.

Candidate No. 7

If, I may add, direct marketing also involves sending mailers and brochures, organizing road shows or events to reach out to customers.

Candidate No. 5

In the beginning of this discussion, somebody mentioned that marketing has become a nuisance these days. I would I like to clarify that it's not marketing which has become a nuisance, but crude advertising which is so. Till a few years back, print media and radio/TV were only used for advertising, but now with the wide usage of mobile phones and internet, advertising has acquired an altogether new dimension. In fact telemarketing has emerged as one of the most irritating part of marketing. It blatantly encroaches upon the privacy of a person and hence rightly, it could be called a nuisance.

Candidate No. 4

Also selling on the internet is being included in the wide spectrum of activities that are related to Direct Marketing.

Candidate No. 1

Yes, another irritating part of advertising is shamelessly covering every empty space on the road side, or else where, with a hoarding and leaving no space for important information which needs to be displayed in these areas. Secondly, obscenity has also become an essential element of advertising, especially projecting woman in an undignified and vulgar manner to attract popular attention to various products. I think, there is a need for a Censor, which must be more strict with these kinds of advertisements. Advertising must involve creativity and good taste to have the right impact on the masses.

Candidate No. 8

But, all said and done, I feel healthy advertising is a part of marketing strategy, and this is definitely here to stay and society will accept it also. These days focused advertising can be converted from a speculative expense to an investment for profit, if organized in a planned and scientific manner. So, marketing will remain exciting for the sheer variety of work that it offers, and successful marketing managers will continue to climb hierarchical ladder in the organisation.

Candidate No. 6

I think, we have discussed some relevant aspects of marketing fairly in details. We all agree that marketing shall remain a very significant aspect of managerial functions, since through marketing, an organisation can achieve its objectives.

It is marketing which enables an organisation to marshal its resources towards its prime objectives effectively and efficiently. That is why many MNCs and business houses recruit MBAs who have specialised in marketing.

Critical Analysis of Candidates' Performance

Good: Candidate Nos. 1, 5 and 6

Candidate Nos. 1, 5 and 6 have displayed good knowledge of the subject. These candidates have shown consideration for other participants also. The group members have agreed with their views and they have displayed good insight of the topic. It is apparent that they have definitely contributed in the discussion in an effective manner. Due to these factors, their performance has been assessed as 'Good'.

Average: Candidate Nos. 8 and 4

Candidate Nos. 8 and 4 have taken part in the discussion, but their knowledge base is somewhat limited. Obviously, they did not prepare well for the discussion and hence could not participate in an effective manner. They did not add much information to attract others' attention. Due to these reasons, their performance has been assessed as 'Average'.

Below Average: Candidate Nos. 3, 7 and 2

Candidate Nos. 3, 7 and 2 did not take part in the discussion as was expected. They did not possess much of information or data on the topic, and hence they hesitated in airing their views. Due to their inadequate information base, they lacked self confidence to come out with their views. These candidates have been merely agreeing with what other participants have been saying. They did not prepare adequately for the discussion. Owing to these reasons, their performance has been assessed as 'Below Average'.

How to Resolve the Kashmir Issue?

Nine Candidates are Taking Part in this Group Discussion

Candidate No. 1

We all know that, problem of Kashmir has been the most controversial issue between India and Pakistan and has made these two largest countries of South Asia the bitterest rivals. For over 60 years, this problem has remained unresolved despite wars, as well as efforts to find a peaceful solution to this waxed issue. Subsequent to India and Pakistan becoming nuclear powers, Kashmir issue has become a very serious problem for the entire world. Leaders from all over the world have expressed their anxiety in this regard and described Kashmir as a flash point of a major conflict. I think, the task before us is to find out whether this issue can be resolved through dialogue or India and Pakistan will have to fight yet another war to find its solution.

Candidate No. 7

Oh, we've tried all this before, but nothing is working out. We will have to try some thing new.

Candidate No. 2

Well, I feel we are jumping the gun. Before we try and suggest a solution to this problem, let us first make an effort to define the issues involved making it so complicated. To really appreciate this problem, there is a definite need to recollect a few historical facts. Let me point-out these facts.

It all started when the process of partition of our country was taking place. The Maharaja of Kashmir, Raja Hari Singh could not make-up his mind, whether to merge with India or Pakistan and kept delaying his decision in this regard. Meanwhile, Pakistan sponsored Kabayalis invaded Kashmir to forcibly occupy it. At this juncture, he sought the help of Indian government to push back Pakistani forces. At the same time, consequent to an agreement, Kashmir formally acceded to India. However, since Hari Singh wanted to seek the opinion of people of J&K in this regard, he also promised to hold a plebiscite. Pakistan has been insisting that a plebiscite must be held to resolve the Kashmir issue.

Candidate No. 7

Absolutely right No. 2. But, we cannot give Kashmir to Pakistan at any cost. Kashmir is now very much a part of India.

Candidate No. 8

I think I would clarify the stand taken by India on this dispute. India maintains that Kashmir has formally and finally acceded to India and the portion of J&K occupied by Pakistan, i.e., Pakistan occupied Kashmir (POK), should be vacated by Pakistan. Kashmir has been given a special status by the Indian Constitution and Kashmir now is an integral part of India. During the past 50 years or so, people of Kashmir have chosen their representatives a number of times and government machinery of the state is fully functional. The very fact that people of Kashmir have been taking part in the election process, shows that they have full faith in Indian democracy, and now they are a part of Indian union. There should be no second thoughts in this regard in our minds.

Candidate No. 9

I fully agree with No. 8. Well said No. 8.

Candidate No. 4

I entirely agree with No. 8, when he says that Kashmir is an integral part of India. Pakistan should immediately vacate POK, and stop claiming that Kashmir is a disputed territory. There is no justification for Pakistan to occupy a portion of Kashmir after an aggression. To my mind, once Kashmir has acceded to India, what claim does Pakistan have on Kashmir and to repeatedly describe it as a disputed territory in all international forums.

Candidate No. 7

But, why is Pakistan doing such things?

Candidate No. 5

As far as Pakistan is concerned, they want to capture Kashmir by whatever means they can adopt. Towards this aim, Pakistan has waged wars against India on three occasions, i.e., 1965, 1971 and now recently in Kargil. On all these three occasions, Pakistanis could not succeed in achieving their goal. But I am sure, despite fighting three wars, we are no where near any solution to this problem.

Candidate No. 7

So, what is the solution?

Candidate No. 9

Yes, that is the problem. What do you suggest No. 2?

Candidate No. 3

We all know the problem. We are looking for a solution now.

Candidate No. 2

I think, wars cannot resolve all issues on a permanent basis, while dialogues can help us reach near permanent solutions to several issues. Consequent to 1965 war, Tashkant Pact was signed between India and Pakistan and both countries had then agreed to solve the problem through bilateral talks and peaceful means. Again after 1971 war, Shimla agreement was signed and both countries had again agreed to rule out any third party intervention. Unfortunately, Pakistan did not go by these agreements and continued to internationalise the issue. This attitude of Pakistan had added fuel to fire and has caused tremendous bitterness in our region.

Candidate No. 7

Yet another problem in Kashmir is the fact that Pakistan has been encouraging terrorist activities in J&K in a big way. This is very upsetting.

Candidate No. 8

Yes, yet another factor, which has been a constant irritant between India and Pakistan, is the well known fact that Pakistan openly instigates secessionist elements in the J&K. In the recent past, Pakistan has been training terrorists and pushing them in India to create disturbances. And these terrorists have been fairly successful in creating numerous problems for Indian security forces. Primary aim of these elements is to keep Indian security forces engaged in low intensity conflicts on a constant basis, and bleed our security forces. On a number of occasions, India has given evidence to prove that Pakistan has been maintaining a number of terrorist camps near the LOC. These terrorist activities have been a major source of tension and confrontation between the security forces of India and Pakistan. Pakistan also has the audacity to call these terrorists as people who want independence in J&K. Pakistani army openly supports their senseless activities like killing innocent Indians, including women and children. I really think, unless Pakistan stops all such negative activities and shows her desire to resolve all outstanding issues through a dialogue, nothing much can be achieved between India and Pakistan.

Candidate No. 7

All these killings must come to a stop now. I think we must discuss the issue with all parties involved.

Candidate No. 6

I wish to agree with No. 8, when he says that activities of these terrorists are a major problem between us. This is the reason, due to which Indian Government had announced that no dialogue will take place till such time all terrorist activities are stopped by Pakistan. There is another side of this situation also. Pakistan army has a major hand in running the government of Pakistan and there are vested interests in Pakistan, who do not want a peaceful settlement of the dispute. As we know, Pakistani economy is in a very bad shape and they also have a spate of other internal problems to solve. Therefore, Pakistani political leaders have found Kashmir, a handy tool to divert public attention from these teething problems. Under these complex circumstances, I don't think the dispute of Kashmir can be resolved through a dialogue.

Candidate No. 9

Yes, I agree with No. 6. I think under the present scenario, there cannot be any dialogue. Therefore, now only a final war with Pakistan will bring peace in J&K.

Candidate No. 1

I think, we have become quite pessimistic about resolving the issue through a dialogue. Yes, in the past, Pakistan had been adamant, but it does not necessarily mean that dialogue will not succeed in future as well. We have not forgotten the initiative of our former Prime Minister Shri Atal Behari Vajpayee to go to Lahore by bus. But Pakistani army did not like it, and soon thereafter, we had the Kargil conflict. Similarly, Agra Summit also could not succeed due to adamant attitude of General Pervez Musharaf. It is well known that, Pakistan is a puppet in the hands of certain western powers and these forces mould the situation as they want. These forces also do not want India to become a powerful nation as per their scheme of things. But, then efforts must be made to resume the dialogue to resolve all outstanding issues between India and Pakistan. I think, we are giving up rather prematurely.

Candidate No. 7

Well, in this direction, we can take the help of SAARC, and resume talks. Things appear brighter for a fruitful talk now.

Candidate No. 3

This is all show biz-total show business. The government of Pakistan is not interested in solving this problem. If this problem is solved-how will the Pakistani government divert the attention of Pakistani people from their internal problems.

Candidate No. 2

Well Gentlemen, I would rather agree with No. 7 that, we must try to resume meaningful dialogue to resolve all issues including Kashmir. You all would appreciate that the world is quite different after the start of Kashmir problem more than 60 years ago. The problem should be viewed afresh with a positive intention to resolve it by all parties concerned. In this regard, Kashmiri people should also be allowed to present their point of view. Fortunately, during SAARC 2004 meeting in Islamabad, both India and Pakistan had agreed to resume dialogue to resolve all issues. Subsequently, assembly elections were held and state government headed by Omar Abdullah was installed with the help of Congress Party. However, this government did not deliver goods as expected by people of Kashmir. During the years 2008–2009, Kashmiri Youth displayed their anguish and came on streets pelting stones on Security Forces. This resulted in many young men getting killed in police/military firing. These developments made things worse, as there are now increased demands for 'Azadi' in the Kashmir Valley.

Candidate No. 9

Let me tell you No. 2, Pakistan understands only the language of war and this time if there is a war, Pakistan should be wiped out from the world map.

Candidate No. 4

Come on No. 9, lets give peace a chance. I am in agreement that Kashmir issue can be resolved by resuming dialogue at the earliest. We should not forget that people of Kashmir have suffered a lot in terms of life and property during the last 70 years. Owing to terrorists activities prevailing in the region, tourism, which is the main source of income for Kashmiri people, has suffered tremendously making them fairly economically weak.

Candidate No. 3

Well, I think our government is also responsible for the present situation.

Candidate No. 8

Presently, there is also a demand to withdraw Armed Forces Special Power Act (AFSPA) from J&K region. This Act provides special powers to soldiers to arrest and conduct investigations on suspects. It is alleged that the Act has been widely misused by Security Forces. However, Armed Forces are not in favour of withdrawing AFSPA. Looking at the turmoil in J&K, the government sent an all party delegation in September 2010 to Kashmir to assess the ground situation. Government of India then announced an eight point peace formula for Kashmir. In addition, the government was also focusing on expanding job opportunities for Kashmiri youth, both within J&K and elsewhere.

Candidate No. 1

I feel, if enough job opportunities are created for the Kashmiri youth, they will not play in the hands of separatist elements. After all, what can Kashmiris expect from Pakistan? Pakistan is a failed state, Sindh and Baluchistan are seething with discontent and what about Kashmiris in Pakistani Kashmir? Do they have any democracy? The problem of Kashmir is a complex one which has other dimensions also. Two of its non-Muslim regions, Jammu and Ladakh will surely demand their own right of self-determination and exercise it to stay with India. The only way is to hold a dialogue with the people of Kashmir. One of the options has been an offer of "special federal relationship". That would fall short of Azadi for the youth of Kashmir, but they would soon realize that Pakistan is no option for them. In fact, for some, Azadi means an end to repressive military rule in the valley. Interlocutors, who were appointed by the Government to initiate dialogue with the people of J&K state, have recommended much more autonomy to the State Government, almost a pre-1953 status for the J&K State.

Part II Mock GDs

Candidate No. 2

I think, we have discussed the topic adequately. As we can see it is a very complex issue with so may groups involved. Hardliner Syed Ali Shah Gealani's call to make Kashmir a part of Pakistan is also not very popular among the youth. Moderate Hurriyat Leader Mirwaiz Umar Farooq has been talking of independence for Kashmir. I think, the need of the hour is to talk to the young generation and address their genuine problems. Youth has been demanding Kashmir for people of Kashmir only. But, the question is, can Kashmir remain an independent country? I am sure, a meaningful dialogue only can lead to a solution, sooner or later. I hope, people of Kashmir would realize that they can lead a peaceful life and also become prosperous by accepting their future with India, and certainly not with Pakistan. In 2015 assembly elections in J&K, people have voted in a record large number for peace and development, while expressing faith in Indian democracy. This clearly shows that majority of Kashmiris trust India and want to remain in India. It was hoped that the new Government of J&K would be able to meet the aspirations of Kashmiris.

During the last 2 years, supported by Pakistan, terrorist attacks have increased manifold in Jammu & Kashmir. Notable among them were attacks on Air Force Base at Pathankot and Army Base at Uri. In addition, Kashmir youths are being encouraged by the terrorist groups to indulge in stone – throwing activities to disrupt normal life.

Critical Analysis of Candidates' Performance

Good: Candidate Nos. 1, 2 and 8

These Candidates brought out the vital aspects of the topic, spoke 3 to 4 times and also countered others, who were incoherent. They brought the discussion to its logical end with an optimistic note. They adopted a logical and pragmatic approach to resolve a very complex issue. They have shown their mature outlook. Therefore, their performance has been graded as 'Good'.

Average: Candidate Nos. 4, 6 and 7

These Candidates were mainly mediators who participated just once or twice. Though their ideas were positive and helped in prompting others into action, they did not take part in the discussion in an effective manner. Their lack of preparation was quite evident. Due to these reasons, their performance is assessed as 'Average'.

Below Average: Candidate Nos. 3, 5 and 9

These Candidates just butted in once or twice, but mostly with negative remarks. Their rebuttal/casual remarks show their superficial knowledge, and casual/ negative approach. They did not make any preparation for participating in the group discussion and, therefore, could not take part in the GD in the desired manner. Therefore, their performance can only be assessed as 'Below Average'.

India and the World Trade Organization (WTO)

Nine Candidates are Taking Part in this Group Discussion

Candidate No. 1

Let me first, give a brief introduction of World Trade Organization (WTO) for the benefit of all. We all know that the WTO, i.e., the World Trade Organization came into being in 1995. Some members of the United Nations had promoted this organization to encourage trade among various countries of the world. WTO has its head quarters at Geneva and this organization has made a huge impact on liberalization and globalization among developing countries, including India. The primary aim of this organization is to conduct international trade in an open and uniform manner ensuring that no discrimination is shown against any country. On the face of it, aims of WTO are quite good. But, there are teething problems with certain rules of WTO.

Candidate No. 4

The WTO's creation was agreed to at the end of the 1986–93 Uruguay Round of International Trade Negotiations.

Launched on January 1, 1995, it replaced the old General Agreement on Tariffs and Trade (GATT), which had acted as an "interim" world trade watchdog since 1948. It is officially defined as "the legal and institutional foundation of the multilateral trading system".

Unlike GATT, the WTO is a permanent organization created by international treaty ratified by the governments and legislatures of member states. As the principle international body concerned with solving trade problems between countries and providing a forum for multilateral trade negotiations, it has global status similar to that of the International Monetary Fund and the World Bank. But unlike them, it is not a United Nations Agency although it has a "cooperative relationship" with the United Nations.

Candidate No. 7

But, may I ask what has India got in return. Most of our so-called rights, were not given. Well, No. 2 what have you to say about it?

Candidate No. 2

I would like to add here that, WTO enforces certain rules and regulations on members, which they have to adhere to. Mostly, countries enter into bilateral agreements, which are between two countries. However, the rules of WTO are such that countries are expected to follow multilateral agreements, i.e., these agreements are to be made by a group of countries together. WTO wants that export and import restrictions imposed by certain countries are also abolished. Thus, there is an emphasis on common agreements among a number of countries to promote trade among these nations.

Candidate No. 7

OK, OK; what do you say about it No. 3?

Candidate No. 3

Let me remind that, World Trade Organization not only controls international trade of goods, but it also controls various services that are provided by a number of nations. It is essential that the members of WTO also adopt suitable laws and policies in order to comply with the WTO stipulations.

Candidates No. 7

OK, if you've finished, let No. 4 speak.

Candidate No. 4

I think after learning the background of WTO, let us now discuss the impact of WTO on the Indian economy. I feel that, WTO provides India a very fine opportunity for trading with other countries, that are also members of WTO. Obviously, we will be able to export our goods and services to other countries encountering much less problems and restrictions from those countries. Secondly, technology from developed and technologically advanced countries would also be available to India at a much lesser price and at a faster pace. This would be beneficial for our country in so many ways.

Candidate No. 2

But, I do not think the same is really happening. In the past, at the WTO meeting at Cancun we saw that the developing nations were kept at bay, when it came to these kind of benefits.

Candidate No. 8

I must add that, most of the trade takes place between advanced countries only, and therefore, India does not really get much of benefit being a member of WTO. To my mind, the major problem is that a number of rules of WTO do not favour developing countries like India, e.g., a number of Indian industries may not be able to face the competition which developed countries offer, and these Indian industries may even have to close down. This in turn would adversely affect employment opportunities for our youth, and as India is already saddled with the problem of unemployment, this issue assumes even greater significance.

Candidate No. 9

Good point, I agree with him.

Candidate No. 6

Let us not forget that WTO certainly interferes with the functioning of internal economy of a country. To illustrate, prices of a number of commodities, including some life saving medicines, may go up due to a series of restrictions imposed by WTO. Further, the WTO agreement on agriculture may also discourage distribution and provisioning of subsidized food grains in India. This is certainly not desirable looking at conditions that are prevailing in India.

Candidate No. 7

What WTO rules are you all talking about? In our country, poor farmers are committing suicides. They don't have the very basic amenities to cultivate their land. I think, WTO stipulations will kill them all.

Candidate No. 9

He has a point. I agree. Any answer to it?

Candidate No. 3

I think, it is quite apparent that a number of provisions of WTO do not favour the developing countries and these have been deliberately designed to suit the requirements of developed nations only. It was in this context that in the WTO meeting, which was held in Cancun in September, 2003, a number of developing countries joined hands to raise their voice against developed nations. As a result, the meeting at Cancun turned out to be another failure for WTO talks, just as it happened in the meeting that was held in Seattle in 1999. It is quite heartening to note that India played a very significant role on behalf of developing nations at Cancun.

Candidate No. 7

But to my mind, this cannot be called a victory. I think, it was a sort of defeat for the developing nations.

Candidate No. 8

In my considered opinion, India took a very correct stand at Cancun. There were mainly two issues involved at Cancun. One issue was pertaining to agriculture subsidies being given by American and European Union countries. We all know that, it is very difficult for developing countries to compete against subsidized products of developed nations. The second issue pertained to the foreign investment without conditions, global competition, transparency in procurement policies and trade facilitation. The developed countries wanted a reduction in import tariff, so that their product could be easily sold in all member countries of WTO.

Candidate No. 9

Very good point indeed. I agree.

Candidate No. 5

It is quite clear that, after two failures at ministerial conferences in the past, the WTO now faces a crisis of legitimacy. Developing countries are now gradually losing their confidence in the WTO agenda. Subsequently, during Doha Round of talks, the issues between developed and developing countries were somewhat resolved, but the differences still remained. Later, in 2013 during the meeting of WTO members in Bali, deadlock was somewhat removed and a 'Bali Package' worked out to adopt a work program to be completed by the end of 2014 to deal with remaining issues of Doha Round. Developing nations also want an end to subsidies on exported food that allow cheaper Western products to flood global markets. At the Cancun meeting, India, China and Brazil emerged as leaders of the developing countries.

Candidate No. 3

But, after the BJP government took charge in India, during the 2014 WTO meeting, India took an extremely rigid stand, which brought an impasse in WTO. India refused to rectify WTO's Trade Facilitation Agreement (TFA), which is so dear to developed nations, without any move to find a permanent solution to India's public food stock holding issue for food security purposes. India's stand has been much criticized by a number of countries. With this stalemate, the future of WTO seemed uncertain. However later, India and US have reached an agreement to resolve the issue, but this needs to be ratified by all WTO nations.

Candidate No. 8

India has now asked WTO to amend norms for calculating agriculture subsidies, which are now only up to 10% of total food grain production, so that the country could continue to procure food grains from farmers at a Minimum Support Price (MSP) and sell them to poor at cheaper rates without violating WTO norms.

Candidate No. 9

Again a very good point, I agree.

Candidate No. 4

I would like to add that, at present WTO is not able to encourage trade among nations as was earlier envisaged. The reason for such a development is primarily the attitude of the developed nations. Now, everyone knows that rich countries spend about 300 million dollars on farm subsidies every year. These subsidies artificially reduce the price of their farm products and render developing countrys' agriculture products internationally non-competitive. It is obvious that in the absence of such subsidies, developing countries could gain substantial benefits from the farm produce.

Candidate No. 1

We may end by saying that impasse in the WTO, which had occurred due to India's tough stand in 2014, was resolved after the meeting of Indian PM with US President in September 2014, where India agreed to urgently start negotiations with other WTO members on a broader negotiating agenda. WTO Chief has been consulting other countries to find a solution to all outstanding issues. Let us hope that in the next WTO meeting, a more pragmatic approach will be adopted by developed nations and this would definitely pave the way for better trade links between the developed and developing countries.

Critical Analysis of Candidates' Performance

Good: Candidate Nos. 1, 3, 4 and 8

Candidate Nos. 1, 3, 4 and 8 were the main speakers who did a fine analysis of the topic. They brought out the finer aspects of the topic and logically countered others. Their knowledge was up-to-date and they made reference to the latest happenings connected with the topic to make it more interesting. Thus, their performance has been assessed as 'Good'.

Average: Candidate Nos. 2, 5 and 6

Candidate Nos. 2, 5 and 6 managed to put across their views along the sidelines. They also enhanced the momentum and kept a positive approach. However, their contribution was somewhat restricted due to lack of initiative and preparation. Owing to these reasons, their effort can only be graded as 'Average'.

Below Average: Candidate Nos. 7 and 9

Candidate No. 7 merely conducted the initial part of discussion—asking others to participate. His own contribution was very limited. No. 9 was only a bystander who appreciated the efforts of good speakers. His own application and contribution to the discussion was negligible. It is apparent that these two candidates did not put in efforts to study the topic or collect relevant data to support their arguments. Owing to these reasons, their performance can be merely assessed as 'Below Average'.

Part II Mock GDs

Should India be Proud of its Democracy?

Ten Candidates are Taking Part in this Group Discussion

Candidate No. 6

Good morning everybody. A very good topic indeed which we will discuss. Please express your thoughts one by one. Let's start with No. 10.

Candidate No. 10

Thanks No. 6. I think, before we discuss as to how democracy is functioning in India, let us try and understand the real meaning of democracy. To my mind, democracy implies the government, wherein, the entire power is in the hands of the people. Democracy could either be a direct or indirect type of democracy. In case of direct democracy, the citizens themselves rule, while in the case of indirect type of democracy, citizens elect their representatives and these representatives form a government, which runs the administration. In India, we have the indirect form of democracy that is functioning presently. But, the issue before us is whether we in India are running a healthy democracy, i.e., a government for the people, by the people and of the people, as was defined by Abraham Lincoln. Other forms of democracy are parliamentary and presidential forms of governments. Obviously, we have opted for the parliamentary form in our country.

Candidate No. 1

Actually to my mind, this democracy has spoilt Indians. Looking at the state of affairs in India, this country needs strict military rule. Politics has really degenerated to very low levels. That is the main issue.

Candidate No. 4

I would like to add that for the smooth running of democracy, political parties must function in a responsible manner. While the ruling party conveys the reaction of a larger number of voters to the government, the parties which are defeated in elections also play an important role. They have to function as the opposition, and as and when required, constructively criticise the government's functioning. Thus, political parties play a vital role in the formulation of public opinion. In India, a person who has attained the age of 18 years can exercise his franchise or the right to vote. The right to vote is an equal right for all citizens. Elections provide an opportunity to the people to judge the performance of their leaders. Another important aspect of democracy is the fact that elections must be conducted in a fair, free and transparent manner, enabling people to cast their votes freely.

Candidate No. 2

Yes, I agree with you No. 4.

Candidate No. 8

Yet, another significant element in the functioning of democracy is the presence of free press and the electronic media which provide information to the people and play an important role in moulding public opinion, especially during the time of elections. The Election Commission must be given a free hand to ensure that elections are conducted in a judicious, free and fair manner. During 2017 elections, several opposition parties have alleged that working of Electronic Voting machines (EVMs) was manipulated by the BJP government to win elections.

Candidate No. 3

But, we have seen elections in the past. By and large, were they conducted in a fair manner?

Candidate No. 4

Well, we have seen what all it takes to let democracy function in a country, but when we talk of India, there are several teething problems which grossly hamper the smooth functioning of democracy. These hindrances are namely illiteracy, casteism, communalism, poverty and linguism. All these factors are obstacles in formation of public opinion in a democracy.

Candidate No. 1

I think, we were better off under the British rule. Everything was so well organised then, and such problems were not there at all.

Candidate No. 8

Let us not forget that, democracy flourishes on government response and consent of the people for this response. In case there is no discussion, no free expression of views and no freedom of expression, there cannot be a real democracy in the country. These factors presume the existence of literacy. There cannot be a discussion, debate and free exchange of ideas, when people are not literate and do not possess adequate intelligence, which makes them decide what is right and what is wrong. Therefore, I am quite sure that democracy and illiteracy cannot coexist. Democracy assumes that people are fully aware of the value of difference of opinion and they have tolerance for dissent in a democratic order.

Candidate No. 4

I fully agree that, people must display their maturity and tolerance in a democracy. If they do not have such tolerance, democracy cannot last for long. Democracy provides a fundamental right to the people to express their opinion under all circumstances. Here lies the true democratic spirit.

Part II Mock GDs

Candidate No. 5

What if we had two party system, I think, democracy would have flourished better and we would have got rid of the bickerings that we now see amongst so many parties.

Candidate No. 8

I think, if we discuss the conditions prevailing in our country, we will realize that there are so many problems which hamper the functioning of democracy. To begin with, we have a multi-party system existing in our country where, except for 3 or 4 central parties, there are a large number of regional parties existing. There is hardly any stability in these regional parties, which makes the entire political scenario very fluid and uncertain. Every time when elections are held, new political equations emerge and this confuses the illiterate masses of the country a great deal. Secondly, a number of political parties have religious, regional and caste biases, which divide the people into a number of segments, which even threaten the unity of our country.

Candidate No. 9

But, the Government is spending quite a big sum on the literacy front. What we need to uproot is the flimsy caste and religion based differences which hinder our progress.

Candidate No. 4

I agree with No. 8 when he says that presence of a number of parties poses a lot of problems. Though certain significant measures have been taken by the Election Commission, no major change to make our elections more transparent and fully representative of public opinion has yet been made.

At present, due to the presence of multiple political parties, it usually transpires that people, who are elected to the State Assemblies or Parliament, receive only a minority of the votes cast in their respective constituencies. As a result, few of these members actually represent a majority opinion in their electorate. This tends to undermine the legitimacy of our democratic process and leads to frustration and negative thinking.

Candidate No. 7

I think, the huge problem which really threatens our democracy is the problem of illiteracy in our country. The situation which prevailed in Bihar is a case in point. The illiterate and poverty stricken people of this state exercised their franchise strictly on the basis of caste. As a result, there was hardly any development in this state and people continued to suffer economically. A number of parliamentary seats have been declared as reserved scheduled caste seats also. A similar situation is also seen in a number of districts of Jharkhand and other states. However, in elections of 2010 in Bihar, the people voted for the development of the state and realised the power of their votes to change the government. As of now, about 35% of our population is still illiterate making functioning of democracy all the more difficult. Under these circumstances, how can we say that democracy is flourishing in our country?

Candidate No. 4

In the six-plus decades since independence, democracy has failed to create a single political community. Instead, we have become more conscious than ever of what divides us: religion, region, caste, language, ethnicity. The political system has become looser and more fragmented. Politicians mobilise support along ever narrower lines of political identity. It has become more important to be a "backward caste", a "tribal", or a religious sectarian than to be an Indian.

Candidate No. 1

Friends, to my mind, in India, democracy has almost failed, we have seen it enough in the last 10 years. Have we not ?

Candidate No. 8

I am sorry, 1 do not entirely agree with my friend when he says that almost everything is wrong with our democracy. Let us not forget that, India is the world's largest democracy and a fairly successful one too. This has been proved every time elections are held. The fact remains that democracy itself is a sort of education for the people. The Indian masses have now acquired enough experience of the democratic system and they know where to cast their vote. The result of Lok Sabha elections held in 2004 has once again established this fact. While, quite a few opinion polls predicted a victory for the NDA government, it did not happen so. Elections of Bihar and Lok Sabha in 2014 and huge win of AAP in Delhi (2015) also prove this point.

Candidate No. 10

I must emphasize that our experience has shown that Indian masses are politically mature, since they have repeatedly rejected inefficiency and falsehood. Quite a few senior political leaders have been rejected by the people since they were corrupt. In this regard the case of Andhra Pradesh and Karnataka during elections in 1983 is still fresh in our minds. Once again in 1977 due to several actions of Mrs. Indira Gandhi, she was rejected by the people and the Janata leaders were allowed to form a government. However, the Janata alliance leaders did not function efficiently. They were also rejected by the people in the elections. Yet again, subsequently Mrs. Indira Gandhi was given a mandate to form a new government and that too by a huge majority. Political activities of UPA Government in 2014 Lok Sabha elections and of Shri Lalu Yadav were totally rejected by the people of Bihar in 2010 elections. State elections held during 2017 also prove the same point. These include elections wins of Congress in Pubjab, BJP in U.P. and JD(U) Ghatbandhan in Bihar etc.

Candidate No. 5

Well, we are the world's largest democracy and during all these years our population has grown by leaps and bounds. As compared to other neighbouring democracies, we are one of the most open, advanced and successful among asian countries.

Candidate No. 8

Interestingly, some people feel that India is perhaps experiencing an over dose of democracy and this is hampering its rapid development. Often, due to prolonged debate and avoidable acrimony, Parliament is not allowed to function and this certainly impedes government's decision-making and functioning. In this regard, India needs to learn a lesson from China where development has taken place at a much faster pace.

Candidate No. 10

I think, we all agree that in India, democracy is functioning in a satisfactory manner. Once, the literacy rate improves in our country, we will get still better results. We must ensure that criminalization of politics is checked forthwith and young, honest and qualified candidates are allowed to win elections. I would like to emphasise that, we need to further strengthen our democratic system by making it truly representative of the views of the people, and therefore, more dynamic. Finally, voting in India, as in Australia and some other countries, should be made mandatory for every Indian adult. Then, only we can say that democracy is flourishing in India.

Critical Analysis of Candidates' Performance

Good: Candidates Nos. 4, 8 and 10

Analytical and positive views of these candidates were heard and appreciated by the group. These candidates were in the centre of discussion most of the time. They politely, yet cluefully, disagreed with others and countered them logically. They had prepared for the discussion, and therefore, their performance has been assessed as 'Good'.

Average: Candidate Nos. 5 and 7

These candidates could get a chance once or twice. But, whatever they spoke was relevant and to the point. They propagated the discussion towards a positive conclusion. However, they had somewhat limited ideas. Their performance has been just about 'Average'.

Below Average: Candidate Nos. 1, 2, 3, 6 and 9

While Candidate No. 1 was very aggressive and negative in his approach, No. 6 was only appreciating others, contributing nothing much from his side. Numbers 1, 2 and 9 were generally quiet. They were observed to be just nodding once or twice to keep themselves in the picture. Therefore, their performance can only be assessed as 'Below Average'.

Part III

Detailed Discussions on Significant Current Topics

US-India Defence Relations

After India attained independence in 1947, we consciously opted to join the group of non-aligned countries. India at that time was not a strong country in terms of economic and military power and not joining any power-group was considered a viable strategy. However, over a period of time due to a variety of reasons, India became close to USSR and a substantial amount of military equipment was procured from USSR for more than five decades. Most fighter planes for IAF and other military and naval equipment has its origins in Russia even today. However, consequent to turmoil and break up of USSR in 1990s, supply and cost of Russian military equipment to India started having several problems. Therefore, India had to look for other sources to procure defence supplies, as India's own defence research and development organizations continued to disappoint and frustrate the Indian armed forces. Currently, India is one of the largest weapon importers in the world and it is expected that India will import weapons worth USD 200 billion in the next decade.

Shift in Sources of Acquisitions

As the cost of Russian military supplies continued to rise and these supplies also become inadequate during the last few years, India procured substantial defence equipment from Israel and other nations as well. Even now, Israel continues to supply vital military items to India and this strategic partnership with Israel is all set to continue. In addition, France is also a significant source of military acquisitions.

However, during the past two years, US-India defence relations have grown manifold as Indian PM paid four visits to US during this period. US President also visited India to become the Chief Guest at India's Republic Day cele-brations. As a result, various proposals for co-production of latest defence equipment, increase maritime security, improve counter terrorism measures and intelligence sharing between the two nations was actively mooted. Meanwhile, China's economic and military power has increased substantially, and it now poses a strategic challenge to the countries of Indo-Pacific region, including India. Since USA considers India a major strategic player in this very region, cooperation between India & USA has markedly increased to counter a dominating China. In this regard, simmering border dispute between India and China and various Chinese aggressive actions in South China Sea have been major issues which are in focus.

US-India Military Cooperation

Currently, besides C-17 Globe master and Super Hericules aircrafts, India buys considerable military items from the US. In view of the above developments, cooperation between India and U.S.A has taken a quantum jump and currently U.S.A has become India's largest weapons supplier, over taking Russia, Israel and France. Defence Trade and Technology Initiative (DTTI), which were first proposed by US in 2012, have been given a relook. Now, there is an increased emphasis on co-production, co-development and transfer of sophisticated technology to India by US. Towards this end, American companies have shown keen interest to cooperate with Indian Defence industry-both in public and private sectors. DTTI now aims to strengthen India US cooperative research, co-production and co-development of capabilities which are needed for continued up gradation of Indian military forces as well as growth of our economies.

Under the renewed DTTI, production of latest Unmanned Arial Vehicles, various modules for C-130 J Super Hercules aircrafts, mobile electric hybrid power sources and production grear for chemical and biological warfare were included. In addition, cooperation will be extended between the two countries on jet engine technology and aircraft carrier design etc. Earlier, India has approved plans to buy 37 military helicopters from Boeing company of U.S.A. These include 15 CH-47F Chinook heavy lift helicopters and 22 AH-64E Apache multirole combat helicopters. This approval has an option to buy additional 7 Chinook and 11 Apache helicopters, making the deal worth $ 3 billion. In addition, contract to buy Ultra Light howitzers has been finalized and 145 artillery guns will be made in India with Mahindra Defence and Aerospace, Mahindra Group as the Indian business partner. India has also expressed desire to buy two intelligence, surveillance target acquisition and reconnaissance (ISTAR) aircraft from US. Even though fairly restricted, US is now agreeable to share defence technology with India while doing co-production of defence equipment. DRDO wants to partner with GE on making engine for Tejas aircraft. All these developments indicate a far greater strategic re-alignment between US and India and this will impact balance of power in own region.

Future Plans for India-US Cooperation

Since US possesses advanced and cutting-edge defence technology, India is mainly interested in technology transfer and subsequent US support to keep the equipment and machinery functional. India wants to co-develop and co-produce next generation equipment and weapon systems and is not in favour of establishing a buyer-seller relationship with US. In this context, the US DTTI and India's 'Make in India' program have much in common.

It is obvious that in the recent years, trust and cooperation between US and India have increased manifold, which have lead to more trade and partnerships between India and American governments and companies. While America wants more trade with India. India looks for technology transfer. USA is quite reluctant to transfer technology and does so to only a few nations, like Israel, Australia and UK etc. India first wants to become self-reliant for its defence equipment like China. It is a well known fact that a few years back China was one of the big importers of defence material, but has now quietly become a big arms exporter. India has similar ambition like China in the field of defence equipment.

Britain's Exit From EU (BREXIT)

Recently, Britain surprised the world by finally deciding to quit the European Union (EU). It was a very close finish in the voting where leave camp won the support of 51.9% votes against 48.1% in favour of remaining in EU. The turnout of the referendum was 72.2% and very strong arguments were exchanged between opposite groups of British people. With this, 43 years old association between UK and EU ended rather abruptly, weakening seven decades of European Unity.

Consequent to the Second World War, since 1945, efforts were made to unite the European Community. Reasons for such unification were both political and financial. However, over a period, right parties all over Europe have been expressing their strong convictions to leave Europe for a variety of reasons, including cultural. So currently, there is a decreasing support for European Union and current polls show that 48% in France and Italy could also vote to exit EU in the near future. Britain's exit from EU has triggered debates whether the concept of a global village is at all a feasible one or, we need to take corrective measures to cure the ailments associated with globalization.

The fact of the matter is that, Britain had easy access to unified market of 27 nations and enjoyed consequent commercial advantages. But, cultural issues continued to haunt British citizens and they have had reservations against supra-national integration with other EU countries. For example, Britain continued to use Pounds to Euros and never gave up Miles to Kms etc. In the recent past, the open door policy announced by Germany and arrival of a very large number of Muslim refugees raised alarms in UK, annoying large number of orthodox British citizens. UK wanted to bar the free movement of labour, which EU countries would never accept. Ironically, economic gains from EU could not control the growing anger and frustration of British people.

An analysis of voting pattern in the recent referendum shows that elderly and not so educated favoured the exit, while the young and progressive voted against leaving the EU. Anti immigration sentiments played a pivotal role and everything from stagnant pay packages to low job opportunities were blamed due to arrival of large number of immigrants. Large Muslim refugees threatened the national identity and sovergnity of Britons.

Exit of Britain from EU is now considered the world's most important event after collapse of communism, which has far reaching impact on world economy. Uncertainty of events would adversely affect the Indian markets as well and initial shock pulled down the Sensex by 600 points. It caused turbulence in the currencies of the world and has severely threatened the EU project of unity. To make things more serious, Northern Ireland and Scotland have voted to join the EU and leave UK as well. Finally, the world needs an urgent and just immigration policy to check the current turmoil in Europe and stabilize the global economy. Sooner, the better.

Part III Detailed Discussions

India's Pride—LCA Tejas

After 33 long years of wait, Indian Military Aviation made history when on 01 July 2016, two Light Combat Aircrafts (LCA) were inducted into the Indian Air force. The project to produce LCA commenced in 1983 and India's then Prime Minister Shri Atal Behari Vajpayee gave the LCA name "Tejas", which means "Radiance" in Sanskrit language. The two LCAs now formed the 45 Squadron of IAF(The Flying Daggers) located in Sulur in Tamil Nadu. According to plans, there will be 10 Tejas by the year end, with total procurement to be 200 aircrafts and additional two seaters trainers. Much to the discomfort of IAF, the LCA project got substantially delayed owing to a variety of reasons leading to huge cost overruns. But, better late than never. Tejas will meet the requirement of Indian Navy as well.

After India became independent, the requirement to have an indigenous fighter aircraft was realized, but we lacked the technical know how. As a result, during all these years, India had to spend huge sums of currency to import a number of aircraft from a number of countries, with Russia leading the way.

Initially in 1969, Hindustan Aeronautics Ltd (HAL) was assigned the task to develop a multi role fighter aircraft, but was soon discontinued due to lack of resources. Subsequently in 1983, primarily to replace the MIG 21 aircraft, LCA programme was restarted. This was felt necessary to reduce India's dependence on other nations in this significant sector of military aviation. Since it was estimated that MIG 21 aircraft, which was the backbone of IAF, would be phasing out by 2005 or so, HAL and DRDO would have around 20 years to make Tejas. Towards this aim, Aeronautical Development Agency (ADA) was formed in 1984 primarily to push the development of LCA. ADA had to coordinate the efforts of various agencies, both civil and military, as no one agency could perform this highly technical task of integrating various aircraft systems. The Gas Turbine Research Establishment (GTRE) Bangalore was assigned the task of providing the appropriate engine called "Kaveri" to power the LCA. However, production of Kaveri engine ran into a variety of problems and ultimately, India had to import an engine for the LCA.

Aircraft Characteristics

Tejas is a single engine multi role aircraft catered to meet the tactical needs of IAF. Its delta wing configuration has been specially designed to increase agility and maneuverability in the air. Its total weight is 8.5 tonnes and it has the capability to carry three tonnes of weapons.

Efforts have been made to keep the aircraft weigh less but strong at the same time. LCA can carry precision-guided munitions, missiles (air to ground, air to air and anti ship), bombs and rockets etc. It can also take required equipment for electronic warfare, drop tanks and could be used for surveillance. The cockpit of the aircraft facilitates the view in all directions and it also has night vision capabilities. LCA has digital fly-by-wire flight control system with excellent integrated GPS and radio communication system. The aircraft is fitted with General Electric engine, while the work to develop Kaveri engine is still in progress. Tejas can fly at a maximum speed of 2205 km/h and at a max altitude of 15200 meters. It has a range of 3000 kms and can be refueled in the air also.

Recently, Tejas displayed its might in an international air show and impressed the audience a great deal. During this show, Tejas pulled more than 8g, and therefore, could be compared with the best in the world in its class. By developing Tejas, India has taken a quantum jump forward in technological advancements in the field of military aviation. In 2014, the government gave out the cost of development of LCA as Rs. 7965 Cr including around Rs. 2500 Cr for the version for Navy.

To conclude, India can now be proud of developing a world-class military aircraft indigenously from scratch. With the induction of Tejas, it is hoped that various other pending military projects would also be pushed forward by DRDO and other agencies.

Part III Detailed Discussions

India and Olympic Games

In Aug 2016, Olympic games were conducted in Rio and as expected, US sports persons collected the largest number of medals, followed by UK and China. However, India's record at the Olympics has been almost heart breaking. The world's second most populous country with a population of 1.3 billion has so far earned merely 28 medals—9 Gold, 7 Silver and 12 Bronze in the Olympic history. Interestingly, Michael Phelps, well-known swimmer of US, has also won 28 medals alone. So one is forced to ponder over India's performance at the Olympic games.

Prior to commencement of games at Rio, there was much euphoria in India and we sent 117 athletes to Rio, the highest number ever, covering 15 disciplines. Four years ago, though we had sent less number of athletes to London, we had grabbed six medals. Since more athletes had qualified for the games in London than ever before, hopes were justifiably high. India's Sports Ministry had set a target of 10 plus medals at Rio. It was expected that India would use the foundation created in London as a springboard, but unfortunately nothing of that sort transpired.

By the time games at Rio ended, India could only talk of the heroics of PV Sindhu and Sakshi Malik and our poor performance was discussed in every nook and corner of India. We had to ultimately console ourselves with only two medals, one silver and one bronze. This clearly was a comedown from the performance of Indian sportspersons in 2012. Perhaps the only silver lining was the talent shown by Dipa Karmakar, who is a gymnast from Tripura. The fact of the matter remains that till Rio Olympics in 2016, only one Indian, Abhinav Bindra, has won Olympic Gold in an individual event of shooting so far.

The above state of affairs namely, India's regression in sports, calls for serious revamp in our sports management. Indians might love sports, but they certainly do not encourage sports. Our problem starts at the basic level; we pay negligible attention to sports, since only 15% of our population is really exposed to organized sports/games. There is an urgent need to thoroughly analyze this situation and initiate proactive measures to redeem the situation.

After the Rio games, Indian athletes complained of gross neglect, where one marathon runner was not even provided water in the hot climate and due to which she collapsed and almost died on the track. Talking of our planning in Rio games, while ₹ 40 crores were sanctioned for the Sports Ministry for Target Olympic Podium (TOP) scheme for Rio 2016, only ₹ 6 crores could be spent by Dec 2015 and ₹ 25 Crores by July 2016. Of course, only spending more money on sports would not resolve the issue and we need to pay focused attention to creating world level infrastructure for sports, besides maintaining and structuring training and other associated facilities. We need to develop an atmosphere of excellence in the field of sports and nurture talent like in countries such as UK and China.

Looking at the countries that have performed well in sports, we infer that while Government should continue to adequately fund sports, Ministry of Sports need not control Indian sports and must allow professionally run sports programme by independent agencies. The time is now ripe for National Sports Council (NSC) to replace Sports Ministry. In this context, recently, Indian PM has announced that a "Task Force" would soon be set up to prepare a comprehensive action plan for Olympic games to be held in 2020, 2024 and 2028. The panel is to prepare a strategy for effective participation and work on sports training, facilities and selection.

We need to keep politicians and bureaucrats away from sports, like Supreme Court has recently done for cricket in India by imposing restrictions on working of BCCI. Study reveals that a nation's wealth and health of citizens, Human Development Index and quality of institutions regulating sports are all relevant to bring up standard of sports in a country. We need to develop a sporting culture and recognize excellence in all fields in our society and openly dissuade mediocrity. Currently to redeem our self-esteem, we must urgently plan a roadmap to spot sports talent early, provide adequate sporting facilities, build infrastructure for training and fair selection of sports persons, besides revamping our sports administration at all levels. Finally, looking at India's performance in Rio, India should focus on limited disciplines to improve medal count, like a number of countries have done in Rio. However, India must provide comprehensive sports science experts for all sports and concentrate on physical fitness and mental strength of our sportspersons. We have plenty of talent, which we must spot, and nurture.

Part III Detailed Discussions

Indus Waters Treaty

Pakistan's proxy war against India has continued unabated for a very long time now. But, India's patience ran out recently, when on 18 Sep 2016, Pakistan based militants killed 18 Indian soldiers at Uri Army Base. Consequently, Indian Army carried out well-planned surgical operations to demolish some terrorist bases across LOC. At the same time, India expressed its intentions to reclaim its right over J&K rivers. Presently, water resources in J&K have been shared between India and Pakistan through the Indus Water Treaty. "Blood and water cannot flow together", Indian Prime Minister said recently.

This treaty was signed in 1960 between India and Pakistan and was brokered by the World Bank. The agreement gives control of the three eastern rivers – Beas, Ravi and Sutlej to India and Indus, Chenab and Jhelum to Pakistan. All the rivers either originate or pass through J&K. The pact is seen as generous to Islamabad, as it gives Pakistan 80 percent of the water of the Western rivers: Indus, Chenab and Jhelum. As Indus was the biggest of them, the treaty was named as Indus Waters Treaty. The treaty gives Pakistan more than four times the water available to India.

Present Situation

Despite the fact that this treaty apparently favors Pakistan, India did not rake up the issue of sharing water resources, primarily to maintain peaceful relations with Pakistan. But, looking at Pakistan's stance against India for a very long time, Pakistan should not expect the Indus Waters Treaty to survive eternally, if it refuses to honour the 1972 Simla Peace Pact with India. Therefore, India may be well within its right to take more water from Indus, and consequently squeeze Pakistan. If India builds infrastructure such as hydel power projects and irrigation canals to optimize its use of rivers, even within the treaty's framework, the water flow to Pakistan farmers will be considerably reduced. The current situation has taken this ugly turn since repeated cross border terrorist attacks and Pakistani establishment's refusal to acknowledge that such strikes originate from its soil, have forced India to use the water treaty as the bargaining tool to force Pakistan to mend its ways. But, the core issue now is whether scrapping of the pact would be a credible deterrent for Pakistan?

Experts opine that India needs to consider the following aspects before taking requisite steps to scrap the treaty:

Firstly, presently India has no infrastructure to hold/divert the excess water. India would take some time to build required infrastructure to hold this excess water.

Secondly, if India walks out of this treaty, our country would lose overall credibility among international community in the long run.

Thirdly, in support of Pakistan, China could also decide to divert waters of river Brahmaputra.Moreso, since India has no water treaty with China pertaining to Brahmaputra river presently, and of late, China is openly favoring Pakistan.

Fourthly, India could utilize the provisions of the Indus treaty more aggressively to favor J&K and other states of India, since considerable unused waters of the eastern water flow into Pakistan unutilized.

In view of the above, within the provisions of the Indus treaty, India could revisit the Indus Treaty to utilize more water for India after taking adequate diplomatic measures to inform the international community, and at the same time, plan a long-term strategy in this regard. Presumably, a strong message has already gone to Pakistan that India could take recourse to hard measures of diverting more water for India, if Pakistan does not mend its ways.

Part III Detailed Discussions

Role of Media in Moulding Public Opinion

In the recent past, the subject 'how media can impact public opinion', has been passionately discussed in almost all public forums. Still a more serious question remains, whether media has been adequately responsible towards our society? Unfortunately, an emphatic No or Yes answer cannot be given to this extremely significant question.

Two well-known incidents in public domain were chiefly responsible for the above intense debate. First was Nirbhaya's case, where a Delhi girl who was brutally raped, died subsequently; and second was the high voltage media campaign launched to project Mr. Modi as India's Prime Minister and the landslide victory of BJP in the 2014 Lok Sabha elections.

Nobody denies the fact that Indian economy needs a vibrant media. People require basic facts to form independent public opinions. One consents or dissents based on available inputs, but the real problem comes to the fore when media is forcefully accused of manufacturing consent or dissent. No one denies the fact that media has the prime responsibility on its shoulders to present facts before the people in a fair and objective manner, irrespective of circumstances. Today, is media above all accusations of distorting evidence to favour some and condemn others? Is so much euphoria built by media on trivial issues justified? Media denies all such accusations vehemently, but can't media be biased due to various constraints?

Let us analyse the discernable rise of media reach in our times. Television arrived in India in early 1970s, but both electronic and print media have grown exponentially during the past few years only. Today, there are thousands of newspapers and hundreds of news channels in so many languages. In this period, broadcast media has reached a significantly large number of people in the last 8–10 years or so. Notably, the media has now reached people who are not quite literate – they can now see the news, because they cannot read it. Immense popularity of mobile phones and internet has given so much extra-energy to media and this reach now is really extraordinary. Additionally, social media with Facebook and Twitter, is now shaping public opinions like never before. Messages are now sent to millions in seconds. Due to this, majority view points are shaped or manipulated and once they are formed, these opinions become quite difficult to alter. Obviously, advantage of forming opinions in early stages leads to much bigger benefits during crystallizing of public opinions in the final stages. Surprisingly, such opinions evolve rather rapidly and remain dominant for a considerable point of time. Currently, political candidates and corporate are taking full advantage of this phenomenon to mould public opinions in their favour and also condemn or bring down others.

Coming back to the two issues mentioned earlier, while highlighting Nirbhaya's story, media came out clearly victorious to attract public opinion and finally ensured that four accused were sentenced to death after trial via a fast-track court. This was terrific, considering the judiciaries deliver justice far too late or never at all. Not only that, government was forced to pass laws making rape punishable with a death sentence. But one really wonders why media does not highlight so many other less-known rape and gang rape cases, where there are no fast-track courts and poor victims still continue to suffer extreme pain and humiliation of our society. It is then one wonders, whether media is really interested in delivering justice to the needy. Apparently, public opinion is very powerful to bring out results, but media remains highly selective in picking up issues due to their own selfish reasons. Of course, one must put on record media's contribution to highlight corruption cases, but there have been heated debates on media trials, where the accused person barely gets an opportunity to defend himself. One notices everyday on News channels, anchors bombard people with so many questions and give them not much opportunity to defend. This certainly is an evidence of a dominating media in India today.

In the case of media's role in creating hype about Mr. Modi during the Lok Sabha elections in 2014, it was more than apparent that media was not only reporting, but was a clear player in politics as well. Media bias in favour of Mr. Modi was so conspicuous and live coverage of Mr. Modi's speeches reached a saturation point. While others were severely and bitterly criticized for even trivial matters, Mr. Modi was barely asked any hard questions and authenticity of his claims through a well-organized media campaign, Mr. Modi was projected as a man who could solve all problems of our country by using his 'magic wand'. Notably, media's treatment of Aam Aadmi Party changed diametrically once AAP started hitting corporate corruption and questioned the 'Gujarat model'.

It is hardly surprising to notice such behavior of the media if one knows who owns these media houses. Since media is big business, big business houses, politicians and political parties are buying huge stakes in media to control sections of the press. Even though media denies any bias and avoids any questions to examine it. We may conclude by saying that while we agree that freedom of media is sacrosanct, distorted news is highly damaging. Finally, media must also be open to criticism as they criticize all others.

Part III Detailed Discussions

Significance of Indo-Japanese Relations

Bilateral relations between India and Japan got a big shot in the arm when Indian Prime Minister visited Japan in September 2014. During this interaction, Japan promised to invest $35 billion in infrastructure in India during the next five years. These include setting up of power plants, purchase of US-2 amphibian aircraft, development of industrial cities and running bullet trains in India, etc. In return, India assured Japan to introduce a speed mechanism for fast-track channel for Japanese investment in India. It would be interesting to trace the background of progress made by Japan and relations between India and Japan.

Traditionally, Japan and India share a tradition of Buddhism, as well as fundamental values such as freedom, democracy, human rights and rule of law. Historically speaking, Japan deserves all praise for remaining ahead of other countries in Asia after defeating both China and Russia in separate wars. However, despite its crushing defeat in World War II, Japan rose from ashes rather quickly to emerge as Asia's first global economic power house. In the Nehruvian 1950s, Japan, Britain and Russia were inspiring role models for young Indians. People in India were star struck by Japanese engineering skills, discipline and glorified status as an Asian super power. Crazy for Japanese goods, Indians loved to buy Sony television, Seiko watches and Japanese toys. Notably, an imperialist Japan did not scare Indians the way overbearing China did. It was then no wonder that we gladly invited Japanese companies to establish car factories, build roads and bridges and sell lots of Japanese goods in India. Maruti Suzuki became the hallmark of Indo-Japanese friendship. As of now, the number of Japanese companies in India has grown to over 1200.

Despite some economic setback in the recent past, Japan has been slowly rising and has now become a crucial economic and security partner for India. Japan can no longer rely on America's security guarantee, given Washington's neutrality on various Asian territorial disputes. In the recent years, Japan and India have markedly improved their cooperation on security matters. Japan has a world class navy and Japan's high-tech arms capability makes it an ideal partner for import-dependent India to build a domestic weapons production base. In addition, both countries have been regularly conducting joint military exercises to improve their military strategy, especially in the context of dealing with a dominating China in South China Sea and Indian Ocean. Close co-operation between India and Japan can only restrict China from dictating terms and maintain a power balance in Asian region.

Unlike in the past, China has been challenging Japan–US alliance and this has considerably dampened the relations between US and Japan. As commercial relations between China and Japan have lost their sheen, Japan is finding India another large market to invest in the near future.

While Japan excels in energy generation, infrastructural and manufacturing projects and launching high speed trains, India needs them desperately to push forward its development agenda. India and Japan have apparent dissimilarities, but these create ample opportunities for strong economic collaboration. While Japan is a leader in hardware, India is charming the world with its software; Japan possesses a heavy manufacturing base, while India boasts of its service-led growth; India has the world's highest young population when Japan is aging rather quickly, and finally; while Japan is strong in terms of economic and technological power, India offers plenty of manpower and a very big market for commercial activities. Japan is willing to assist India to develop as it did for China by large investments and transferring of technology.

However, as Japan and China are drifting apart owing to socio-political tensions, India fortunately has no such tension with Japan, and therefore must seize this opportunity to industrialize itself much as China has done. Strong relations between Asia's richest and largest democracies can fundamentally transform power balance in the region and help India to fulfill its dream of fast-track development. Moreover, cooperating with Japan would help India become a globally competitive manufacturing economy. All said and done, by developing strategic and commercial ties, India and Japan must lead the attempt to make Asia more prosperous and stable. India should do it in its own interest also.

Is Naxal Movement India's Greatest Internal Security Threat?

India, being a country of many religions, languages, castes and tribes, has faced a number of internal security threats ever since she became independent. In fact, Indians have become used to living with conflicts on a daily basis. Fanaticism of various kinds has continuously disturbed the peace and tranquility of people of India. However, in the recent past, internal security threat due to Naxal movement emerges as one of the most serious security threats that independent India has so far encountered.

In September 2010, former Indian Prime Minister Mr. Manmohan Singh declared that Naxalism is the single biggest internal security challenge India has ever faced. Earlier in 2010, the Home Ministry admitted that 83 districts in nine states are virtually being run by the rebels in what they call the 'Free Zone'. Here, they operate as a parallel government with their own courts and administrative machinery. The Naxalites also have influence on over 220 of 626 districts across the country, the Ministry found.

The Naxalite movement began in the Naxalbari area of West Bengal in 1967, claiming to defend the rights of tribal groups and landless workers. Its current avatar dates back to 2004, when a number of splinter groups merged to form the Communist Party of India (Maoist).

The movement, whose aim is violent revolution and eventually over throwing the Indian government, now has a force of about 20,000 soldiers and is spread across parts of West Bengal, Bihar, Orissa, Chhattisgarh, Jharkhand, Maharashtra, Madhya Pradesh and Andhra Pradesh.

Since November, 2009, the government has officially begun bolstering anti-Naxalite counter insurgency efforts with a strong development agenda. Known as 'Operation Green Hunt', the effort also aims to ease "the sense of deprivation and alienation among the rural populace in these regions".

In Aug-Sept, 2010, Naxalites also kidnapped a few security personnel from Lakhisarai in Bihar and demanded release of some Naxalites, who were in police custody. While, the negotiations were still in progress, one security officer was brutally murdered by the Naxalites. In 2013, the Naxalites killed almost all senior leaders of Congress party of Chhattisgarh in a single well-planned brutal attack in Sukma, which shocked the entire nation. During the period 2015–17, Naxalites continued to attack security forces regularly and killed a large number of security personnel.

In view of display of such brutalities by the Naxalites, a debate is now on to decide whether Indian Armed Forces, with their sophisticated weaponry, should be called upon to counter Naxalites. It appears that while, the Government is inclined to use the Armed Forces in a limited manner, some social activists are of the opinion that it would be highly inappropriate to call Armed Forces against our own people. They argue that, after all Naxalites are not our enemies but our countrymen, who have been deprived a livelihood by incorrect policies of our governments for a very long time now. Despite this, in October 2011, Government finally gave two UAVs (Unarmed Aerial Vehicles) to security forces involved in anti-naxal operations for intelligence gathering in Chhattisgarh, Orissa and Jharkhand.

In this context, if we analyse the reasons due to which Naxal movement has acquired its present size, we would conclude that, by most accounts, it is the government's own industry friendly policies, corruption and resultant failure to develop these areas–despite thousands of crores pumped in expressly for this purpose–that have seen the Maoist, left-wing, guerilla rebellion spread from one district in West Bengal to 220 district across 28 states.

The fact remains that, Naxalite movement has spread since a large number of tribals were displaced and their mineral-rich lands were handed over to giant corporations and even government PSUs, such as NTPC, etc. Tribals were thus forced to leave their habitat and were also denied a livelihood. If one looks at a number of burning problems that we face today in a broad way, we would surely discover that the problems in Kashmir, the north-east and the tribal regions can all be traced back to corruption. In many of these regions, the local leadership has been co-opted through corruption. Massive resources have been siphoned off, leading to inequality, and disenchantment with government. The state is perceived to be insincere, so that the issue moves from economic to political and social. Everything that can go wrong, does go wrong, and the leadership is left only firefighting. Interestingly, a survey conducted in September, 2010 in Andhra shows that people think Government is worse than Naxals, and Naxalites were good for their area.

In view of the above, the Central Government as well as State Governments must initiate a series of positive measures to resolve this problem without losing any more time. These measures would include developing the areas occupied by Naxalites as well as providing rehabilitation to the youth of these areas. Government has to ensure that essential development does take place and the money spent is not eaten away by the middlemen. The development must necessarily take place at the grass root level. In the recent past, there has also been a demand to recruit the youth of these areas in the army and the police. This step would give them an opportunity to positively direct and utilise their energies as well as give them rehabilitation. It goes without saying that, there is an urgent need to win confidence of these people and somehow draw them to the mainstream by giving them opportunities to earn and lead a

Part III Detailed Discussions

normal life. Government must implement effective employment generation policies geared to reduce casualisation of labour to empower poor people of areas that are now affected by this problem. After all, growing disparities between the rich and poor and large-scale displacement of poor people necessarily leads to social tensions. Naxal problem is certainly an issue, which does not augur well for Indian democracy and puts a big question mark on the governing capabilities of Indian bureaucrats and politicians.

Finally, quoting the famous Lawrence of Arabia, "Making war upon insurgency is messy and slow–like eating soup with knife".

Can Sri Lanka Resolve the Problem of Tamils?

The ethnic conflict in Sri Lanka has been hogging the headlines for several years. For more than 35 years now, Tamils have been struggling to establish an identity for themselves in Sri Lanka. Initially, it was a peaceful movement but under the aegis of Liberation Tigers of Tamil Eelam (LTTE), it acquired the shape of a full scale war between the LTTE and Sri Lankan Security Forces. Historically speaking, the problem in Sri Lanka was triggered by gradual alienation of Tamils for sometime due to a number of reasons.

As of now, Tamils constitute about 19% of the population, which includes Tamils, both of Indian origin and Sri Lankan origin. Sinhalese constitute 70% of the population, Muslims 7% and other ethnic groups are 4% of the population. At the outset, let us look at the origin of this problem.

The Beginning of Indian Migrations to Sri Lanka

Since, the 2nd century BC, kingdoms of South India started invading Sri Lanka and a large part of northern Sri Lanka came under their rule. Tamil migration, which started during this period, continued for more than a thousand years down to the period of the Chola King Raja Chola I and later his son Rajendra Chola I, who brought almost the entire island under Chola control. Another major wave of Tamil migration happened when hired labourers were taken to the central highlands of the country by British tea planters.

Reasons for Conflict between the Sinhalese and Tamils

Owing to conspicuous differences of religion and language, these two groups never quite integrated—but, experts believe that the present conflict started after Solomon Bandaranaike's Sri Lankan Freedom Party (SLP) came to power in the 1956 elections and the 'Sinhali Only' bill was passed. This Act made Sinhalese the only official language of the island country and also provided state support to Buddhism and Sinhalese culture. The Tamils, who were also largely Hindus were deliberately ignored and thus got alienated. At that time, the English-based civil services had a significant number of Tamils. The new rule meant a large number of these Tamil civil servants lost their jobs. The Act was opposed by the Tamil MPs who staged a non-violent protest which received a violent response from Sinhalese mob. The violence turned into riots and thousand of Tamils were killed and forced to flee and relocated in north of the island. These developments marked the beginning of conflicts between the Sinhalese and Tamils.

Actions which Brought things to a Boil

Consequent to the riots and various Tamil movements, the government banned the import of Tamil language films, books, magazines and journals from India. The long established practice of Tamil students going to Indian universities was also stopped. In 1971, the policy of standardization of marks was implemented, which meant higher qualifying marks for Tamil students for the university entrance examinations. The situation further worsened when the government introduced quota system in 1972, to push the enrollments of students of unprivileged districts, who were largely Sinhalese. As a result, the enrolment ratios of Tamil students started falling and it angered the Tamil population a great deal. The rule was finally abolished in 1977, perhaps too late.

Status of Indian Tamils in Sri Lanka

Apart from the Sri Lankan Tamils who live in the north and eastern parts, there is a significant population of Indian Tamils in the central highlands. They are descendants of the Indian indentured labourers. These people, most of whom still work in the tea industry, are usually considered a separate community. Immediately after independence, the Sri Lankan government stripped them of their citizenship in 1949. The denial of citizenship to Indian Tamils meant reduced Tamil voting power and hence, a lower level of opposition to pro-Sinhala policies in the country's parliament. Then PM Sirimavo Banadaranaike (wife of Solomon Bandaranaike, who was assassinated in 1959) signed agreements with Indian government and 600,000 of these people were to be sent back to India over a 15-year period, while the remaining 375,000 would be restored their Sri Lankan citizenship. But, a significant number of Indian Tamils did not actually return to India. Their full citizenship was finally restored in 2003.

The Onset of Civil War

After the 1977 elections, the United National Party (UNP) formed the government and the Tamil United Liberation Front (TULF) became the leading opposition party. There were serious communal clashes in August that year. As a result, the UNP government agreed to grant most of the demands of the Tamil population. But dozens of armed Tamil groups had already come into being. In July 1983, LTTE attacked a Sri Lankan military base and killed 13 soldiers. This enraged Sinhala nationalists, who retaliated by massacring Tamilian—this was the beginning of the civil war.

Role of Indian Government

In 1980s, India gave support to LTTE in terms of training, weapons and equipment. The Sri Lankan government accused India of openly supporting the rebels. The Indo-Sri Lanka Peace Accord was signed on July 29, 1987, by late Rajiv Gandhi and then Sri Lankan President Jayawardene. The Sri Lankan government made several concessions to Tamil demands. India agreed to help in restoring order by sending in a peace keeping force, IPKF. Though most rebel groups were for the Indian move, LTTE started attacking the Indian forces, which ultimately withdrew in 1990. Rajiv Gandhi's assassination by LTTE in 1991 indicated that the final break away of the Indian government with the LTTE was complete.

Situation in the Recent Past

In the 2001 elections, Ranil Wickremasinghe, came to power campaigning for peace. In February 2002, an MoU was signed between the government and the LTTE and Norway was named as the mediator. There were six sessions of peace talks between 2002 and 2003 and the situation started improving. After the Tsunami of December 2004, both the government and LTTE were involved in relief work. But since 2005, the situation again started deteriorating. During 2008–2009, full scale war broke out between LTTE and Sri Lankan Security Forces. Eventually, in 2010, Sri Lankan forces defeated the LTTE and took control of the entire region, which was the stronghold of LTTE. Prabhakaran, who was the leader of LTTE, was presumably killed in this operation.

Civil war is over now. Indian Government recommends more autonomy for Tamils in Sri Lanka, but is not in favour of a separate 'Eelam'. During his visit to India in August 2010, the Sri Lankan President assured India that his government will take adequate steps to rehabilitate the Tamils. Subsequently, after Sri Lanka elections in 2015, the new President, who is known to be pro-India, has assured that displaced Tamils will be duly rehabilitated, and in turn, Indian government assured that Tamil refugees now in India will be given needed help to go back to their homes in Sri Lanka. It is also hoped that the new government will not pursue pro-China polices and now strategically cooperate with India, unlike the previous government. As of now, the problem of Tamil refugees and the nature of a political solution remain hanging.

Recently, Indian PM visited Sri Lanka to ostensibly celebrate the Buddhist Vesak Day Celebrations, which is commemorated by millions the world over to mark the birth of Buddha in 623 BC, the day he attained enlightenment and also the day he left this world in his 80th year. However, his visit has noteworthy political connotations as well in view of some recent developments in the foreign policy of Sri Lanka. Prior to this, since 2015, Sri Lankan PM, Ranil Wickremsinghe has visited India thrice and so has Sri Lankan President Srisena. In fact, Indian PM has also now visited Sri Lanka twice during the last 3 years.

Relations with China in the Immediate Past

The previous Rajapakse government in Sri Lanka had much closer relations with China in the recent past, and China was known to supply arms as well as provide huge loans to Sri Lanka for its development. To shake up India, in 2014, Sri Lanka even allowed docking of a Chinese submarine in Colombo harbor. Since Sri Lanka is only half an hour away by sea and only a few seconds by air from India, this development did send alarm bells to India. China also invested sufficiently in the infrastructure of Sri Lanka, which included building of Colombo international container terminal by China Harbor Corporation. Therefore, during the regime of the previous government in Sri Lanka, China could make her presence visible in Sri Lanka. Even today, Sri Lanka considers China a friend, since China provided equipment and weapons to Sri Lanka even when there was an official arms embargo. However, in the recent past, Sri Lankan government has become conscious of Chinese military interest in making Sri Lanka a forward base to aim India and gain more strategic influence in the region.

Recent Developments

Clearly, while previous Rajapakse government in Sri Lanka preferred to deal more with China, the present government now considers equally significant to have good relations with India. At the leadership level relations are quite cordial, but they have to be translated into action and presently there is some rebalancing in Sri Lanka. The present government feels that after the conflict in Sri Lanka, even though India had a development portfolio of over $ 2.6 billion, built 50,000 houses and railway tracks, some people in Sri Lanka thought India was only helping Tamils in North Sri Lanka. India's efforts did not receive adequate publicity, which led to certain misunderstandings among Sri Lankan population. Now, the new Sri Lankan government wants that some Indian companies build Colombo Port's East Terminals after China's earlier effort in this region. On the other hand, Sri Lankan government needs to initiate adequate steps to rehabilitate displaced Tamils, who are still in India after the earlier conflict in Sri Lanka.

It has been reported that recently, Sri Lanka refused permission to China to dock its submarine in Colombo port, which has been well appreciated in India.

During his recent visit to Sri Lanka, Indian PM also inaugurated a 150 bed-hospital built with Indian assistance and also interacted with Indian origin Tamil tea-workers. The Sri Lanka government feels that there is a need to have more cultural and religious interactions between the people of two countries to build more trust and faith.

India has been for long Sri Lanka's biggest trade partner and has played a significant role in rebuilding Sri Lanka. Since India cannot match China's economic power, India needs to focus on its traditional values of Buddhism and Ramayan to improve relations with Sri Lanka. At the same time, India can supply electricity to Sri Lanka and further improve its trade and economic relations by introducing easier visa norms etc. There is an urgent need to start ferry services between India and Sri Lanka to improve people to people linkages. Finally, India needs Sri Lanka strategically as well, to ensure security in her neighborhood.

Part III Detailed Discussions

How should India Deal with China?

India and China are two undisputed Asian giants and the 21st century belongs to these two in the background of receding American influence. The geopolitical landscape of the world is likely to transform accordingly. Unfortunately, instead of adapting a cooperative posture, China tends to dominate over its neighbors, with whom she has numerous disputes. For India that fancies itself as an emerging superpower, learning to live with an assertive China is one of its greatest foreign policy challenges. As of now, India is still a lesser power than China in terms of its economic and military might, both conventional and non-conventional.

Indian policy makers find China's approach to India quite perplexing. On the border, China has vastly superior military machinery. Its economic muscle is much bigger. And yet it appears keen to avoid any major confrontations along the 4,056 km undemarcated border. But on many issues of bilateral import, China takes a far more belligerent stand-like seeking to check India's bid for a place in the UN Security Council; trying to keep India out of an Asian economic community; blocking ADB from giving Arunachal money for a water project; denying Arunachal residents Chinese visas; not allowing India to join nuclear supply group of nations etc.

Major Issues between India and China

The steady emergence of India as a powerful player is not looked upon favourably by China. A theme dominant in all Chinese commentaries is that India's growing power-backed by US-would bring about a shift in the Asian balance of power which may not be favourable for China. In the past, China has been trying to prevent clashes with its neighbours but the situation seems to be changing with India recently.

India-China boundary dispute is a major problem between India and China. The India-China territorial dispute is a 4,056 km long problem that stems from British expansionism in the early 20th century. Imperial Britain tried to push its line of control and carve buffer zones around the jewel in the crown. Sir Henry Mc Mohan, the foreign secretary of British India at the time, drew the 890 km McMohan Line as the border between British India and Tibet. The so-called McMohan Line, drawn primarily on the highest watershed principle, demarcated what had previously been unclaimed or undefined borders between Britain and Tibet. The McMohan line moved British control substantially northwards and became something the Chinese never accepted. Independent India inherited the dispute and despite Nehru's bhai-bhai, a full-scale war erupted in 1962. China occupied the Switzerland sized barren area of Aksai Chin in North-Eastern Ladakh and the PLA stomped into Arunachal Pradesh. Since then, there has been discomfort on both sides of India-China border.

Beijing claims approximately 90,000 sq. km in the Middle Sector of the India-China boundary. Beijing does not recognize Arunachal Pradesh. The border has never been officially delimited and none of it features in the mountainous area marked on a map. Recently, China is insistent upon its access to Tawang.

China's defence-budget and Armed Forces are more than double of India's and China possesses 250-500 Nuclear war heads compared to less than 100 of India. China maintains almost four times the Fighter jets India has. Though, India cannot match China's military might, yet its forces are capable of giving a big blow to China in a battle. And China is well aware of this reality.

On the business front, despite promises and agreements, China's foreign direct investment in India is very low. China can become India's number one trading partner. India complains that its manufactured goods cannot enter China because of tariffs. But, China has similar problems with India due to security measures taken by India. India's success in information technology, English language skills and widespread poverty are endlessly discussed in Chinese media. It is often said that China is still the biggest exporter and importer. In India's case, we want to be the biggest exporter but not the biggest importer. There is a popular saying: China is a closed society with an open mind and India is an open society with a closed mind.

Tension over Tibet has been yet another issue between India and China. China thinks that India has problems with domestic succession, particularly in Tibet. China is afraid that India could play a problematic role in Tibet. Even though India allows the Dalai Lama to pursue his spiritual mission, China feels India will use him for geopolitical ends. Indian still considers Dalai Lama an honored guest. But, China considers him a "Separatist".

In the recent past, China has become more dominating and a protector of Pakistan. The fact remains that China is the main provider of Pakistan's missile and nuclear arsenals, and with the purpose of balancing that country against India. There are reports that China is increasing its influence in Nepal by extending its rail link to the Tibet-Nepal border, which will extend right up to Kathmandu and reduce Nepal's dependence on India. Rail link will enable China to supply combat readiness material to airports built at high altitudes in Tibet. China is all set to establish rail links between Afghanistan, Pakistan and Uzbekistan in Central Asia. Further, India's plan to build a railway network for Afghanistan had been off set by China.

Part III Detailed Discussions

New Delhi has not been pleased with Beijing's hardened stance on Kashmir; and about the increasing Chinese strategic presence in the Indian Ocean. The most recent irritant for China has been India's project to explore for oil and gas in the South China Sea in partnership with Vietnam.

Recent Problematic Issues

Recently, China has come up with the idea of extending the 'BRICS PLUS' Bloc by inviting other developing countries to join the BRICS group of nations. India views this development as an attempt to dilute Delhi's role and to expand China's influence by inviting its allies to join the group. India will obviously oppose this idea floated by China.

It has been reported that China will deploy 1 lakh marines at ports in Gwadar and Djibouti to increase its control and keep a check on all movements in the Indian Ocean. Even though Beijing denies that these would be military bases. Gwadar port is in Pakistan and Djibouti is a country in East Africa, all these actions of China demonstrate its dominating attitude which India has to cope with.

In view of the above factors and the fact that India cannot wish away its neighbours, there is a growing realization in both nations that the simmering tension just cannot be allowed to get out of hand. After the election of new US President, US has shown a soft attitude towards China. Recently, China granted approval to 38 Trump trademarks, a full sweep approval which is surprising. Chinese President is also likely to visit US soon. India needs to build the kind of interdependence with China that will give both nations increased stakes in each other. China would like to have a foothold in South Asia and India has to reflect on this reality. After all, world is quite big for both India and China to cooperate and compete at the same time.

Is Creation of Smaller States Desirable?

At present India has 29 states and 7 Union Territories. But, the issue before is, whether there is adequate justification for carving smaller states out of larger ones? Absence of requisite infrastructure to run governments of smaller states was one of the many arguments that were put forward disfavouring formation of smaller states. It was also argued that administratively, it was much easier to deal with a few states rather than a large number of small-small states. At the outset, let us understand how were these states established when India became independent in 1947.

British India had been divided into princely states under the control of local hereditary rulers, and provinces, which were directly governed by British officials. Upon Independence, the British colonial power dissolved the treaties they had with nearly 600 princely states, letting them choose which side they wanted to join, India or Pakistan. Most joined India and a few went to Pakistan. Sikkim choose to become independent with special protectorate status (and later merged with India in 1975). During the period 1947–50, the princely states were absorbed into various provinces.

When the Constitution came into force on January 26, 1950, India became Union of states (earlier called provinces) that had extensive autonomy, and Union Territories, which were administered by the central government. Under the Constitution, there were three kinds of states—nine Part A states, eight Part B states and ten Part C states. Part A states were former governor's provinces in British India. Part B states were the former princely states. Part C states included a few princely states as well as former provinces governed by Chief Commissioners.

The Basis for Organizing States was Language

The movement to create states based on language gained momentum in the early 1950s, starting with the demand for a separate state for Telugu speaking people. Jawaharlal Nehru remained unconvinced about a linguistic basis for states as he felt that after partition, any further division of the country would weaken it. However, the movements demanding linguistic autonomy became stronger with Kannada, Marathi, Malayalam and Gujarati speakers demanding separate states.

Language, ethnicity and administrative convenience led to further breaking up of states. In 1960, Bombay was split into Maharashtra and Gujarat,

Nagaland was carved out of Assam, while Punjab was split to form two more states— Haryana and Himachal in 1966. More changes took place when Meghalaya, Manipur and Tripura were granted statehood in 1972 and former UTs, Mizoram, Goa and Arunachal were elevated and became states in 1987. The most recent reorganization was in 2000, when three states of Uttarakhand, Chhattisgarh and Jharkhand were created and later in 2014, Andhra Pradesh was divided into Telangana and Andhra Pradesh.

The Case for Creating Small States

Assuming 20% population growth since the last census, Uttar Pradesh has 198 million people, more than Brazil, Russia or Pakistan. Maharashtra has 106 million, West Bengal 96 million and Andhra Pradesh 90 million. All are much bigger than France or Britain. At the other end of the scale, Sikkim has just 0.6 million people, Mizoram 1.1 million and Arunachal Pradesh 1.3 million. Clearly, statehood has been determined by political expediency not logic.

Is there a case for carving smaller states out of large ones? Some analysts say small states won't be economically viable. Others believe small states will fare better, since, ordinary people will have better access to power elites. Consider the record of three states carved out of larger ones in 2000— Jharkhand, Chhattisgarh and Uttarakhand. Ignore data for the first few transitional years. Instead, focus on to average growth rate of gross state domestic product for the last five years, from 2004–06 to 2008–09. Amazingly, all three new states have grown fabulously fast. Uttarakhand has averaged 9.31% growth annually, Jharkhand 8.45% and Chhattisgarh 7.35%.

The Central Government exempted industries in Uttarakhand from excise duty, a concession already applicable to other hill states such as Himachal Pradesh, Kashmir and the north-eastern states. Many big industries rushed to Uttarakhand for the tax break, giving the state's growth an artificial boost. Still, Uttarakhand easily out-performed Himachal Pradesh (8.47%) and Kashmir (5.98%). Remember, Uttarakhand was once backward part of UP. After statehood, it has become a growth champion.

Jharkhand and Chhattisgarh were the most backward parts of Bihar and Madhya Pradesh, which in turn were among the most backward states of India. Yet, after becoming separate states, Jharkhand and Chhattisgarh have emerged as industrial dynamos. Both have large tribal belts with pathetic infrastructure. In Chhattisgarh, four-fifths of habitations lack road access. Both states have ample minerals like coal and iron ore. But, this was not an economic advantage when they were part of larger states. Rather, their mineral revenues were diverted to state capitals. This diversion ended after they became separate states.

Their rapid economic growth has been tainted by massive corruption. Natural resources from coal to the telecom spectrum are constantly gifted to favoured parties instead of being auctioned, and this enables politicians to amass fortunes. But just as the telecom revolution has been good for India, despite corruption, so has private entry into mining and processing.

Jharkhand and Chhattisgarh are not growing fast simply through mining, they have also experienced a manufacturing boom. Read what research firm Indicus Analytica has to show: "Since 2001, Jharkhand and Chhattisgarh have moved up into the top 10 (industrial states), displacing Rajasthan and Punjab... The phenomenal growth in these two states has seen the share of manufacturing in their GDP rise dramatically as they have attracted industrial projects. Looking at the share of income that originates in the manufacturing sector, these two states have shown higher levels than Maharasthra, Haryana and Tamil Nadu... Being newer and smaller states, they responded more rapidly than their larger– and in some cases better endowed–neighbours... Raipur in Chhattisgarh has now entered the top 10 districts of India in manufacturing, with two industrial estates at Urla and Siltara".

The neglect of tribals and consequent rise of Maoism is a blot on the record of Jharkhand and Chhattisgarh. The two states account for 68% of all Maoist attacks. That's bad for civil rights and security. Yet, achieving fast growth amidst such insurgency is a major economic feat. It highlights, the dynamism created when backward regions become separate states. Hopefully, this economic dynamism will help mitigate the backwardness on which Maoism thrives. Thus, we may say that though forming a large number of small states may not be a very good idea, good governance is essential to run even a small state.

In the recent times, apart from simmering demands of new states in north-east, Andhra Pradesh experienced violent demonstrations to press the long pending demand to create 'Telangana' out of Andhra Pradesh. In Nov, 2011 UP Chief Minister Miss Mayawati declared that she had recommended creation of four states out of UP for better administration. However, political observers feel that this demand is an exercise to check-mate and embarrass the Central Government and Congress party before forthcoming elections in UP in 2012.

Let us now, briefly discuss the procedure to create a new state as enumerated by existing laws on the subject. By law, Parliament can form a new state by separating territory from any state, by merging two or more states or parts of states. Parliament can also reduce or increase the area or alter the boundary of any state or even change its name. But first, a bill on the matter has to be referred by the President to the legislature of the affected state so that the legislature can express its views within a certain period.

Once, the President has ascertained the views of the State Government, a resolution is tabled before the assembly. Once, the resolution is passed by the assembly, it has to pass a bill creating the new state. Finally, a separate bill on the matter is introduced in Parliament on the recommendation of the President. Once, this bill is passed by a two-third majority and ratified by the President, the new state is formed.

Part III Detailed Discussions

42 After Information Technology, is Medical Tourism All Set to Boom in India?

'Health is wealth', goes the old adage. But, unfortunately, Indians are not among the healthiest people around and Government of India spends only 1 percent of GDP on health, while private spending on health sector is 4.2 percent of GDP. The public health care sector caters to just about 26% of total cases of ailment in India, though the private sector is clearly more expensive. This clearly shows that people have to go to private doctors, since they have no way out.

In India, government primarily focuses on basic health care, though quite inadequately. But, a country of one billion people, definitely requires much better care for the sick. More so, there is a gross inadequacy of specialised medical aid in the public health care sector. A large number of poor who stay in rural areas die before they can receive specialist treatment or reach a hospital.

In view of the above scenario, the business of healing the sick and taking care of them is obviously set for an explosion. Therefore, as per current estimates, hospital beds, jobs and facilities including equipment and laboratories will mushroom in India in the decade ahead. The fact remains that a poor person would even borrow money to save the lives of his kith and kin and provide best possible medical aid.

If, we look at the history of a developing nation, we realise that consequent to satisfying the needs of food, clothing and accommodation, there is always emphasis on health care. It is expected that by 2012–13, health care will grow by 20–25 percent in India. Due to the work culture in the Indian corporate sector, life style diseases like hypertension and diabetes, etc., are making even young Indians suffer from such ailments. In addition, increased awareness of Indians also leads to more demand on health care issues. Due to all these factors, health care sector has acquired increased significance. Corporate India is all set to grab huge benefits from medical tourism due to cost-friendly Indian medicare. It is logically hoped that foreigners will be attracted to India to undergo world class medical treatment at almost half the cost than they would incur in their own country. Obviously, corporate India aided by global capital and entrepreneurial zeal is set to pump in hundreds of millions of Dollars, eyeing growth and profits. Groups such as Fortis, Max (offshoots of Ranbaxy founders) and Apollo Hospitals have been joined by hot start-ups such as cardiologist Naresh Trehan's Medanta group in a boom that makes some say that, this is India's next IT: with foreign exchange earnings and job opportunities to match.

Apart from doctors, nurses and paramedics, the industry is also throwing up jobs in activities like clinical trials, in which India is emerging as a new base.

According to an international survey conducted in September 2010, while so far, India has been resting on its medical laurels, in reality the country's healthcare system has failed miserably in almost all parameters when compared to six developed and developing nations such as the US, UK, China, Brazil, UAE and Singapore. Though India has presently 10.8 lakh beds, but in terms of beds availability per thousand people, it is not doing well at all by having just about one bed for every thousand people. WHO norms require three-beds for every thousand people. India's burgeoning population, say experts, can not be used as an excuse, given that China has 40.63 lakh beds, and meets WHO's norms. Similarly, India has the highest number of medical and nursing colleges, but when it comes to colleges per thousand people, we are not doing well. Factually speaking, a minimum of one lakh beds have to be added to the country's existing kitty over the next 30 years and about two-third of these beds have to come up in rural areas to ensure an even development of health infrastructure.

The Indian healthcare market is expected to grow from US$ 35 billion in 2006 to $77 billion in 2012, according to YES bank and ASSOCHAM reports.

"The opportunities are huge and the profit will be good in India's health care in the coming years," said Shiv Raman Dugal, Chairman of Institute for Clinical Research in India (ICRI).

Malvinder Singh, Chairman of Fortis Health care, said "India currently has 1.2-beds per 1,000 citizens compared to the world average of 3.96. As a country we need to add 1.7 million beds by 2025 to get closer to the world average, and I see the growth trajectory momentum accelerating". Accordingly, health care companies are providing facilities and comforts to suit every budget.

Apollo hospitals plan to provide better healthcare facilities in smaller towns at much lower costs than the Metro ones. Similarly, Max Healthcare plans to double its bed count in National Capital Region. Thus, private players are catering to lifestyle diseases in a big way, especially for the affluent of other countries as well as Indians. Along with medical tourism, health insurance is expected to drive demand on a large scale. According to a report by consulting firm Deloitte, Indian medical tourism sector is expected to grow 30% annually. Thus, we can summarize by saying that health care is really the next IT in the booming economy of India.

Right to Information Empowers Aam Aadmi

In the knowledge age of today, information is power. Any information that affects the larger common good should be made public and the masses should have free access to it for their use. This is particularly relevant with reference to the use of taxpayers' money by the government for developmental purposes. In this context, the Right to Information Act demands a special mention.

The Official Secrets Act, a legacy of the British Raj, which should logically have become redundant by now, still holds good. It is widely misused to hide and withhold even the most harmless piece of information. Everything seems to be in the category of 'classified' and 'top-secret' information. Only money speaks. But money cannot be the answer to all our problems. For true democracy to function, information should be available for free to everyone alike, and flow without barriers. And this can happen only if the citizens are aware of their rights.

The long-oppressed masses of our country have been conditioned to live in a culture of silence. What rights and awareness are you talking about? Whoever, dares to speak about corruption or any wrong doing pays for it with her/his life. It is very easy to get away with murder in times of lawlessness and painfully slow judicial trials. In such an insecure atmosphere, even if someone has the requisite information about any misuse of taxpayers' money or inaction by the concerned authorities, he/she would not act foolish by raising an alarm.

The word 'transparency' is perhaps the most widely used word all over the globe to describe democracy, or an ideal form of governance. Despite their popularity, words such as 'transparency' and 'accountability' are hardly operational in government-public interface. It was in this context that National Campaign for People's Rights to Information (NCPRI) was launched and consequently RTI Act passed in 2005. In this development, Aruna Roy and Arvind Kejriwal and others made valuable contributions.

The RTI Act 2005 empowers all Indian citizens to seek information from public authorities. These include central, state and local governments, parliament and state legislatures, judiciary, police, security forces and all bodies substantially financed by the government. Under the RTI Act, one can ask questions or seek information, take copies or inspect official documents, inspect government works, and take samples of any government work. It is essential to ask specific information from the Public Information Officer (PIO) of the department concerned. The information one can seek includes records, documents, memos, mails, opinions, advices, press releases, circulars, images or any other computer-generated material, orders, log books, contracts, reports, papers, samples, models or electronic data. The concerned authorities are required to reply within 30 days.

The RTI Act has drastically changed equation between citizens and government. It has given the ordinary Indian a tool to exercise his/her sovereignty and to ask questions and demand answers. From public toilets to ration cards to drinking water and road repairs, ordinary people are not satisfied in letting those people get away with shoddy service. People are now using RTI to force authorities to mend their ways. The RTI application has forced panchayats, states and the centre to disclose the information, and has initiated an era of citizen-driven transparency and accountability.

From the beginning, the RTI campaign has strongly advocated that all institutions that use public money and affect public interest must be brought under the ambit of the Act. This includes NGOs, political parties, the media, trade unions, cooperative societies, religious institutions and the like. It was felt that even private sector should be coming under the purview of the RTI Act in so far as it affects public interest. Recently, the Central Information Commission (CIC) has brought six national political parties under the purview of RTI, which is considered a master stroke.

Interestingly, awareness about RTI has spread more rapidly than most laws in India. However, it is not enough. RTI has the potential to change the culture of exclusion and secrecy to one of openness and inclusion. Citizens have displayed courage, commitment, and creativity in putting RTI to use. Before the enactment of RTI in 2005, only MPs were authorized to put questions to the Central Government and MLAs to their respective State Governments. In a revolutionary change, any of the 1.25 billion citizens of India is now legally empowered to put questions, which the public authority concerned would have to reply within 30 days. Thus, democracy is no more about just exercising franchise at the time of election. More importantly, it is about constantly engaging with the government through the RTI mechanism. RTI has emerged as an anti-corruption tool for whistle-blowers. It has been so effective in unearthing corruption that it triggered off a wave of fatal attacks on RTI activists. RTI has forced the government to come up with bills to protect whistle-blowers, to reduce public grievances and to set up Lokpal or Lokayukta to deal with corruption allegations.

Right to information is perhaps a powerful means to get justice for the poor, who do not have the financial resources to bribe the corrupt and only have truth on their side. It can be used for both individual and collective good. For example, in the elections in 2004, it was the right to information of the masses that pushed the candidates to declare their assets. They may not have been completely true about the disclosure of their personal wealth and assets, but the point had been made. Nobody is allowed to take the common man for a ride, and the voter has the right to know the antecedents of the candidate contesting for a seat.

RTI can be effectively used to obtain legitimate pending work with the government, like issue of passport, any type of licence, certifications like marriage, death, birth, inclusion of name in voters list, etc., without having to pay bribes to get the work done.

To ensure effectiveness of the RTI, an Information Commission has been established in Delhi, which is the final court of appeal with regard to complaints in respect of Right to Information Act. It is heartening to note that a number of NGOs have come forward to help out citizens in exercising their legitimate right under this Act. If this is not an evidence of the power of information, what else could be? If one is optimistic about the future of democracy, the right to information cannot be sidelined.

Should Students Participate in Active Politics?

During India's freedom struggle against the British rule, students took an active part and organised various activities against the British Government. Even after India attained independence, students in India continued to take part in politics for valid or invalid reasons. A number of well known present day politicians were student leaders in younger days and they took pride in their activities while they were in students' politics. Despite this fact, often the issue whether students should take part in politics or not is being widely debated.

It is argued that during the days of our freedom struggle, the entire nation was required to protest in a cohesive manner for the just cause of our freedom, which is why students' participation at that time could be perhaps justified. However, subsequently, there is no reason why students should continue to waste their valuable time in taking part in politics. It has been experienced that more often than not, student leaders work to serve their own vested interests by organising various political activities in the university campuses. At the same time, political parties also openly fund and support student groups for their own interest. A case in point are the activities in the campus of Delhi University, where political parties openly fund and support student unions. Senior political leaders even make statements in support of the student unions they patronize. The situation in BHU at Varanasi is no different. Similar conditions prevail in a number of other universities as well.

Politicians feel that students cannot and should not remain aloof from political activities, therefore, it would be futile to keep students away from politics. With the lowering of age for voting rights in India, students' interest in political affairs has further increased. Political parties now realize that senior students are positive vote banks, who should be exploited for substantial political gains. Therefore, student leaders are formally cultivated and provided wide media coverage to project them as future political leaders. It has been observed that a number of student leaders do have political background or backing and they treat their student life days as a period for their grooming or training to acquire more confidence, so that they can become effective political leaders subsequently. To name a few, Mr VP Singh, former PM, was an active student leader of Allahabad University in 1950s, Mr. Chandrashekhar, also a former PM, was again a top student leader of Allahabad University in

1940s. Laloo Prasad Yadav was President of Patna University Students Union in early 1970s. Mr Prakash Karat, CPM General Secretary, was the first President of Jawaharlal Nehru University Student Union in 1970s. Sitaram Yechury, CPM Leader, was also the President of JNUSU for three terms in 1970s. Arun Jaitley, BJP leader, was President of Delhi University Students Union in 1977 and Mr ND Tiwari, Former Chief Minister of Uttrakhand, was the President of Allahabad University Students Union in 1945. There are many other political leaders in this category.

On the contrary, people who oppose participation of students in politics strongly feel that, students unnecessarily misutilise their time in politics, while they must adequately focus on their studies. It has been seen that political activities create considerable tensions and stress and even bring violence to colleges, causing long disruptions in academic activities. Students can ill afford to indulge in such activities at this juncture of their lives.

Specially poor students, who come to attain higher education in colleges, which their parents can barely afford, are the worst hit. These parents feel that their hard earned money, which they had invested on their sons/daughters, had certainly gone waste, if their wards were not able to acquire requisite knowledge during their college days. Further, unfortunately most of our politicians do not transmit higher moral or ethical values to students, which definitely does not help in their character building.

When parents spend so much of money on the studies of their wards, their primary goal is obviously to complete studies and become economically independent and not get involved in petty politics. It is now common knowledge that politics has generally corrupted almost all spheres of our lives and in all fairness, politicians should not be given yet another opportunity to corrupt the minds of our young students, which are still in their formative years. Moreover, such activities also bring down the names of our prestigious educational institutions. If students are permitted to play in the hands of politicians, there would definitely be a down fall in the standards of education being imparted in our colleges and universities.

Yet, another aspect of this problem is the fact that most student leaders try and justify their existence to the cause of welfare of students and to fight injustice done to the student community. While, in fact there are very few student unions, who are sincerely working for this cause. Most student leaders are bad students, who pay hardly any heed to their studies, much less to the needs of other students.

It has been seen that, of late, student politics in India is changing and campuses are becoming more sensitive to larger issues of society. Take the example of JNU, where students from every nook and corner of the country are studying. As reported in The Sunday Times of India dated November 11, 2007, polls in 2007 show that student politics is changing. And the issues are changing too. A few years ago, the issues were more local in nature: hot water in bathrooms, half-burnt chapattis in hostel mess, leaking taps, cheaper bus passes and eve-teasing on the campus. Now, it's a bit different. They are debating class conflict and affirmative action. Students are showing sensitivity towards the issues that do not affect them directly. They are looking at the bigger picture and student activism is becoming progressive. The signs are everywhere. Even the recent Delhi University Students' Union election, known for its high glamour quotient and money power, could not escape the real issues.

In a developing country like India, there is always an intense competition to grab respectable jobs and one needs tremendous efforts to secure such jobs. Unless our students work assiduously in a focused manner, it is fairly difficult to become successful in life. With the number of jobs decreasing in the public and government sectors, the problem has become all the more acute. All this requires that students do take their studies extremely seriously and do not while away their time in infructuous activities. One may not though oppose the very existence of students unions, but these unions must not distract the attention of our students from their main occupation, i.e., studying and gaining knowledge of the subjects they are taught. The unions may take-up only genuine causes of welfare of students, but the role of these unions must be clearly defined and given a strict code of conduct. Politicians must not interfere in the college/university affairs and should allow the students to concentrate on their studies, and let them fulfill the ambitions of their parents.

Part III Detailed Discussions

Can Reservation in Jobs Solve Problems of Our Society?

In May 2006, the proposal of the government to introduce reservation in higher education had led to widespread protests from the student community. These protests were mainly led by doctors who demanded that merit should be the sole criteria for admissions to medical and engineering colleges. In view of these developments, this hot topic is once again being debated in almost all forums.

It is brought out to remind that, reservation is not at all a new concept in India. In Kolhapur state and in the state of Mysore, reservation was introduced in as early as 1902 and 1921 respectively. French Revolution in the year 1789 also brought about significant socioeconomic equality in Europe and eliminated social injustice. Even now, there is 50 percent reservation for blacks and women in the medical faculty of Harvard University.

The less privileged in a society do need reservations or special privileges to do away with previous injustices. That is what a good society is all about, taking extra care of the weakest so that they can survive to be fit and competitive. In the case of India, through a shameful past of caste based divisions, the fact also is that the upper caste people exploited people of lower castes ruthlessly, and kept them completely marginalised. So, the moment we became a sovereign and secular democracy, our first job was to do away with the shameful concept of castes and make up for our past mistakes. At that time a reference to SC/ST/backward castes, etc. was perhaps still justified.

Despite more than six decades of independence, Indian society still has discernible social inequalities. While, rich continue to become richer, large number of poor have become more poor. Caste based reservations were introduced to help out the real downtrodden, so that they could be given an opportunity to lead an economically improved life. However, it is argued that really poor population has not been given much of relief by providing reservation in jobs on caste basis. On the contrary, reservation has disintegrated our society. Since, the poor were not in a position to educate their children due to lack of educational facilities or poor economic conditions, reservation in jobs was perhaps the only way out to help them at that stage. Reservation was only a concession given to socially and educationally backward people, and certainly was not a solution to the problems of our society.

But, it is so disappointing that after so many years of independence, our successive governments have not been able to ensure even basic education to all sections of our society. And this pathetic situation has brought us to the present dilemma.

It is certainly one of the most shameful failures of our governments. Yet, another interesting repercussion of the reservation policy has been the fact that the so called 'backward' became richer by virtue of their cast, while the economically backward have not benefitted much during all these years.

To quote Shashi Tharoor, "Caste, which Nehru and his ilk abhorred and believed would disappear from the social matrix of modern India, has not merely survived and thrived, but has become an instrument for highly effective political mobilisation. Candidates are picked by their parties with an eye toward the caste loyalties they can call upon; often their appeal is overtly to voters of their own caste or sub-caste, urging them to elect one of their own. The result has been the growth of caste-consciousness and casteism throughout society. In many States, caste determines educational opportunities, job prospects, and governmental promotions; all too often, people say you cannot go forward unless you're a backward".

In view of the above developments, today's youth demands that we should do away with caste based reservations and higher education must be based on merit and not on quota system. Sometime back, Supreme Court of India had asked the government to justify the criteria it uses for identifying particular categories as OBCs, as well as quantum of 27%, it has reserved for them in central services and proposed to introduce in the centrally funded educational institutions from the year 2007. Supreme Court also pointed out that this has serious social and political ramifications and may even cause to divide the country on caste lines. It may be recalled that Mandal Commission pegged OBC population at 52%, which led to quota quantum being fixed at 27%. However, this figure has been questioned by a number of surveys. This dispute over numbers can be sorted out by launching a caste based census for the first time since 1931.

It is widely opined that OBCs in India are around 30%, since rest are not discriminated by our society. Therefore, reservation for the rest would be without much justification. Economically backward people may be provided with free education and hostel facilities, etc. but not jobs. In today's environment of global competition, we cannot afford to compromise on quality of people, working in an organisation, as this will certainly reflect on its output.

Yet another impact of this policy would be obvious encouragement to brain drain since intelligent young men and women would get discouraged and leave India for better career prospects abroad. The whole idea has political repercussions and aims at capturing the vote bank. It may also eventually adversely affect the development of our country and may even impact the overall efficiency of the government, which, as we know, is not quite commendable presently.

Part III Detailed Discussions

In view of the above, we may conclude by saying that the government must consider the social and economic repercussions of the reservation policy and not try to introduce the new policy in haste. Even though social equality should be encouraged, merit based selections for higher education cannot be wished away. In any case, reservations should be gradually and rationally removed to pave the way for merit based selections in a developing country like India. India plans to develop at a fast pace to become a developed country by 2020, and towards this aim, merit based selections must be encouraged. The government must view the problem keeping the interest of the entire society in view, and not appease a particular section of the society to procure votes for their selfish ends. A merit based selection for higher education and jobs will certainly provide India better governance as well as efficient corporate management. This, in turn, will ensure desired progress and prosperity for the people of India.

Is Knowledge of Financial Management Essential for All Managers?

Financial management has a pivotal role in the over all functioning and growth of a business organisation. Most business activities do have financial ramifications, and therefore, significant business decisions cannot be taken unless corporate managers are provided with requisite financial inputs. These inputs are called 'Corporate Finance' or 'Managerial Finance' or 'Financial Management'. While analyzing a financial decision situation, knowledge of these inputs forms the basis for various corporate decisions.

During the last century, Financial Management has taken the shape of a distinct field and its changing relationship with economics and accounting is noteworthy. It is quite evident that scope of financial management has distinctly broadened during this period. Another development has been the fact that approach of financial management has now become more analytical and quantitative. Managing working capital and handling of capital budgeting and dividend policy, etc., are now being done with much detailed analysis and accuracy for the over all gain of the business enterprise. At least, basic knowledge of these financial aspects is now considered quite essential for all corporate managers.

Most commonly, share holders invest money in corporates to maximize their wealth in the shortest possible time period. Similarly, objective of a firm is to maximize the net value of the firm for the ultimate benefit of share holders. This is achieved by a company by strategically managing its finance and ensuring highest market value of its equity shares. Financial management achieves these goals by efficient allocation of all resources of the company to safeguard adequate economic growth of the organisation. Since, equity share holders incur considerable risk by investing money in a new business, finance people have to adopt suitable measures to look after the interest of share holders. Thus, we may safely state that maximization of the wealth of equity share holders remains the most desirable goal for financial decision-making.

Till recently, majority of Indian companies did not pay adequate attention to safeguard the interest of share holders, but things are fast changing for the better. Due to liberalization in the business scenario, corporates are expanding their business and they need more capital to invest in new ventures. Therefore, they have to adopt policies that favour share holders in general. This has increased the role of Financial Management in a big way.

To achieve the aforesaid goals, financial management people need to undertake a number of activities which include financial planning, analysis and control. These involve forecasting the financial future of the organisation keeping in view the financial needs of the firm and subsequently adopting sufficient means to control the financial goals of the company. These will include preparing profit and loss account, balance sheet and various other statements to ensure strict financial control. Another role of a financial manager is to manage firm's asset structure, which includes preparing capital budget and looking after the liquid resources of the firm. Yet, another role of financial manager is to frame a viable credit port folio and control levels of inventories.

Some other financial management activities which have long term repercussions on the financial structure of the firm include establishing the debt equity ratio and devising the dividend policy of the firms. Financial Management people also negotiate with suppliers of capital as well as selecting the appropriate instruments of financing the firm. Managing foreign exchange of the firm is yet another important function of a finance manager.

Financial management has acquired additional significance in view of the fact that, a number of financial decisions also affect operations and quite a few other aspects of a firm. To illustrate, financial decision to select the capacity of a plant to be installed would directly influence quite a few other functions of the organisation. This decision may also involve risk-return connotations, installing a bigger plant may involve higher risk-return factor. Similarly, debt-equity ratio may affect the cost of capital and lead to varying risk factors involved.

In view of the above, we may conclude by saying that, due to the present economic environment in the business world, job of a finance manager has become fairly complex and demanding. And since financial decisions are so very important, all managers must have the basic knowledge of financial status of the organisation. No wonder, we so often find management training courses with the title "Finance for non-finance executives" being frequently conducted in the corporate world.

How Relevant and Effective is SAARC in the Present Day?

Asia is the largest continent, which occupies almost one third area of the world. Asia was the motherland of some of the world's earliest civilizations. As of now, Asia accommodates more than 60% of the world population. There is tremendous potential for consolidation of business and trade relations between the Asian nations. It was in this context that eight nations of South Asia have now joined together to form SAARC (South Asian Association for Regional Cooperation). Headquarters of SAARC have been established at Kathmandu in Nepal. SAARC was founded in 1985 in Dhaka.

For the present, the foremost concern of these South Asian countries is to develop their economies. Once they succeed in developing the economy, other things will automatically follow. Japan could be quoted as one example in this regard. Thus, India has embarked on an ambitious programme of comprehensive economic cooperation through these dynamic South Asian countries. Participating nations of SAARC are India, Pakistan, Afghanistan, Bangladesh, Nepal, Sri Lanka, Maldives and Bhutan. By joining SAARC, India also wants to fulfil her endeavour to try and maintain peaceful relations with her neighbours and other countries of the world as well.

Despite the fact that, SAARC nations were more than willing to develop cooperation between them, the progress in this direction was curtailed for want of stepwise planning and follow-up action. If one looks at the results consequent to a number of SAARC meetings, it emerges that the main stumbling block has been the lack of trust and political tensions between India and Pakistan. Unfortunately, even though Pakistan has agreed with India to resolve all issues through bilateral cooperation and discussions without third party involvement, Pakistan has been displaying a habit of raising the issue of Kashmir at almost all international forums, rather indiscreetly. Once, Pakistan raises such issues during the meetings of SAARC, India also uses these forums to put across her point of view on the subject. As a result, the whole atmosphere of SAARC is vitiated and issues between India and Pakistan occupy the centre stage, putting all other issue on the periphery. The problem boils down to the fact that Pakistan is unable to resist her intense temptation to highlight the issue of Kashmir at all international forums, including that of SAARC. India has been warning SAARC nations on this issue. However, the result of irresponsible behavior on the part of Pakistan is there for everyone to see. A number of SAARC nations have been showing their concern in this regard.

In the past, despite the commitment, SAARC nations have not been able to operationalise the South Asian Preferential Trade Area (SAPTA), which is an important step towards strengthening trade relations between the SAARC nations. Similar problems have been encountered with regard to other steps towards better economic cooperation as well.

During the past few years, there has been increased awareness with regard to regional cooperation among countries of South Asia, as has been the case in respect of WTO, EU and ASEAN, etc. SAARC nations, which are mainly developing nations, are now realizing that trade opportunities in these countries are being increasingly grabbed by developed countries. In countries like India and Pakistan, MNCs of developed nations have already captured markets of a wide array of products, including food and other consumables. SAARC countries, have a large number of people below the poverty line, and therefore, cannot afford to lose business opportunities to developed nations.

In view of the above mentioned realization, prior to meetings of SAARC heads of states, which are held at regular intervals, Commerce Secretaries of SAARC nations meet to sort out differences on the South Asian Preferential Trade Agreement (SAPTA). Consequently, a general consensus was achieved to operationalise SAPTA to provide much needed fillip to economic cooperation among SAARC countries. Yet, another issue of South Asian Free Trade Agreement (SAFTA) was also discussed during these meetings.

Subsequently, a number of crucial agreements were signed to promote regional cooperation. SAARC summit, which was held in Islamabad in 2004, ended with leaders of the seven nations hailing the three-day meeting as a watershed for the region. The atmosphere during this summit was extremely cordial and India and Pakistan also exercised restraint and did not vitiate the atmosphere. Agreement for free trade pact was also signed at this meeting of SAARC. An important development that took place was the breakthrough in talks between India and Pakistan on the sidelines of the SAARC summits. During this meeting, India and Pakistan agreed to resolve all issues including the issue of Kashmir through bilateral talks. Detailed programme for progressing such talks was also drawn and this has been hailed as an important step towards normalization of relations between India and Pakistan.

During subsequent SAARC meetings also, Indian and Pakistani officials met to resolve a number of issues. Now, a SAARC University has been established in Delhi/Gurgaon for the benefit of students of SAARC countries and encourage educational and cultural exchanges.

It is, therefore, apparent that SAARC can really play a pivotal role in encouraging even bilateral relations between two SAARC nations, besides hopes of better trade interaction among SARRC countries.

48 Is Advertising an Art to Promote Goods or an Instrument to Mislead Unsuspecting Customers?

Advertising is an art of successfully marketing a product. Certain companies and manufacturers have established their names in the market to the extent that it is enough to sell their goods without any active promotion.

In a larger context, one still needs to promote goods through advertisements to capture the imagination/fancy of a prospective customer. In the age of cut-throat competition in the industry, manufacturers and sellers are beginning to realise the significance of utilising the art of advertising to win over customers. The market is flooded with numerous brands selling the same basic item and such a wide variety of options can easily confuse a prospective buyer. All other factors remaining constant, what ultimately increases the probability of a specific brand scoring over others in terms of sale is the niche that a particular brand carves for itself through advertising. Gone are the days, when the decision regarding the purchase of an item was dependent solely on its utility and its quality or standard.

Advertisements help highlight the distinguishing features of a product. This helps the consumers to decide better as she/he is able to figure out as to which brand meets her/his specific requirements.

Assuming that all brands are:

1. easily available
2. competitively priced
3. boasting of a good quality
4. having their goods in demand

What makes the actual difference in the acceptance of one brand and rejection of others, is the advertisement and active promotion the winning brand enjoys. Advertising is about successfully convincing an Eskimo sitting in an igloo to buy ice.

In other words, advertisements help the consumer to make an informed choice and receive true value for money. On the other hand, unscrupulous advertising may be used to mislead people into buying low quality and expensive goods. Attractive advertisements and promotional campaigns have the ability to lure unsuspecting people into buying poor quality products by creating an aura about them.

In the recent past, consider the following advertisements:

- Complan claims to make children taller, stronger and smarter with 23 vital nutrients

- Use of Parachute advanced hair oil means "aapke bal badhe teen guna zyada"
- Sugar Free D'Lite says it's a 99% calorie-free drink.
- Tide Plus maintains that its "powder lage aadha" while giving "safedi zyaada"
- Maggi offers complete nutrition for your hungry child in "2 minutes"
- LG air conditioners help you "breathe healthy"

In addition, there are ads wherein a soap will ward off the Swine flu virus, a fairness cream that can change your complexion in seven days, an AC will improve your love life, a fridge will pep-up the veggies to keep them extra fresh and nutritious, etc. Such ads are obviously based on half-truths and false claims to mislead innocent consumers, who are finding it more and more difficult to segregate fact from fiction. Even though we agree that— advertising thrives on exaggeration, no doubt. But of late, a slew of misleading and deceptive advertisements is constantly aired on television to influence consumers to pick up the products advertised. Especially, targeted are impressionable kids; employing pester power, advertisers know, always pays.

The companies themselves may not be entirely wrong about what they claim, but it has been proved often that some of their advertisements are full of half-truths. And it's the race for market share and a focus on the top line in an increasingly competitive market place that drives companies to go over the top in their sales pitch. A number of times, companies are excited about their products consequent to research inputs and many dramatise their claims. However, advertising professionals defend their assertions by saying that advertisers are conscious of their 'societal' responsibility and try to win the confidence and trust of consumers.

Senior advertising professional Prasoon Joshi explains the "exaggeration" as "creative interpretation" or putting across facts in an interesting manner to attract eyeballs. "The client knows that the consumer is the audience, and no client would want to lose that trust," he says.

World over, there is a crackdown on food advertisements with rising obesity and increase in related ailments. Recently, in the US, the Federal Trade Commission's Bureau of Consumer Protection asked Nestle to stop claiming that its Boost Kids Essential can strengthen the immune system of children, help fend off illness and reduce the number of days that children are absent from the classroom. Nestle's claim did not stand up to scrutiny and so it had to agree. Other than penalties, many countries take disciplinary measures against false claims such as corrective advertising. For instance, in 2009 in Australia, Coca-Cola ran "myth-busting" ads claiming that the soft drink did not make children fat, and was not packed with large amounts of caffeine. The Australian Competition and Consumer Commission came down hard and the company had to carry corrective ads titled "Setting the Record Straight" in seven newspapers.

However, unfortunately in India very few companies are penalized for making impossible promises. In fact, so far and few between are the instances of advertisers being hauld up for false claims that when a case is registered against a company, it makes headlines. Case in point is the controversy involving the health drink, Complan. The Maharashtra FDA took its manufacturer, Heina, to court over the claim that Complan can add two inches to children's height.

Advertisements, with the influence they exercise over the thoughts of a prospective buyer, give an iconic status to the brand that they are promoting. Throughout the campaign, the necessity to own the said product is asserted, so much so, that it becomes a status symbol to own a product of the particular brand. Most of these goods come in the category of luxury goods and leave a buyer's pocket visibly lighter.

Advertising is about playing with human emotions and psychology to the extent that people relate to it or are forced to relate to the message inherent in the advertisement. Once, a dent is made in the memory of a consumer, repeated viewing of the same advertisement helps secure a long-lasting place in the consumer's memory. The person then becomes more receptive to the message and displays readiness to try out the product. Advertising, thus, helps to convert non-consumers of a certain commodity into consumers and also to brainwash consumers of rival brands to change/swap sides.

Harmful goods/substances such as cigarettes, tobacco and liquor are promoted unabashedly through eye-catching advertisements. The statutory warnings that are required to be clearly mentioned as per the law, are hardly given their due importance and get camouflaged in the larger than life ad campaigns associated with promoting these goods.

It is therefore, most crucial for consumers to carefully scrutinize the hidden messages in advertisements to avoid being misled or even cheated. The thumb-rule for consumers should be to use one's common-sense. But, unfortunately, commonsense is not-so-common. All said and done, ballyhoo must be avoided.

Chapter 49

Leaders are Born, Managers can be Trained

The topic in simple terms would imply that leadership qualities are not much trainable, while on the other hand, managerial skills could easily be developed in an individual. Before discussing the core issue, it would be pertinent to elaborate the role and job requirements of a manager as well as a leader.

Interestingly, a number of social scientists have opined that roles of a manager and a leader are almost similar. While others feel that such roles are easily distinguishable. A leader need not belong to an organized group of people, but managers belong to organized groups, which have a defined structure. More often than not, a manager achieves his/her goals by exercising authority and allocating the resources to his/her subordinates. This is generally not the case with a leader and a leader has to earn respect of the people who work for him and also assist him in his work. A leader invariably puts himself as a model for others to emulate.

It must be emphasized that, while a manager gets his work done through the authority that he has, a leader has to motivate people to follow him by setting example of his own conduct. The keen desire of the people to follow a leader emanates from within, and not due to any kind of pressure or authority. The tasks performed by a manager are mainly reactive, while that of a leader essentially proactive. It is also an accepted fact that, all leaders can be trained to become managers, but all managers may not be able to become leaders.

The knowledge and behavioural pattern of a leader are the most significant qualities that make him a person, who is naturally admired by people. The functions of a leader include his ability to induce and persuade his subordinates or followers to willingly contribute towards predetermined goals. A leader by virtue of his charisma drives people to give their best. Thus, a leader utilizes the full potential of his subordinates or followers to attain the best results in the shortest possible time.

It therefore, emerges that a leader would become extremely effective, if he is able to motivate people by identifying as to what precisely motivates them. This involves his ability to know his followers rather well through analysis of their personality traits. Subsequently, based on this knowledge, he has to devise a plan of action to motivate people. It is being realised that the ability of the leader to know the personality of his followers could be scientifically developed by focused training and guidance. However, the ability of a leader to plan requisite action to motivate his followers is more a matter of art. This precisely is the reason due to which it is stated that leaders are born and cannot be trained. This could also be the reason due to which some leaders are extremely effective while others are not. Due to this very reason, it is aptly said that powerful leaders are able to motivate ordinary people to perform extraordinary tasks.

Owing to inspirational abilities of the leader, the followers feel that they have close inter-personal relations with their leader, even though they do not have any face to face contact with him. Examples of Sir Churchill, Napoleon and Gandhi could be quoted in this context. We all know that in India, Gandhi could inspire the entire Indian population to revolt against the mighty British empire forcing them to quit India. Eventhough Gandhi had no official authority of any kind, he was certainly most effective and a very powerful leader, who could sway public opinion. Of course, it goes without saying that the typical environment in which, the leader operates also contributes a great deal towards his effectiveness.

A leader must not only be able to create a vision, but should also possess the requisite skill to achieve results by careful planning and execution. A leader should necessarily be able to look far ahead and innovate and enthuse people around, to go for higher aims. All said and done, a leader should teach and not always preach.

On the other hand, a manager helps mobilize human and material resources to achieve targets in an efficient and effective manner. The word "efficient" implies that he must utilize his resources in an economic manner to attain desired results. While the word "effective" means that he must achieve the desired target. Since most of our social goals are achieved through organized group effort, role of a manager assumes increased significance, especially in a developing nation like India.

In a business environment, distinction between good managers and good leadership is often discussed. Any business organisation which has good leaders with it, will always be way ahead of its rival business organisation, since leaders will provide the requisite on-ground inputs, data and advice that assist the organisation to adopt better strategies to move forward. At the same time, it is also essential to look after the human resource and enhance managerial capabilities at all levels to ensure improved customer delight. This would help the organisation meet the new challengers of globalisation and growth—thus achieving the organisation's long-term targets.

We know that, managing is both a science and an art. While, learning the theory of management is a science, its application is more of an art. Management training is now being imparted to develop skills that make a manager efficient as well as effective. This training is now fairly well established and meets the essential requirements of a budding manager, almost

Part III Detailed Discussions

entirely. It is largely based on practical experience gained over the years. The lessons learnt from these experiences are so significant that apprising managers of these experiences is considered most critical and hence the need to train managers. These training programmes for the managers are tailor-made to facilitate this learning process. People who are specially selected are now trained in a scientific and well organised manner for specialist job requirements of a managerial job. Managerial training is the process of personalised growth that is aimed towards optimum utilisation of managerial capabilities of the individual and its utility is now not only desirable, but considered essential. Management training is now being organised to focus on the fact that management is not about power or authority, but about persuasion and team work and that a manager should adopt a people-centric management style.

To summarise, we may say that, while managerial qualities can be learnt through management training, most leadership skills come as a part of the personality of a leader. By careful grooming and organised training, the leadership personality traits can be enhanced that make a leader more effective. Leadership now has been widely recognised as the "Force Multiplier" of business and the hallmark of leadership is successful execution of difficult tasks.

Can Corruption be Eliminated from India?

It may not be a matter of some pride for an Indian to know that India ranks among the most corrupt countries of the world. While India has developed on a number of counts and shown discernible economic growth, yet rampant corruption that prevails in our country, considerably tarnishes its image in the eyes of the world. As corruption has become clearly so deep rooted in India, some people frankly opine that corruption can merely be controlled and not altogether eliminated from Indian soil.

Major scams routinely grab the nation's attention. But the minor ones hardly draw public attention, even though they affect citizens every day. Among the recent scams that made headlines are the Commonwealth Games, illegal mining at Bellary, the IPL manipulations, the Medical Council of India fraud, the Sukna Land Scam, the allotment of 2G Spectrum, Coal Gate, Adarsh Building Scam and bribes in purchase of Augusta Westland Helicopters etc.

While the Bofors files are on the verge of being closed for obvious reasons, cases against Mulayam Singh Yadav, Mayawati and others have been put on back burner. Today, black economy is more than 50% of our GDP. This leads to ineffectiveness of schemes for the poor like NREGA and Mid Day Meals, etc. Black money leads to colossal waste. We repeatedly repair our roads due to poor quality of construction. Thus, money for making new roads is always inadequate. India has been losing more than 6% of its rate of growth since last forty years or so.

After gaining independence more than 60 years back, while India's industrial base expanded and our cities grew both vertically and horizontally, corruption also grew at all levels and in all spheres of Indian life. It would not be untrue to state that in India corruption has become an institution by itself. In fact, an honest person starts considering himself an out-cast and a misfit in the Indian society. He/she is labelled as an eccentric or a crazy individual, who should be better left to himself/herself. Such persons are in gross minority, who are put against the wall and they somehow manage their mere survival.

It is really amazing to discover, how the mindset of our recent day politicians is so markedly different when compared to those who sacrificed their every thing to give us freedom. While, our elder politicians gave up lucrative jobs and large business establishments to become freedom fighters, the present day politicians grab all kinds of jobs for their kins and make money from whatever opportunity comes their way. They invest huge amount of money to become an MLA or MP or a Minister, and once they grab power, they earn many many times more. Thus, politics has undoubtedly become the most paying business, which one enjoys during his/her life time and then passes on to his/her next generation. Today, most politicians ensure that their sons or daughters join politics and continue to enjoy the friuts of their status and power. A good number of our politicians themselves present the best example of how corruption has taken its roots in India at the highest level. MLAs and MPs cross floors to change governments after taking huge sums of money. During such transactions black money changes hands in plenty, while we claim democracy is functioning quite satisfactorily in our country. The system is further polluted due to the entry of a large number of known criminals into politics. This variety of politicians certainly does not have faith in adhering to any ethics or lawful procedures. One really wonders when people at the highest level have embraced corruption, where does the ordinary man go to complain? Obviously, he is fighting a losing battle.

One would recall that at one time, almost the entire cabinet under the then Prime Minister Narasimha Rao was charged with corruption. In the recent past, Tehelka exposures are still fresh in our memories. One could keep quoting the number of scams that have occurred in our country. A few years ago the Chairman of Punjab Public Service Commission was caught for recruiting officials in Punjab State after taking hefty sums of money from a large number of candidates. Even though public memory is short lived, one vividly remembers Bofors scam, Enron scam, Fodder scam, JMM bribery scam, Telecom scam, Urea scam and Stamp papers scam, etc. Interestingly, Hyderabad-based NGO, Solus Media has created the 'A to Z' of scams under various Indian governments. This NGO has undertaken this task to tell people about those who seek their votes. The list of corrupt officers and politicians in India is long and never ending. Names of a number of top IAS, IPS and other officials are included in this list. These include two Chairpersons of the Port Trust, Chief Secretaries, Directors General Police, senior bureaucrats and and host of other officials. All such cases only indicate the tip of the iceberg of corruption that exists in India and goes to show that the cancer of corruption is extremely widespread and deep rooted.

While the Delhi Development Authority (DDA) was named as one of the most corrupt departments of our country, in most government departments, no file moves, unless palms of the concerned officials are greased. This state of affairs is prevalent in almost all offices of central and state governments. The corrupt continue to find novel means to cheat the government and the public alike and the existing system supports such rogue elements of our society. Interestingly, in certain activities, corruption has really been well organised. These include ticket-less travel in trains and corruption in departments of civil supplies etc. States of UP and Bihar deserve special mention in this regard. In certain areas in these states, travellers do not buy tickets and instead pay some money to the middle men who manage everything to ensure that journey of the client is completed without any hassles.

Happenings at Karanja Irrigation Project in Karnataka provide yet another glaring example of an organised corruption racket. This project was delayed enormously since almost all officials had been making money due to a number of corrupt practices that existed there. Cost of the project eventually went up from 9.6 crore to 340 crore, causing immense loss to the government.

To correct the above state of affairs, several organisations such as CBI, CVC (Central Vigilance Commission), Anti-corruption Wings and Vigilance Departments in most establishments do exist, but their effectiveness has been quite minimal. The fact that, the entire system is corrupt has ensured that such organisations are not allowed to function in the desired manner.

In view of the above, former CVC, Mr. N. Vittal had floated a suggestion that the right to corruption-free service be included as a fundamental right, so that it can be enforced upon by the courts of law. Consequent to introduction of this provision, an honest citizen would be in a position to initiate appropriate action against a corrupt official. Yet another measure proposed was the appointment of a powerful Lok Pal at the centre, and Lok Ayuktas in states. While some states did appoint Lok Ayuktas, Jan Lok Pal bill was finally passed by the Parliament in 2012 following agitation by social activist Anna Hazare in August 2011, which received tremendous public support. However, it is alleged that Lok Pal under this Act does not possess the required teeth to bite the corrupt in high places.

However, thankfully Indian judiciary has delivered some very bold judgments against corrupt politicians in high places. These include imprisonment and disqualification of high profile politicians like Lalu Yadav, Madhu Koda and Om Prakash Chautala. Recently, Court sentenced then sitting CM of Tamil Nadu, Jayalalithaa to 4 years' imprisonment and also slapped a fine of 100 crore for accumulating money due to alleged corrupt practices.

About two years back, Arvind Kejriwal launched Aam Aadmi Party (AAP) mainly to fight corruption and convincingly won Delhi elections in 2015. AAP did expose a number of corruption cases and also took them to the court. While during the 2014 Lok Sabha elections campaign, BJP loudly promised to fight corruption, once it came to power, the present government at the Centre has more than 30% of the ministers who have corruption/criminal cases against them. Under such circumstances, the common man does not know where to look for honest politicians. But, huge victory of AAP is very encouraging.

The above discussion indicates that, it may not be feasible to remove corruption altogether from our society, but we will do well if we adopt adequate and effective measures to keep it under control. This will definitely help India to project a better image of herself and redeem our national honour to some extent. We must encourage honest people to enter politics to clean our political environment, and at the same time, outrightly reject corrupt and communal politicians. Use of technology would help us reduce corruption in official procedures in a big way. Be honest and applaud those who are honest.

Will India ever Get Rid of Terrorism and Insurgency?

Acts of terrorism pose a very serious law and order problem for our society and may even become a cause for its disintegration. Acts of terror include various incidents of killing, kidnapping, torture, rape and creating an atmosphere of panic and fear in our society. Terrorist acts are extremely inhuman, since mass killings and torture include civilians, women and even children. Further, frequent conflicts between security forces and terrorists also cause tremendous loss of life and property. The relationship between terrorists and other anti-social elements encourages illegal transfer of money, smuggling and such other types of crimes.

In the twenty first century, terrorism has emerged as the biggest threat for the humanity. This unfortunate trend has registered a marked change during the last two decades. While in India, due to various reasons, terrorism got encouragement in some states, 11 September, 2001 attack on the twin towers of World Trade Center in New York, USA and subsequent terrorist attack in Mumbai depict the current state of affairs in this regard in the world. Now, terrorism has become a global phenomenon and developments in the field of Information Technology have given it teeth to bite even harder. Due to international funding and support to terrorist outfits, terrorists are in a position to acquire advance technologies to develop even weapons of mass destruction. It goes without saying that, terrorism poses a serious threat to humanity and democratic functioning of a country.

In the recent past, religious terrorism has been given substantial impetus. Under the garb of their religion, fanatics plan and encourage communal violence threatening peaceful life of our citizens. However, the fact remains that irrespective of the so-called noble cause that terrorists may support, terrorism should not be justified under any circumstances. The primary aim of terrorists is to violently disturb the law and order of a country. Yet, another reason to denounce terrorism is the fact that terrorism brutally opposes functioning of democracy and preservation of human values.

We may thus define terrorism as the use of violent means by a group of misguided individuals, who want to bring about certain political changes through unlawful and inhuman means. More often than not, terrorists aim to create a psychological impact on the society to ensure achievement of their goals. While terrorism and insurgency may have similar objectives, it needs to be clarified that insurgency is largely visible within the national boundary of a state and is directed against one's own government. On the other hand, terrorism can easily cross national boundaries and may not have the support of local population. We may, therefore, summarise by saying that insurgency in a larger form may or can acquire the status of terrorism.

It needs to be clarified that Maoists threats is essentially a domestic phenomenon, which can be contained with improved governance. On the other hand, terrorists threat is much more serious and would threaten our political structure and economic stability irrespective of the measures that we may initiate. The Maoists have a guerrilla army of approximately 10,000 men, but Jihadi foot soldiers are far too many to count.

Let us now take a stock of terrorist activities in our country. During the British rule, some Indian patriots indulged in violent acts, but these were mainly directed towards certain British officials who were known for their rude and atrocious behaviour. These revolutionaries never directed their activities towards the public or the innocent. Independent India experienced Naxalite terrorism, which was mainly inspired by Chinese revolution under the guidance of Mao. This movement commenced in 1967 in West Bengal and later encompassed Bihar as well. Subsequently after 1972, it even spread to Kerala, Orissa, Tripura and Andhra Pradesh. Even today, terrorist outfits such as People's War Group (PWG) and Maoist Communist Centre (MCC) are active in various parts of our country.

In the north-eastern region, insurgency has been persisting ever since India became independent. In this regard, insurgency activities in Nagaland have been the most predominant. Formation of Nagaland in 1963, did witness a decline in these activities, but, the demand for a separate independent Nagaland has been persisting. The National Socialist Council of Nagaland (NSCN), a militant outfit in Nagaland, Manipur, Myanmar and Arunachal Pradesh, continues to remain active. In Tripura the National Liberation Front of Tripua (NLFT) and All Tripura Tiger Force (ATTF) are the main tribal groups which are fighting for the ouster of non-tribals from this region.

In Mizoram, Mizo National Front (MNF) had been demanding creation of a state comprising areas of Manipur, Tripura and parts of Assam. These activities got substantially curtailed consequent to formation of Mizoram in 1987. However, Assam has been most affected due to terrorist activities of the United Liberation Front of Assam (ULFA) and the United Minorities Front (UMF). The activities of these two organisations have adversely affected the economy of Assam. At the same time, Bodo movement has been demanding a separate homeland causing substantial violence. In this regard, Bodoland Liberation Tiger Force (BLTF) is yet another militant outfit which has been demanding a separate Bodoland.

If one looks at terrorist activities in Punjab, these activities commenced in

Part III Detailed Discussions

Nineteen eighties in pursuance of a demand for a separate Sovereign State of Khalistan. However, consequent to an army action, terrorists were flushed out from places of religion and all such activities were brought under control.

India saw the ugliest face of terrorism in Jammu and Kashmir, where large scale terrorist activities are being conducted by Pakistan. These activities have seen serious repercussions since 1988. Such activities have forced a large number of people to leave their homes and become refugees in other states. Militant activities in this state include kidnapping, killing of innocent people and extortion. Most terrorist activities in J & K have been sponsored by Pakistan, where terrorists are trained and armed to create disturbances in India. In this respect, the terrorist attack on the Indian Parliament in 2001 and subsequent terrorist attack in Mumbai deserve specific mention.

For long, India has been a victim of terrorist activities. We cannot forget the sacrifices of Mrs. Indira Gandhi and Mr. Rajiv Gandhi, who had ironically taken a pledge to fight terrorism in our country. The agony of people is beyond description where terrorist activities have been prevailing. There is a need to consolidate public opinion against such activities and suitably equip our security forces to face the brutal acts of terrorism. Unless, India is in a position to control such activities, our economic development would be affected substantially. It is hoped that the terrorist activities would be controlled, if relations between India and Pakistan improve and a political solution to the problem of Kashmir is ultimately found.

Is IQ More Relevant than EQ for Success in Management?

For quite some time now, almost everyone believed in the age-old paradigm that IQ is solely responsible for success in life. One would vividly recall being repeatedly told by parents and teachers that unless you do well in studies, there would be no success in life and so on and so forth. But at the same time, one could also come across some people who, without having a good academic record card in their pocket, still managed to become successful and even achieve very high targets. The problem became somewhat more perplexing, when after completing the studies one got a job but was surprisingly told that success was not directly proportional to academic excellence. Also, one could notice that there were a large number of people, who had very commendable academic report cards under their belts, yet could not achieve much during their life span. Thus, the concept that IQ is the sole determinant of success had to be accepted with a pinch of salt.

It was during late '70s-early' 80s, that validity of IQ as the only measure of a person's intelligence, was formally questioned. Further, the popularly assumed correlation between IQ and success was also found somewhat suspect. The term "Emotional Intelligence" was perhaps first used by Peter Salovey of Yale University and John Mayer of New Hamshire University to describe a set of personal and social abilities of an individual. It was realised that there is definitely much more to success in life than possessing a high IQ and this realisation eventually brought the concept of EQ to the fore. Consequently, it is now being widely accepted that to realistically define success and effectively mange oneself and others, the EQ component needs to be amalgamated with that of IQ.

Emotional intelligence being a multi-dimensional ability of a person can be defined as "the ability to command respect by building relationships" or "the ability to get along with people and situations" or "a positive and proactive attitude towards all aspects of life". It is now acknowledged that there are three essential or basic components of EQ:

a. Motivating oneself

b. Motivating others

c. Emphathising with others

It could be noted that the first component, i.e., motivating oneself, involves our own feelings and thoughts that help us to remain in control and also inspire ourselves. The other two components, namely, motivating others and empathising with others, pertain to interpersonal skills. One needs to match other people's wavelength to ensure best results in a work situation or in personal relations.

Research has revealed that EQ encourages a person to aim high and ultimately become more result-oriented in life with discernible emphasis on human relations. Equipped with a high EQ, one can increase his areas of influence markedly and become more contented by acquiring an increasingly purpose-oriented outlook. Emotional intelligence can be fruitfully utilized to make flexible and multi-skilled teams and even to handle a plethora of adversities in a better way. It does help to assist people in becoming more dedicated to their jobs and provide them a constructive feed back. Utilising the benefits of EQ, one can ensure that a team operates smoothly and weeds out any internal conflicts to achieve results. A manager needs these tools everyday to interact with others and more significantly, to meet his targets. No wonder, it is often opined that with a high IQ, you may perhaps get a good job, but to go up the ladder, you must also have a high EQ. Thus, EQ makes a manager manage himself as well as others in a meaningful and proactive manner and guides him to achieve higher goals.

Studies have also established that emotional intelligence plays a prominent role in group effectiveness of an individual. In the present day context, when almost all jobs invariably entail monumental team effort with an ever-increasing time and resource crunch, a manager must be competent enough to motivate and influence his team members adequately to optimise results. This role of a manager necessarily demands that he must be equipped with sufficient emotional intelligence to become an effective motivator for himself and for others around him.

Acknowledging the impact of EQ on behavioural patterns of individuals, a number of companies and armed forces have purposely laid much emphasis on these aspects, and therefore, EQ forms an integral part of the selection criteria being used for induction of managers in these organizations. It has been noted that EQ plays a pivotal role in defining the behaviour of an individual, more significantly under stressful and trying conditions.

Mercifully, research also brings out that EQ ingredients are by and large fairly trainable and one is never too late to improve himself in this field. While, studying the ramifications of EQ on human behaviour, one cannot help feeling somewhat awestruck by the contemporary relevance of the subject, where stress seems to adversely affect most activities of our lives. It would be interesting to note that some of the critical areas where EQ has tremendous potential to contribute include:

a. Inspiring yourself and others around you—it multiplies your achievements.

b. Adopting an empathetic attitude towards others—it works like magic.

c. Controlling negative thoughts—they invariably spoil you.

d. Learning optimism—see the dough'nut, not the hole.

e. Developing trust—you only get it, if you give it.

f. Complex decision-making and emotions—essentially, logic is not everything.

g. Managing conflicts—resolving to resolve.

h. Building stress immunity—adjusting your sails to meet challenges of the wind.

i. Controlling anger—it really helps.

j. Increasing sensitivity—surveying the emotional landscape.

k. Building and maintaining a cohesive team—you cannot do without it.

l. Handling diversity successfully and so on.

It is needless to emphasise that the alpha and omega of the argument is that there lies an urgent and inescapable need to organize formal and focussed training for managers on EQ aspects so that, they can reap an optimum harvest for their efforts and can create a harmonious environment at their place of work as well as in their homes.

Part III Detailed Discussions

Should We Import Management Techniques to Manage Indians?

The ancient culture of India always boasted of its knowledge packed compilations of principles such as the Vedas, Arthashashtra, Mahabharata, Ramayana, Gita, Panchtantra and several other sources of wisdom. These revered books present simple, concise yet stunningly practical solutions to our day to day problems and they continue to remind us of our rich cultural heritage and its sheer practical relevance in the present day world. After all, human nature and social relationships have not altered much through these long years, while we presumably are far more modernized today. But somehow, over the years, while others took some lessons from us, we got caught in our own whirlpool of confusion. Willy nilly, we rushed towards the West to tell us how to manage our own people. Busy, the way we are, in importing foreign management techniques, the most essential requirement to develop an indigenous style of management that gels with our culture and upbringing, was conveniently overlooked or ignored. While, one must keep oneself abreast with the latest advancements in the field of management studies all over world, there is a positive need to exercise caution while applying them in practice at some specific location.

Culture, powerfully and persuasively guides our thoughts, actions and general behaviour. Today, international business involves close interaction and movement of people across national boundaries. Therefore, an appreciation of cultural differences, especially when these differences become critical, is most essential. It is common knowledge that most Indians attach discernible credence to emotions, close bonds, long lasting relationships, commitments and opportunities to grow in a conducive environment. These preferences obviously emanate from the socio-cultural environment that prevailed and still exists in India. Close social bonds and structure of family system were mainly responsible for this situation. Quite clearly, unlike West, human bonds were always allotted the uppermost priority in our relationships, dealings and even business transactions. Indians are very strong in the element of personal devotion; they can annihilate themselves for the sake of a parent, a brother, or a friend. People of the West have the distinct capacity of acting in concert with persons for whom, perhaps they may have the greatest personal dislike, merely out of regard for the organisation to which they all belong. This power of self-suppression for the sake of an ideal is a virtue, which the Indians have to learn. To evolve and then sustain an effective management style for Indians, it is essential that this socio-cultural scenario and typical behavioural traits of Indian culture should be taken into account.

India is one of the biggest exporters of knowledge workers. Unfortunately, we do not have the required mechanism to utilize this knowledge bank for developmental work of our country. It may sound somewhat ironical that even though India has the distinction of having some of the best management institutes and highly talented and technically trained manpower, there is a conspicuous absence of indigenous management techniques that should enthuse Indian companies to out-perform others in the international market. At present, our management schools continue to rely heavily on Western business concepts and management strategies. For training purposes, even case studies are hijacked from companies of USA, which may not have any relevance in the Indian environment. Apparently, such management training would be markedly devoid of practical ground realities of the Indian set-up and peculiar situations of business transactions that take place in India.

Thus, adopting the local culture could be the key to success, whereas imposing management techniques of other countries may not yield the desired results, or at times may prove to be somewhat counter-productive or even hazardous.

Keeping organisations healthy and viable in today's world is a daunting task. Individuals in organisations likewise face multiple challenges that include among other things, finding contentment in and through work and discovering dignity and purpose in pursuit of organisational goals. As individuals strive hard to perform better, expectations of organisations continue to snowball, causing extra stress on an individual. International management experts now refer to Bhagavad Gita to seek the Gita-inspired philosophy for guidance. Gita is quite logically considered a significant storehouse of valuable information that encompasses management techniques for all occasions. The wisdom that Gita contains is not only practically applicable, but also functionally effective to manage organisations, even under most trying circumstances. The leadership and management styles of Lord Krishna are considered most apt for handling complex problems of situational management. It is now widely believed that the success of Lord Krishna was largely attributed to his smart and flexible approach in dealing with varied situations and people. Gita suggests improvement of organisations through planned, systematic, long-range efforts, primarily focused on the culture of an organisation and its human and local processes. Above all, it provides a comprehensive yet concise exposition of theory and practice. Management consultants now realise that most management principles eventually date back to the teachings of the Bhagwad Gita. Lord krishna, while exhorting Arjuna to take stock of things of the present, literally gave him the philosophy of action to work for

Part III Detailed Discussions

excellence without permitting the anxiety for results to distract his attention and energies. It stands to reason that such controlled behaviour enables a person to focus one's attention on work in a stress-free environment to deliver best results in a given situation.

Reports now assert that a number of foreign corporates operating in India prefer to chart their ethical programms based on the philosophy enshrined in the Bhagavad Gita. Recent reports also unveil that a number of companies have preferred to adopt leadership styles that are propagated by the Vedic principles. Corporate giants like Tata Tea, Hughes India, Modi crop, Hero Group and Jindal Strips are some of the firms that have opted for this kind of management training for their senior managers. Perhaps, gradually we are realizing and acknowledging that our own Vedic principles are far more relevant to manage our people than going by the lessons given at foreign business schools. Further, increased emphasis on individual development through focus on introspection and emphasis on working in a stress-free atmosphere, has attracted the modern managers in a big way. The Maharshi Institute of Management has a department that exclusively deals with development programmes for corporate managers on the "Vedic Style of Management" and has clients such as Reckett and Coleman, Oriental Bank, ACC, Indian Petrochemicals Corporations, SRF Ltd., Tata Tea and Tata Chemicals etc. Specialised programmes based on Yoga, meditation and Vipasana etc., have scientifically proven capabilities to alleviate stress and propel the ability of leading a healthy life, even while working in a stressful environment. These techniques have found acceptance the world over for quite some time now.

In the last few years, all over the world, psychologists have attached noteworthy significance to Emotional Quotient along with Intelligence Quotient for effective performance of managers. It is now appreciated that along with high IQ, one needs a matching EQ to become truly successful in life. EQ provides a fresh approach to maximize productivity, manage change and resolve conflicts at home and at work place. Another interesting area recently discussed has been the relationship of EQ with leadership. Now, very recently, Spiritual Quotient (SQ) has also been added as a new dimension to enhance performance and also appraise employees. Spiritual Quotient mainly refers to the capacity of a person to view life from a larger, more objective perspective. It also points towards the fundamental capacity of an individual to develop ability to select behaviours. It can moderate our interactions with others and ourselves; it can redefine the goals we pursue and so on. SQ aspects indicate our awareness and faith in religion that can ease tensions, worries and anxieties and provide strength for meeting stressful situations of life, especially in a business scenario.

Thus, attaching importance to Spiritual Quotient once again brings the subject of cultural balance to the fore. It makes us sit-up and give a second thought to the fact that indiscreetly importing management techniques, particularly to manage Indians, who have such a rich culture to fall back on, may not be a very bright idea. It is high time that Indian industry and management institutes join hands to critically study these aspects and develop indigenous management styles and optimize the potential of Indian workforce.

Part III Detailed Discussions

Is Capital Punishment Necessary in 21st Century?

Capital punishment implies death penalty for a criminal who has committed a heinous crime such as betrayal of a nation, murder or rape etc. This punishment has been prevalent throughout the world since time immemorial. Several methods used were crucifixion, drowning, burning alive, impalement, hanging and so on. However, for sometime now, a number of civilised countries have stopped awarding capital punishment to criminals due to a number of compelling reasons. Strong views have been expressed in support of capital punishment and also for imposing an immediate ban on this so-called inhuman act.

It is argued that, the chief aim of awarding a punishment is not only to penalize a criminal, but to convey a message to the society that if any one commits a similar offence in future, this example would act as a deterrent for others. This would ensure that no one else dares to behave in that manner. It is felt that such an action does help in containing crimes over a period of time. As a result, a number of countries including Arab countries believe that taking life for life or killing a person by way of extreme torture, chopping of hands for committing a theft, removing a person's genitals for rape and pulling out an eye for committing certain other category of crimes, have the desired effect on the society, and therefore, such punishments must be enforced in full public view to guarantee their intended impact. In earlier times, criminals were flogged and often publicly stoned to discourage people from committing acts of crime.

It is felt that if hardened criminals are let free, they may not feel any remorse and may even commit some more crimes against the family of the victim. This could further aggravate the situation and make the lives of the victim's family worse and more pitiable. For this reason, it is considered appropriate to take the lives of such criminals as a necessary immediate step to prevent people from taking law into their own hands and inflicting avoidable violence on the society. Nevertheless, history has shown that on countless occasions, dictators or fundamentalist elements have used capital punishment brutally to eliminate opposition. In this regard, imposing of capital punishment on the Prime Minister of Pakistan, Zulfiqar AH Bhutto by military ruler, Gen. Zia-ul-Haq of Pakistan in 1979 is still fresh in the minds of people. He was hanged to death subsequent to imposing of certain charges, which were vehemently denied by him. This punishment had astonished people around the entire civilised world. Capital punishments are still being imposed by a number of Muslim nations, especially Iran, Pakistan, Iraq and Saudi Arabia, etc. In India also, Courts impose capital punishment. However, the Courts announce such punishment in the 'rarest of rare' cases and a number of measures are introduced to ensure that such punishments are not imposed arbitrarily by Courts under any circumstances. As a last resort, in some cases, the President grants pardon to criminals, thus avoiding imposing of capital punishment.

Yet, another way of looking at such a punishment is the fact that God grants life to human beings and it is not Human to take away the life of a person due to whatever reasons. If man cannot grant life, he has no business to snatch it away also. Due to this reason, a number of developed countries have imposed a ban on capital punishment. These countries have come to realize that despite imposing this punishment, the crime rate had not shown much of a decline. Therefore, they consider it futile to carry on with this kind of a barbaric punishment, which is so traumatic for the family of the criminal.

In 2013, at least 778 executions were reported in 22 nations, 96 more than 2012. Iran led the list with 369 executions, followed by Iraq, Saudi Arabia and US etc. However, these figures do not include China, which also has a large number of executions. By the end of 2013, 98 countries have abolished death penalty for all crimes. Most of these are in Western Europe and Americas. More than two-thirds of all nations have abolished death penalty in law or practice, while 58 countries have retained it in their legal system. Countries which retained death sentence include US, India, China, Japan, Pakistan, Arab countries, North Korea, Singapore and Nigeria, etc.

In India, only 55 persons have been executed since independence, even though 132 death sentences were given between 2001 and 2011. For almost 8 years, between 2004 and 2012, no executions were carried out. Only in 2013, 26/11 terrorist Ajmal Kasab and Parliament attack accused Afzal Guru were hanged. Following *Nirbhaya* case, Parliament changed the law to make a second charge of rape punishable with death penalty. Recently, in August 2014, Law Commissioner of India, has embarked upon an exercise to review the issue and has asked public views on whether India should abolish death penalty?

In view of the above discussion, we must conclude that in order to regulate our society, we must ensure that the rule of law prevails and people do not take law into their own hands. Towards this end, we must ensure that justice is neither delayed nor denied and no barbaric action is taken against any individual. These actions will go a long way in providing redressal to people by the help of judiciary and do away with the need of imposing capital punishment.

Part III Detailed Discussions

Are Women in Defence Forces a Misfit?

A modern society guarantees equal rights and responsibilities for both men and women. Women have justifiably availed multifarious opportunities offered to them in all spheres of life. They have come a long way in establishing their identity and rightful place in the society. A modern woman does not merely stay at home but comes out to share all kinds of jobs along with men. Till recently, women performed a range of duties and responsibilities except for sharing work at the last male bastion– working in the armed forces as a combatant. In 1990, the armed forces in India opened their doors for women in their officers' cadre. Despite this development, a heated debate still continues as to whether women are fit enough to successfully perform their duties and responsibilities as active members of our armed forces?

Modern age requirements and life styles have made it abundantly clear that women are not inferior to men in terms of physical health as well as mental fitness. In the 21st century war scenario, there are hardly any battles that are fought face to face where soldiers are required to show their chivalry and courage in the face of the enemy. Gone are the days when men folk used to display their masculine power in battles. In today's times, wars are fought with intellect, displaying far reaching strategic and tactical planning. Wars are now fought with ICBMs (Inter-Continental Ballistic Missiles) and other weapon carrying systems using atomic, biological and chemical arsenal. Weapons are launched utilizing mental capabilities much more than physical strength. In such a situation, women are considered equally competent as their male counterparts due to their matching intellectual capabilities. It is obvious that gender considerations become almost irrelevant under such circumstances and women are recognized as equally competent to realize the desired results.

Even in earlier times, when women were not allowed to step out of their houses, Indian history is replete with examples of display of valour on the part of women folk. In this context, names of Laxmi Bai, Razia Sultan and Chand Bibi deserve a mention. In our age, when women are being considered as equal to men in all activities, would it be justifiable to deny womenfolk of an opportunity to participate in the functioning of armed forces?

So far, it was considered that the rightful place of a woman was only at home. The all-important role of women was to cook food, rear children and keep their menfolk in good humour. It was felt that if women were allowed to work outside the confines of home, it would harm the domestic culture of our society and neglect of children will become an everyday reality. God has created women as the weaker sex and therefore, they should be given jobs that are not physically demanding. Besides, responsibilities of running a home require undivided attention and time, which women can devote only, if they are free from all other engagements. Working in the Army is essentially a trying job and entails staying in far-flung and climatically hostile areas for long duration without any support. It would be rather difficult for women to stay at such places while having the responsibility of taking care of children and related domestic chores. Women are basically gentle and not adequately motivated to lead a harsh life, which is a trademark of armed forces. During the time of war and low intensity conflicts, presence of women may cause grave problems of distraction for the menfolk of the army and even mar their efficiency of functioning under such difficult circumstances. There is also a lurking danger of sexual crimes being committed by soldiers, if women are present with them under stressful and frustrating conditions. Hence, it is felt that women are best suited to work as doctors and nurses in the armed forces rather than as regular soldiers,

Some argue that women lack the key eligibility criteria of a soldier, such as mental and physical stamina and courage. Therefore, deployment of women in real-time warfare may lower the fighting capability of our armed forces. Keeping all these factors in mind, it was considered that women are best suited in supporting roles in the armed forces and not as rifle-carrying soldiers. However, the last almost ten years' experience of having women in the armed forces has shown that numerous constraints notwithstanding, they have been discharging their duties in a proficient manner.

So far, women have been inducted into the armed forces mainly as short service commissioned officers. Also, for sometime now, women have been serving the armed forces as doctors or nurses on a permanent basis. Today, women pilots are flying various transport and fighter aircraft of the Indian Air Force with equal efficiency and courage. Women of course, were not inducted as PBORs (Personnel below officer rank).

During the years 2002–2006, some women officers of the Indian Air Force complained of sexual-harassment by their male counterparts. One lady officer in the Indian Air Force was Court Martialled on charges of indiscipline and corruption, while she alleged that male officers had been harassing her for quite sometime. In the Indian Army, one lady officer committed suicide in 2006, alleging disliking for her job and harassment by her senior male officers. Consequent to all these developments, the debate whether male armed forces officers have accepted lady officers as their fellow officers, has assumed new impetus.

Subsequently, remarks by a few senior officers of the army that army can

Part III Detailed Discussions

do away with women officers in combat units, invited sharp comments about the apparent mind set of male officers of our armed forces. A number of senior politicians and activists raised the issue that army was still not ready to accept women in fatigues. It was brought out that though merely 3% of forces comprised lady officers, women lack physical and mental stamina, need better facilities to function and enemy would be brutal with them during a war. Countering these arguments, it was argued that in a number of other countries like USA, UK, Israel and Norway etc., women have been assigned varied roles in their Armed Forces, while in India, women officers were largely utilised to arrange parties for senior officers and their intellectual capabilities were not utilised by the armed forces.

Canada, New Zealand, Denmark, Norway, Portugal and Luxembourg allow combat roles for women. Women in UK and US can serve in all wings, but not allowed in direct ground combat missions. Israel allows women in frontline combat units, but it's voluntary. If, they decline a specific mission, it's not a negative. Malaysia, Sri Lanka and Bangladesh deploy women on warships. The US has even allowed them on submarines. Even Pakistan has seven women fighter pilots. The fighting units of the Peoples' Liberation Army of Nepal, the LTTE in Sri Lanka and the Naxalites in India, all have women members.

In India after women were allowed to join Armed Forces in 1990s, there were 1436 Army, 1331 Air Force and 413 Naval women officers till 2016. In 2010, court allowed permanent commission for lady officers. Women pilots were inducted in 1991 for choppers/transport aircrafts. In Feb 2016, government announced that India will open all combat roles to women in the future. In June 2018, for the first time, first batch of women fighter pilots was to be commissioned.

Several countries like US, Israel, UK, Germany and Sweden have woman fighter pilots. If, women can fly helicopters and transport aircraft in IAF, why not fighters? All male and female IAF trainee pilots, after all, undergo the same basic Stage-I training at the IAF Academy at Dundigal. It's only in Stage-II that male pilots are 'trifurcated' into fighter, transport and helicopter streams, while women are 'bifurcated' into only the latter two. With the top US military brass now even thinking of lifting the ban on women from ground combat roles, in the backdrop of the wars in Iraq and Afghanistan, it was time India at least allowed women to fly fighters and serve on warships?

In June 2017, Army chief announced that army has plans to have women in combat roles as well. This is big departure from attitudes that so far prevented women from being assigned combat duties in the Army. This can be taken as Army's salute to gender parity.

Is the Internet a World of Hidden Opportunities or a Den of Dangers?

In the world of today, the saying that 'geography has become history' has virtually become a reality. Communication network has clearly revolutionized our way of life. In this context, internet has played a pathbreaking role, by becoming the biggest communication network, encompassing several networks in its fold. Internet has linked tens of thousands of organisations, business houses, educational institutions and research establishments etc., and millions of individuals located the world over.

Historically speaking, it was in 1968–69, that American military authorities used this system in connection with seeking information pertaining to nuclear war. The American engineers had designed a system that could keep working even, if a nuclear attack came knocking and some of the computer signals could be automatically rerouted through the servicing computers. However, its usage could spread in a very short spell of time and by late 1980s, it became a very strong computer network, which reached all corners of the world. Its usage was no more confined to American military purposes and extended to civilian networks for a wide variety of purposes. The internet began to grow in reach when the 'world wide web' was made available to everybody in the year 1993. The internet is often called 'cyberspace'– a word first used in 1984 in William Gibson's science fiction novel 'Neuromancer'. Today, the internet is a globe spanning computer network, giving people rapid access to information, knowledge, entertainment and opinions from around the world. Internet allows vast amounts of information to stream around the world from computer to computer, letting the general public have convenient access to it. Due to its mass usage and access, internet is popularly referred as the 'Information Superhighway'.

Internet has emerged as a big boon for exchanging information, especially in the field of education, science and technology and medicine etc. And, as the number of people who have access to Internet multiplies manifold, the opportunities offered by its usage also continue to grow. In the recent past, a major use of the internet has been for exchanging electronic mail or e-mail between computers, irrespective of the geographical distances involved. Additionally, an e-mail message can include pictures and audio chips, apart from words, and can be sent to thousands of computers within a matter of seconds. In a modern world, one finds it difficult to establish an identity for himself/herself, unless one has got one's own website or one's visiting card has an e-mail ID.

Another usage of Internet in the realm of business is that, goods can be displayed and inspected on the net and purchased while sitting at home. All kinds of payments for various services can also be made on the Internet, making business transactions much easier and life more comfortable. Today e-commerce is all set to dominate retail business in India. E-commerce sites like Amazon, Snapdeal, Flipkart and Jabong etc. are doing extremely brisk business by selling goods at much cheaper rates. Now all kinds of transactions on the net can be done without much physical effort.

Social networking on Twitter, Facebook, Youtube, Whatsapp and Google+ etc. has become immensely popular to share information in the form of messages, videos, photos and the like. These platforms have opened new vistas to communicate to a large number of people instantly. Notably, social networking has shown its magical impact during the Lok Sabha elections in India in 2014 and social network is considered a major factor in the landslide victory of Mr. Modi and the BJP. In the new era of technological interconnectedness, everything from garage doors to health systems will be linked and controlled through computer networks. Thus, innovations on the internet are now enabling conduct of surgeries with precision robots located far away from the surgeons.

Even though Internet has been widely utilized for exchange of information worldwide, its usage has not been without some problems and even lurking dangers. The flow of information is so spontaneous that a large chunk of undesirable information also flows via the Internet, which may cause damaging impressions, especially on children. Among other things, this information includes pornographic material. Excessive use of internet is threatening to make our youth brain dead. While it encourages only speed reading of opinions of other people; it certainly does not promote original/deep thinking and problem solving. Physical activity and social interactions become quite restricted if we remain on the net all the time. It is detrimental to health and is soon becoming a serious health hazard. In addition, as our children are using social media uncontrollably, parents must be careful about the websites the children are browsing, which might lead to cyber-bullying and violence. Security firms are now warning about injuries and possible deaths caused by cyber attacks on critical safety equipment, and first online murder could happen very soon. Therefore, teachers must guide kids how to use the internet for their benefit and avoid becoming a victim of cyber crimes.

Various kinds of cyber crimes are being committed that range from illegal reproduction of software to infringement of copyrights. Of late, a large number of cases of impersonation, cheating and unauthorized access or hacking have also come to light. In India, cybercrimes grew by 2,400% in last 10 years. Besides crimes for financial gain, the motives also included cheating, insulting women, sexual exploitation and personal revenge or settling scores. Most financial fraud cases involve hacking of bank accounts, fudging accounting records etc. People using Internet also do not follow a disciplined conduct leading to numerous other problems, including excessive browsing of the Net. After such experiences, governments the world over are in the process of making various conduct rules and regulations to regulate usage of Internet.

In India, the Information Technology Act was passed in the year 2000. With it India, in a way, entered the domain of cyber laws. Despite its several advantages, the Act needs to be further strengthened to include clauses for safeguarding the rights and interests of the consumers, who run the risk of getting cheated by unscrupulous entrepreneurs while making monetary transactions on the net. Efforts are on to make the internet a safer way to explore the world by limiting the spread of misleading and harmful information.

It is hoped that nations all over the world would extend cooperation in cyber policing and in streamlining cyber laws in the near future. We must make sure that, the cyber crimes are reduced to a minimum and internet is fruitfully utilized for knowledge building and information dissemination for the good of the humanity.

Part III Detailed Discussions

Should Right to Recall be Given to Indian Voters?

Subsequent to his fast on the Lokpal issue, social activist Anna Hazare declared that after a while, he will be agitating to bring in the provision of 'right to recall' the elected candidates who do not perform or are corrupt. In effect, right to recall is a powerful democratic instrument to remove non-performing or corrupt legislatures from office before their term expires. It provides an opportunity to people to recall representatives whom they feel are not doing a good job.

Why Right to Recall is Needed?

Even though Indian democracy is more than 64 years old, over the years, there is a growing mistrust between the people and their elected representatives. The fact remains that once the legislatures are elected, they don't keep in touch with electorates and are not at all answerable to those who elected them for five years. Thus, the so called 'representatives' hardly 'represent' their people. This fact was amply highlighted during the massive support that was received by anti-corruption movement in our country recently. Despite of the fact that Indian democracy provides an opportunity to all citizens to reach at the top of Indian Government, legislatures have very often failed to live up to the expectations of the people. And, it is precisely this reason, due to which there is now a loud demand for a provision to recall the elected legislatures.

Why Right to Recall is Justified?

- Right to recall is a totally democratic process that empowers citizens to re-activate the politics of elections and democracy for a better two-way contact between the people and the elected.
- In case legislatures fail to perform their role, citizens must have the power to remove/replace them with more capable legislatures.
- Without recall, the electorate are made to wait until the next scheduled election to voice their opinions on an incumbent's performance.
- The threat of recall may act to focus the minds of elected representatives and encourage them to meet minimum standard of behavior.

Why Right to Recall may not be Justified?

- Some people have apprehensions that due to lack of education and backwardness, some citizens may not be mature enough to exercise the right to recall in India.
- Whilst recall may encourage elected representatives to undertake popular decisions it also applies in reverse. Some have expressed concern that recall discourages certain decisions from being made because they may be unpopular.
- If political decisions are restricted by circumstances beyond the control of elected representatives, then recalling those that make unpopular decisions does not guarantee that their replacements will be able to reverse them.
- There is also some concern that recall could be abused and used as a political tool with some marginal seats becoming the target of organized campaigns.
- There is a cost associated with maintaining recall readiness because election authorities must be prepared to handle recall petition requests whenever they may arise.

Existing Position of Recall Provisions in India

As of now, Indian Constitution does not mention anything specific about such a provision. Similarly, no such provision exists in the Representation of People's Act 1951 also. However, in India, provisions for recall of legislators exist at the level of local bodies in Chhattisgarh, Madhya Pradesh, Maharashtra and Bihar. Section 47 (recall of president) of the Chhattisgarh Nagar Palika Act, 1961, provides for holding of elections to recall elected presidents due to non-performance. The process of recall is initiated when three-quarters of the total number of elected representatives in the urban bodies (councilors) write to the district collector demanding a recall.

After verifying the circumstances, the collector can report to the state government. Once the report has been considered, the government can recommend to the state election commission to conduct a poll to recall presidents. Unlike in Chhattisgarh, in Bihar the recall process begins with the voters of urban civic bodies who can remove the elected representatives from office, if two-thirds submit a signed petition to the urban development department. In the Bihar model, there is some democratic improvement, as the power to recall is vested directly with the voters. In Chhattisgarh, the recall process starts from the councilors, and therefore, can be politically motivated. Nonetheless, neither of these models are foolproof.

Recall Procedures in Other Countries

In a number of countries, provisions to recall already exist. Some noteworthy provisions are enumerated below for easy reference.

Part III Detailed Discussions

- In Canada under the Recall and Initiative Act 1995, the requirement is of more than 40% of the voters.
- The Constitution of Venezuela enables the recall of an elected representative, if at least 20% of the registered voters are signatories.
- In Philippines, the number required is at least 15% of the registered voters from the last election.
- The number varies in different states of the United States of America.
- In Switzerland, six of 26 cantons in Switzerland have recall provisions. A certain number of voters must sign the recall petition but is not based on a percentage of the electorate.

Part IV

Suggested Topics for Preparation and Revision

Some Suggested Topics for Preparation

In the previous chapters we have discussed 10 topics to illustrate as to how a candidate should present his ideas in a group discussion. In addition, background material for 26 current topics has also been provided to update the knowledge base of the students. A glance at these topics would suitably assist candidates in their preparation. Some additional topics for exhaustive preparation should also be prepared by the candidates, such as topics on political scenario, social issues, management, economy, science and technology, education and training, sports and games, environment and ecology, defence and other miscellaneous topics.

Consequent to going through the list of all suggested topics, based on their choice, students should pick up as many topics as feasible for preparation. It would be advisable to select topics from all categories of topics and not from only one category to ensure sufficient coverage and confidence building of the candidates.

Topics on 'Political Scenario'

1. In view of elections in 2014, is Indian Parliamentary Democracy becoming a Presidential one?
2. Who won the Lok Sabha Elections in 2014 – BJP or Mr. Modi?
3. Are ISIS (IS) terrorists fighting for a country or a religion?
4. In your opinion, what matters most in international relations–economic might, military power or goodwill?
5. Reasons for tax evasion in India: corrupt tax officials, higher tax rates or cumbersome tax procedures?
6. In your view, which is the best method to check *criminalisation of politics* in our country?
7. In your opinion, which is the best way to check price rise in our country– stop export of essential goods, increase agricultural output or give more subsidies to farmers?
8. What do you think is the main reason for increasing crime rate in our country–unemployment, glorification of criminals by media or strong nexus between criminals and politicians?
9. Is UNO competent to handle global issues?

10. Will unification of India and Pakistan ever be feasible?
11. Should we give more autonomy to our states?
12. What is the best way to deal with river water disputes of various states?
13. Indian Government has been ignoring North-Eastern States of India in the past. What should be the course ahead?
14. In your view, which is the foremost problem which will hinder India's progress in the next millennium—corruption, illiteracy or criminalisation of politics?
15. Should we abolish Article 370 to solve the Kashmir issue?
16. Should Trade Unionism be banned in India?
17. Repeated elections—why should taxpayers pay for it?
18. Indian bureaucracy—foundation strength or a colonial hangover?
19. If Sarder Patel were the first Prime Minister of India?
20. Are we unfit for democracy?
21. Should strikes be banned?
22. Why cross border terrorism cannot be totally stopped?
23. Present state of Indo-US relations.
24. Should Article 365 be abolished?
25. Going nuclear was a mistake?
26. Would Middle East problem be ever resolved?
27. Does coalition politics have a future?
28. Borderless world—a dream or reality?
29. Do we need a global policeman?
30. Does America need to be Uncle Sam in all matters?
31. Has communism lost its relevance with the breakup of the Soviet Union?
32. In today's unipolar world, has non-aligned movement lost its relevance?
33. Post of a Governor has lost its relevance ?
34. Smaller states can be governed better.
35. India and China are set to rule the world in the 21st century.
36. America's unilateralism signifies the end of UN's multilateralism.
37. Should India change from a multi-party system to a bi-party system?
38. Pen is 'not' always mightier than the sword.
39. When will 'Space Tourism' start?

Topics on 'Social Issues'

1. Should the age of juveniles be reduced to serve as a deterrent against heinous crimes?
2. How is bullying on social networking sites affecting adolescents?
3. Role of social media to mobilize public opinion.

4. Is English a need of the 21st century or a British legacy?

5. Is offer of MNCs like Apple and Facebook, asking young girls to freeze their eggs to improve company efficiency justified?

6. Casteless India—is it a pipe dream ?

7. Materialism—have we sold our soul to the devil?

8. Role of ethics in tobacco industry, liquor industry etc.

9. Should gambling be legalized in India?

10. Should doctors be tried in Consumer Courts?

11. Abortion or Euthanasia—is it morally right for the society?

12. The relevance of Gandhism today.

13. Is India moving away from a secularist state?

14. Indian customs—are we in a time wrap?

15. The role of NGOs in dealing with social and moral issues.

16. NGOs—do they serve people's interests or are they merely pressure groups?

17. Death of socialism in our country is in the offing?

18. In your view, is contribution of urban areas to India's economy greater than that of rural areas?

19. Who is best suited to impart sex education to our youth–parents, teachers, friends or anybody?

20. In your opinion, who suffers most, children of unhappy parents, children of divorced parents or children of working mothers?

21. What is the best way to check overpopulation in our cities?

22. Should reservation be given in our society? If so, to whom?

23. Working women have created an imbalance in our country. Do you agree?

24. Who should be blamed for the rise in senior citizens' seeking solace in Old Age Homes?

25. What is the most effective way to control eve-teasing?

26. What is the main reason for an increase in divorce rate among Indian couples?

27. In your view has the western culture been detrimental to the progress of our society?

28. Has joint family system outlived its utility?

29. Contribution of a non-working woman (house wife) is more than that of a working woman towards our society. Do you agree?

30. Do we need prohibition throughout India?

31. What do you think is the best way to check the hazards of sexually transmitted diseases in our country—educate the masses, legalise prostitution or anything else?

Part IV Topics for Preparation

32. Which is the best way to check exploitation of child labour in our country?
33. Illiteracy in India.
34. Child marriages should be banned immediately.
35. People responsible for dowry deaths and rape should be awarded death penalty.
36. India's fight against AIDS has not been adequate.
37. Are TV channels killing our culture?
38. Position of women in this male dominant society.
39. Are Khap Panchayats taking law in their hands by organising 'Honour Killings'
40. Dowry still haunts Indian brides.

Topics on 'Management'

1. Is quality a myth in India?
2. Success is all about human relations.
3. Relationship is important in team work.
4. Impact of BPO on world economy.
5. Indian ethos and modern management.
6. Leadership excellence is needed for professional excellence.
7. Kill stress before stress kills you.
8. What it takes to be a world class organisation?
9. Moving from brain-drain to brain-gain.
10. One land, one billion minds.
11. Mind-sets shape performance, mind-sets limit performance, mind-sets are difficult to change.
12. One need not be big to be ethical, but one has to be ethical to be big.
13. Modern management is not about authority, but about persuasion and concensus.
14. All is fair in love and business.
15. Is India having appropriate business relations with her neighbours?
16. Is management a science or an art?
17. Quality necessarily means increased costs.
18. Business competitiveness and creativity cannot be achieved without benchmarking.
19. Women as top managers and CEOs.
20. Corporate Board rooms should not become family battlegrounds.

Topics on 'Economy'

1. Which of these should get maximum importance—heavy industries, small scale industries or cottage industries?

2. Should there be more government control on multinationals operating in India?
3. Should Asia, like Europe, also change over to a common currency?
4. India's role in the WTO?
5. Agrarian economy in India—boon or bane?
6. Role of women in development of India?
7. Globalisation is a boon or curse?
8. Who is responsible for the rising prices?
9. Do we need the help of MNC's for our economic development?
10. How to keep inflation under check?
11. Is permitting subsidies the right step?
12. Discuss salient aspects of this year's budget.
13. Greed is good.
14. What does FDI hike in organized retails mean for consumers, companies and politics?

Topics on 'Education and Training'

1. Private educational institutions have been more harmful than helpful in building the career of students. Do you agree?
2. Have examinations killed education?
3. Education and success—is there a correlation?
4. Ragging in college should be banned?
5. Get better or get beaten.
6. Computers and computer training have added to India's unemployment problem.
7. Management education—is it necessary to succeed in business?
8. Primary education and not higher education, needs to be subsidized.
9. Indian education system does not encourage creativity.

Topics Related to 'Sports and Games'

1. Considering the immense popularity of IPL and football clubs like Manchester United etc., has materialism invaded the arena of sports?
2. In your opinion, the deterioration in the standard of sports in India is attributable to inherent lack of talent, politics in sports, extra importance to one particular sport or any other?
3. Is Boxing a barbaric sport?
4. Match fixing in sports is here to stay.
5. Can we avoid betting in sports?
6. What ails Indian sports?
7. Can India host Olympic Games in the near future?

8. Are we paying too much attention to Cricket at the cost of other sports?
9. Why India has lost its past glory of excelling in the game of Hockey?
10. Are we not keen to encourage the game of Football in our country?

Topics pertaining to 'Environment and Ecology'

1. Protection of wildlife.
2. De-forestation is inevitable?
3. "How green was my valley"? Is nature paying the price?
5. Pollution is more hazardous than War?
6. What is the main reason for the decline in tourism in India?
7. Should Archeological Survey of India (ASI) continue with the task of preserving heritage monuments in India, or should it be allocated to someone else?
8. To meet ever-increasing demand for energy, India should look for alternative fuels.

'Defence' Related Topics

1. Present state of India's missile programme.
2. Do we need a cut in the defence budget?
3. Over-involvement of media in the Defence related and National Security matters has done more harm than good.
4. Was induction of women in Armed Forces a mistake?
5. Should there be any reservations in the Armed Forces?
6. Should India go for privatisation of Defence Forces?
7. War is the best solution for peace?
8. Should India have a Chief of Defence Services?
9. Should military be used to solve Sino-Indian border dispute?

Miscellaneous Topics

1. Can technocrats be the prominent faces of bureaucracy?
2. Health and nutrition.
3. Does God exist?
4. Reservation and quota system in India.
5. Youth is a blunder, if not taken care of.
6. Generation gap shall always remain.
7. Hazards of living in a metropolitan city?
8. Is honesty still the best policy?
9. Is Panchayati Raj essential in India?
10. Has religion helped or harmed India?
11. Should Lotteries be banned?

12. Should one go for love or an arranged marriage?
13. We do not learn from history, we repeat it.
14. The world is a stage.
15. Survival tools for the new millennium.
16. Are beauty pageants necessary?
17. Which of these will pose greater problem to our country—over population, illiteracy or communalism?
18. Judiciary often comes with a heavy hand on the government. Is it justified?
19. Do you agree that women today are being truthfully portrayed in the world of advertisement?
20. In your views, can the opinion polls be used effectively to find solutions to various issues concerning the public in our country?
21. Do you think, the press has a right to interfere in the private lives of eminent personalities?
22. Ignorance is no more a bliss.
23. Are media-trials justified?

Part IV Topics for Preparation

Basics Recapitulated

Let us recall that group discussion is an interactive exercise, where a small group of candidates get-together to discuss, respond and reflect on a given thought-provoking topic. The coordinator merely facilitates the progress of this exchange of ideas and closely observes the behaviour of candidates under varying conditions.

It would be worth while to recapitulate what all goes in the minds of the panel members who observe these discussions. Some major points are reproduced below for the convenience of students and should always be kept in mind while preparing to participate in a group discussion.

(a) Initiating the GD: Remember that, if you have adequate confidence in yourself, you may decide to initiate the discussion, but in case you are not so confident about yourself, it is quite prudent to wait and watch the situation and contribute at the earliest opportunity. Do make a positive contribution towards the discussion.

(b) Coming out with ideas: If one has to do well in his sphere of activity, he must be able to generate relevant ideas about such an activity. Therefore, either due to your knowledge about the subject or your ability to generate ideas on the basis of what others say, you should be able to adequately contribute towards the progress of the group discussion. Your knowledge base and preparation comes handy here.

(c) Managing stress: The situation, where 9–10 candidates have to speak in a 12–15 minutes GD, creates tremendous amount of stress on all the participants. The way you react to this situation, will reveal a lot about your stress management. It is a real and practical test of your temperament to check, whether you remain cool or are prone to creating panic under stressful situations. So, try to remain calm and collected despite the chaos around you.

(d) Ability to communicate: It is not good enough to possess a good idea, one should be able to convince others about it also. Communicating with others is an important managerial skill, which is quite easily tested during a group discussion. Ability to communicate may not be sufficient to get you through, but it is definitely a necessary condition.

(e) Adjustment with others: In a situation, where 8–9 candidates enthusiastically aim to clear a test within a very short span of time, behavioural pattern of the participant becomes fairly apparent. The way a candidate displays as to how he is better than others, speaks a lot about his personality and a number of other qualities. A candidate should display that under stressful conditions as well, he can live in harmony with others and this is considered a positive aspect of his adjustment with others. Usually, candidates' team-spirit and quality of cooperation emerge clearly during a group discussion.

(f) Leadership abilities: In a group discussion, leadership abilities are also tested in a subtle manner. The manner in which a candidate manages diverse opinions expressed by other candidates would broadly reveal his leadership qualities. A candidate is expected to respect opinions expressed by others, and at the same time, refine ideas so that these are accepted by the group in an amicable manner. A leader should know that, if he would respect others, he would, in turn be respected. In addition, a leader must be able to keep his team as a cohesive group to achieve the desired results. A leader should be in a position to reach a consensus despite diverse views expressed by participants on a subject.

(g) Non-verbal inputs: Do not consciously display negative body language. In brief, while a slight lean forward displays your keenness to listen to others, an excessive lean forward may convey that you are a bit nervous about the proceedings. Similarly, a lean back posture suggests that, you are not much involved in the ongoing discussion. Keep your hand movements under check. Therefore, make a deliberate effort not to give any negative inputs about your personality and attitude.

(h) Contribute appropriately: In this regard, it is not essential to speak excessively or raise your voice, but you must add a few new ideas or add something significant. In an unfortunate but common scenario, when some over-zealous members of the group shout or speak together, do try to divert the focus of attention to something else to get over this odd situation. This will help in putting the proceedings back on the rails without loss of precious time and your assessors will definitely appreciate this effort.

All the best and happy discussing

■ ■ ■

Part IV Topics for Preparation